NOBLE SOUNDS

A SIMPLE GUIDE TO JAZZ AND BLUES

J STRAUSS

Genius
Music Books

Published by Genius Music Books, an Imprint of Genius Book Publishing, PO Box 250380 Milwaukee Wisconsin 53225 USA

https://GeniusMusicBooks.com

ISBN: 978-1-958727-48-5

240919 Trade

To Serian and Shanna,
the most musical names I know.

CONTENTS

PART TWO
THE BLUES AIN'T NOTHIN'

FIRST OFF

A few people provided invaluable assistance in bringing what you're about to read into the light of day whether they liked it or not.

The lovely Antujaeli Kiondo Marche put all the handwritten scribble on to computer diskettes because this dumb author had not learned how to use a computer yet. Three IT experts helped with computer juju once I learned—namely Boris Petit and Harry Burris, both rightly insisting on lots of back-up copies. Giovanni Di Piazza (GDP), a Tanzanian IT hotshot, updated the technology and helped in too many ways to list.

Three gentlemen made many helpful comments: Dr. Peter Petit, Kevin Mulqueen, and Anders Moller. Dr. Petit knows next to nothing about jazz and blues so was the ideal reader. Mulqueen knows as much as the author but fortunately we hardly agree on anything. Moller, aka Skywalker, made his comments rhythmically since we played together in bands.

And a special shout-out to Darrell Knuffke (Baba K) who painstakingly edited the draft manuscript—word by word, sentence by sentence, page by page, adding numerous useful and often inspired suggestions. As he lives in the Four Corners of Colorado and the author lives in Tanzania, there is no way to know how many beads of sweat or tears of anguish he shed. But as the song goes: "that's what friends are for."

Finally, it is usually stated that any errors are those of the author.

For reasons not entirely clear, jazz and blues have been plagued by sloppy research. No doubt the author made errors, but many come from other authors from whom this particular author tried to steal some facts. Birth dates, recording dates, names of personnel sometimes vary from one source to another. Choosing a fact became epistemological roulette. However, most of the important stuff is probably close to correct and what really counts is the music.

—J. Strauss
Dar es Salaam, Tanzania

BORN TO BOOGIE

I heard Papa tell Mama
    Let that boy boogie...
    It's in him and it's got to come out.
    - John Lee Hooker

I firmly believe we are all born to boogie. Music is as natural to humans as eating and sleeping. All babies sing. It doesn't matter whether they live in mud huts or penthouses. All babies dance. When they hear music, some part of their bodies starts to move. All babies drum. Give any six-month-old on the planet two spoons and a pot and see what happens. No one tells babies to sing, dance, or drum. They just do it... naturally.

Some of us develop this natural part of ourselves; some of us don't. A few claim to be tone deaf. A few become professional musicians. Most of us sing in the shower, shuffle along at a party, and maybe pick out a few tunes on a musical instrument. Nearly everyone listens to music every day and many have some sort of music collection—albums, tapes, CDs, and now digital. Why? I believe we need to have music in our lives, just as we need air to breathe.

This book is aimed principally at those who don't listen to jazz and blues or want to gain a better appreciation of this music. A lot of people I've come across over the years have messed around the edges of jazz and blues but have felt confused or—even worse—intimidated. If you fit that description, you've got the right book in your hand. No need to feel intimidated or embarrassed—you listen to watered-down versions of this music all the time: pop, rock, R&B, television themes, movie soundtracks. Many are based on jazz, blues, or both. Why not try the real thing?

Many potential listeners get turned off because they think they have to become experts to appreciate jazz and blues. Bull.

Here's a hypothetical conversation between jazz fans Bo and Joe. Joe is with his friend Moe who doesn't know anything about jazz. *What Moe is thinking is in italics.*

Bo: Hey man, have you heard that Christian McBride just put out a big band album?

Joe: I'm not surprised, he's played with just about everybody.

Moe: Who is Christian McBride?

Bo: Not as many as Ron Carter… he's been on over 10,000 albums.

Moe: Who is Ron Carter and how has he managed to be on 10,000 albums?

Joe: Carter's good all right, but as far as I'm concerned nobody tops Mingus.

Moe: Mingus who?

Bo: Mingus could play okay but what about Ray Brown?

Moe: Who is Ray Brown?

Joe: Sure, Brown was technically great, but Mingus created all those classics like "Goodbye Porkpie Hat."

Moe: What does that mean?

Bo: Did you know that it has another title—"Theme for Lester Young"?

Joe: Of course, everybody knows that.

Moe: I didn't know that.

Joe: What made Mingus great was his musicians.

Bo: What are you talking about? The only really great musician he had was Jackie McLean.

Moe: Who is Jackie McLean?

Joe: That's my point. These cats were great because they played with Mingus. Take Dannie Richmond. He only ever played with Mingus and Mingus made him great.

Bo: Come on now, Dannie Richmond great? You've got to be kidding. What about Roy Haynes?

Joe: True, Haynes has played with everybody.

Moe: Mind if I ask a question? If Christian McBride has played with everybody and Roy Haynes has played with everybody, have the two of them ever played together?

Bo: Gee, I don't know.

Joe: That's a good question. I'll get back to you on that.

This is not a book for the chosen few. You and I are born to boogie. Jazz and blues—first and foremost—are for enjoyment. I propose to write a book about the music I enjoy in a way you will enjoy. And I bring to this task a number of qualities which may help me (and you). While I can wallow in the trivia and minutiae with the cognoscenti, I will try really hard not to. I am not a convert to jazz and blues; I've listened to this music all my life, so I can dig styles from all periods. I started playing music at six years old, and doing it for money in front of live audiences from the age of 15 on a variety of different instruments (I make up in quantity what I lack in quality). I usually understand where musicians are coming from—well not always but most of the time. Because I am a musician rather than a manqué, I don't have any points to prove. When I use musical terms in this book, I will do my best to explain them to you, just in case you don't know them. Furthermore, I am not a professional writer—which may be obvious by now—so I don't feel the desire to dazzle you with my prose. This book is not a history or a critical review of jazz and blues. We'll listen to some music together. I'll give you some background and try to explain what's going on as the song plays. It's like friends talking about a subject you are interested in and that I know something about.

If you listen with an open mind and open ears, I believe you may begin to enjoy it as much as I do. You don't need to be an expert. You can dig "Salt Peanuts" by Charlie Parker and Dizzy Gillespie without knowing it's based on the chord changes to George Gershwin's "I Got Rhythm." You don't even need to know what chord changes are. To dig jazz and blues, all you need is a soul.

Let me end this beginning back where we started, with John Lee Hooker.

Some years ago, I was visiting a friend in the U.K. For his birthday I took him to the London Blues Festival. We found a spot on the grass about 40 yards from the bandstand and sat down to listen to an afternoon of blues. In mid-afternoon, out comes John Lee Hooker. John Lee is approaching age 74 and on this particular day, he is really off. He fumbles around on guitar. He doesn't remember the lyrics. That deep voice, sounding as if it just rose from the bottom of a Mississippi well, booms out strong as ever, but he only mutters blither-blather as he wanders aimlessly about the stage for half an hour or so. Then his band kicks into that familiar Hooker riff to "Boogie Chillun." John Lee tells everybody to get up and boogie. And around 20,000 people in the baking sun in south London England rise to their feet and begin to move. They are paying homage, whether or not they know it, to an institution. This is JOHN LEE HOOKER. This man is the creator, the human retainer, the living embodiment of BOOGIE. And something about boogie burrows deep down, down inside the guts. My friend and I boogied our respective buns off. And it felt soooo goooood. Because we all need to boogie. We all got to boogie. Yes chillun, all eight billion of us on Planet Earth were born to ... ... BOOGIE.

—J. Strauss
Dar es Salaam

PART ONE
CLOSE ENOUGH FOR JAZZ

It is tough to use words to describe music. How do you put in words the trumpet of Bix Beiderbecke, the drumming of Art Blakey, the piano of Thelonious Monk, the alto sax of Charlie Parker? Music is sound and movement. Words are just... words. Using words to describe music is like using an umbrella to describe rain.

The purpose of writing, my high school English teacher told us, is to communicate. We can't communicate unless we understand each other. And to describe the sound and pulse of music, I have to use certain terms. You don't need to know these terms to listen to and enjoy music. But I can't describe music without using a bit of technical language. So before we get started, I need to lay some terms on you.

Let's start with rhythm, which is where jazz starts anyhow. Just as a writer puts letters together to form words, a musician puts beats together to form *bars* (or measures). The most common is four beats to the bar. A 12-bar blues is simply four beats repeated 12 times. A 32-bar standard ballad consists of two similar eight-bar verses, an eight bar "bridge" (which the British call the "middle eight" even though it doesn't come in the middle, but that's the British for you), followed by a repeat of an eight-bar verse like the first two. Some experts like to call this "the A-A-B-A form." You can play three beats to the bar like waltzes, or two beats to the bar like marches. You can play all sorts of beats to the bar. But you always have bars if the music follows strict rhythm. Sometimes musicians don't play in strict rhythm; they speed up or they slow down the tempo. Sometimes they forget rhythm altogether (the musical term is "rubato"). Sometimes they play two or more rhythms at the same time, which is called *cross-rhythm* or *polyrhythm*. A complete run-through of the song—12 bars, 32 bars, or any other number of bars—is called a *chorus*.

I will likely use the terms *scales, octaves, and chords*. Do-re-mi-fa-so-la-ti-do is a scale. (Remember: "Do, a deer, a female deer/ Re, a drop of golden sun...?) The interval between the first "do" and the second "do" is an *octave*. A *chord* is minimally three notes played simultaneously. Do-mi-so form a chord. Many songs have several chords and as a number is played, the musicians move through a set of chords. This set is the chord progression, sometimes called the *changes*. Different songs may have the same changes—I already mentioned that "Salt Peanuts" has the same changes as "I Got Rhythm;" ditto "Ornithology" and "How High the Moon." Many blues have the same changes.

I will refer to *riffs*. A riff is a repeated musical phrase. If you are familiar with Keith Richards' instrumental opening two bars of "Satisfaction" by the Rolling Stones, you already know what a riff is, even if you have never heard the term used. The seven notes that make up that phrase are repeated throughout "Satisfaction." *Counterpoint* will probably come up. Sometimes referred to as a counter melody, it is a second musical line that complements the main melody. Bach fugues are based on counterpoint. Traditional New Orleans jazz is also based on counterpoint.

I'll only lay a few more terms on you before we get down to the good stuff. Jazz, and other types of music also, incorporate *syncopation*. The accent doesn't always fall directly on the beat. Jazz rhythm doesn't necessarily go: ONE-TWO-THREE-FOUR, or ONE-two-THREE-four, or even one-TWO-three-FOUR. Sometimes the accent falls before or after the beat. The rhythm is syncopated. Syncopation helps create a rhythmic feeling called *swing*, that thing that makes you tap your foot, nod your head, or snap your fingers. Duke Ellington and Ivie Anderson explained jazz in 1932 this way: "It don't mean a thing, if it ain't got that swing."

Finally jazz musicians *improvise*. They spontaneously create musical lines out of their heads, hearts, and guts. Some jazz is composed but much of it is made up on the spot. Great jazz musicians seldom play a solo twice in exactly the same way. When Dave Brubeck was asked why he never played a song the same way twice, he answered: "I have a poor memory." A friend transcribed one of saxophonist John Coltrane's solos note-for-note and asked him to play it. Coltrane said, "I can't; it's too difficult." That's jazz.

No one has ever really defined jazz but the characterization I like best is also the title of a book by Whitney Balliet: *The Sound of Surprise*. That pretty well gets to the core. You will only be surprised by Haydn's "Surprise Symphony" the first time you hear it. But good jazz is different every time. Using another Coltrane example, his drummer Elvin Jones relates how the John Coltrane Quartet spent 12 hours recording a television program in Germany. "We must have played 'My Favorite Things' about 50 times. But it was never boring. I think the last take was probably the strongest."

Inventiveness is the hallmark of great jazz. I expect many of us know Beethoven's "Ode to Joy" from the *Ninth Symphony*. Stan Getz might turn it into a bossa nova. Jazz organist Jimmy Smith might funk it. Count Basie's band would definitely swing it. Free jazz pianist Cecil Taylor might tear it apart and reconstruct it. And it's anybody guess what Thelonious Monk or Rahsaan Roland Kirk would do. Beethoven might dig it or might not. YOU might dig it or might not. But it certainly wouldn't be S.O.S.—Same Old Sound. Mark Gardner describes pianist Elmo Hope's style as "quirky and unpredictable." In jazz that's a compliment.

This quirky unpredictable music was developed by African Americans in the latter years of the 19th century in the southern part of the United States. It mixed brass band music, creole, ragtime, blues, church music, and other elements. We won't get into which elements or how much of each make up jazz. Others, particularly Marshall Stearns, have covered that subject much better than I can, and we don't need to know about it to enjoy the music.

By 1900 the music that would soon take the name jazz was centered in New Orleans. Many musicians played in the jazz style, the most famous being a legendary cornet player named Charles "Buddy" Bolden. (Bolden went insane in 1906 before he could be recorded, so we will never know exactly how his music sounded.) Jazz hit the West Coast as early as 1907 and made a stir in Chicago a bit later. The first jazz record was cut in 1917 by a bunch of white musicians calling themselves the Original Dixieland Jass Band. By 1920 jazz had spread across the U.S. like wildfire and the Jazz Age had begun.

Today people all over the world listen to jazz. I used to tune in to BBC-London to hear "Jazz for the Asking," a half-hour request program. The requests were often more interesting than the music. Boris Badinov in Russia wants a song by Louis Armstrong for his friend in California. Soso Fulani in Timbuktu requests "All the Things You Are" for his wife on their 20th wedding anniversary. Jose Canuse in Tierra del Fuego sends greetings to all jazz fans and please play something off the latest Paquito D'Rivera album. My late friend Emile Katona, a fine sax-playing Hungarian professor of economics, used to be in a jazz group in Lesotho with a Basotho pianist and a Japanese bassist. America gave jazz to the world and now it belongs to everyone. Jazz belongs to you.

You don't need to be a musical genius to appreciate jazz. You don't need to know about all the various styles. The labels people put on jazz can be useful when writing or talking about the music, but they won't make the slightest difference when listening. Jazz has great variety. It incorporates blues (a lot of blues). Some of it sounds like classical music. Some of it has heavy elements of Latin, Indian, and of course African music. Some of it mixes in rock music, which is sometimes called Fusion. All jazz is inherently fusion of one sort of another. Duke Ellington detested labels. He said, "There are only two kinds of music: good music and bad music." Good jazz is in the ear of the behearer. Jazz, as I've mentioned before and will again because it's important to keep in mind, is for enjoyment.

Go get yourself some jazz, sit back and listen. Those musicians are talking to you. They're telling you a story, if you can dig it. They're telling you about happiness, about pain, about love, hate, oppression, and occasionally ecstasy. Mainly they're telling you about freedom. Freedom underlies all jazz: the freedom to create, to express yourself, to tell your story. And when you listen to that story, really listen, you, too, are liberated. For those moments, you are no longer poor, no longer hassled, no longer old or young, beautiful or ugly, no longer white or black or brown, yellow, or red. You are free from all that. You listen to the music and the music will set you free. And that's close enough for jazz.

CHAPTER 1
JOHN COLTRANE
"MY FAVORITE THINGS"

https://www.youtube.com/watch?v=qWG2dsXV5HI

John Coltrane cured my headache. I listened to "My Favorite Things," and before the cut had finished, my headache was gone. Don't be surprised. People have made all sorts of miraculous claims for Coltrane's music; some even claim to have seen God while listening to Trane. This would have made Coltrane very happy, for that's exactly what he was after— nothing less than the vision of God.

Coltrane, nicknamed Trane, didn't start his musical career looking for God. He just wanted to play music. The Vision appeared later. First came the years of struggle. Trane, by jazz standards, was a slow developer. Many who believe he was one of the greatest jazz musicians (if not *the* greatest) forget how many years it took him to master his art. He was almost 30 years old before most people heard of him, when he joined the Miles Davis Quintet in 1955.

A musician who decides on a life in jazz is like the monk who dedicates his life to unending prayer and takes a vow of poverty. You hear about gold records ($1 million in sales), platinum (one million units), and even multi-platinum. A jazz album is a big hit if it moves 10,000 units. And jazz gigs are so few that most musicians have day jobs—sometimes as music teachers but often any sort of work they can get. If they strike it lucky, they might be offered a fairly steady job in a club but often they take whatever there is.

A fellow sax player walking into a club in Philadelphia was horrified to see the very studious, shy, almost introverted John Coltrane "walking the bar." This occurs when a musician, usually a tenor saxophonist, is supposedly gripped with such passion that he loses control of himself, jumps up on the bar and begins to honk and wail on his horn, head bobbing, eyes closed, shuffling from one end to the other, while the drunken patrons yell encouragement. No doubt, Trane needed the bread. Critics write about musicians as artists, which is fair enough. They forget these musicians are also out to make a living. Almost every jazz musician has had his time "walking the bar," or its equivalent. Musicians say: "You got to pay your dues if you want to play the blues."

John Coltrane spent more time than most paying dues. He spent six or more hours a day practicing. If a musician friend came by his home to visit, Trane would invite him down to the basement to practice for a few hours. He would even practice in his dressing room between sets at a club. When you hear Coltrane and maybe think he plays like a man possessed, you're right. He was on a quest: first for Excellence, then for Beauty, then finally for The Love Supreme.

If you want to hear Coltrane's Excellence check out the album *Giant Steps* or a number like "Chasin' the Trane." If you want to hear Coltrane's Beauty, I highly recommend "In a Sentimental Mood" off his album with Duke Ellington or "My One and Only Love" with singer Johnny Hartman. For his Vision, go directly to the album *A Love Supreme,* which I love supremely. I've taken the easy way out and selected his most famous song, "My Favorite Things." I believe it illustrates Coltrane's excellence, beauty, and vision.

Jazz has always taken music composed in another style and done something different with it—"jazzed" it up. "My Favorite Things" comes from the Rodgers and Hammerstein musical *The Sound of Music*. It's a fine little tune and fits nicely within the context of the overall show, but does it really qualify as the all-time greatest Richard Rodgers composition? Coltrane turned it into a classic. He did this on three levels: sound, rhythm, and interpretation.

The sound on "My Favorite Things" is—for want of a better word—haunting. It stays in your head long after the track has finished. This haunting quality comes from Coltrane's choice of performing the number on a then-recently acquired soprano saxophone. In 1960 when Coltrane's version of "My Favorite Things" came out, the soprano was seldom heard. Only a few musicians played it. The most notable was New Orleans jazz great Sidney Bechet, a contemporary of Louis Armstrong's. After Coltrane, many sax players began using the soprano as a second horn. The soprano produces an "oriental" sound absolutely right for the trance-like meditative mood Trane wishes to convey.

However, even before you hear Coltrane's soprano, the rhythm sets you up. McCoy Tyner (piano) and Steve Davis (bass) introduce the number in waltz time. But this is not your ordinary waltz. I had trouble convincing a friend of mine who plays classical music that "My Favorite Things" is really done in 3/4 time. Maybe she was expecting something by Strauss for students at the Arthur Murray Dance Academy. This is no Bavarian oom PAH PAH or Viennese DUM dah dah waltz. Davis on bass acts as the rhythmic anchor. He starts off accenting the first beat but not exactly on the beat. Sometimes he's ahead, sometimes he's behind. After the first few minutes, he moves the accent all over the place. Elvin Jones would probably rather poke a drumstick in his eye than go oom PAH PAH. No sir, Elvin does what he does best—cross-rhythms. He plays clear and for Elvin, known as a power drummer, rather subdued, relying on his cymbal and snare drum with some subtle bass drum accents here and there. Meanwhile Tyner lays out easy-going block chords (chords played simultaneously with both hands). The combination of Davis-Jones-Tyner creates a hypnotic meditative mood. Simultaneously they provide a fluid rhythmic reservoir for Coltrane to float in, pleasant musical waves on a calm, clear lake.

And in floats Coltrane. He plays the first 16 bars pretty much the way Richard Rodgers wrote them. Well not exactly because Coltrane plays jazz so the notes don't fall exactly on the beat and since no one is playing on the beat; anyhow, it all blends together. Anyway, you know right off what you're listening to—"My Favorite Things." And you also know right off this is no ordinary version of "My Favorite Things"; something special is happening. Coltrane is one of the most lyrical ballad musicians in all of jazz. He played only ballads he loved and had the ability to convey that love to the listener.

Tyner-Davis-Jones does eight bars of what is now becoming hypnotic rhythm and back comes Coltrane for a repeat of the first half of this 32-bar song. In fact, you won't hear the second 16 bars of the Rodgers melody until the ending of Coltrane's version. After this second statement of the theme, Trane flashes some of his fantastic technique at you for 24 bars. Then two more repeats of the theme where he begins to unwind with a few flurries of notes at the end, after which comes another 16 bars of technique.

All this, at its most elementary level, is building and releasing tension. You hear the intro in a minor scale with beats falling every which place and the tension starts rising. What is this all about, you wonder. Coltrane plays the melody in a major scale and you begin to relax. Then the minor scale and cross-rhythms—tension. Statement of the melody— release. Then Trane does some serious BLOWING— tension. Restatement of the melody— release. And so it goes.

Coltrane turns it over to McCoy Tyner's piano. Tyner's job is to put you in a euphoric trance. At one point Tyner plays the same right-hand note for 16 bars while his left hand keeps the chords going. Then 16 bars of moving off that note and returning: up and back, down and back, up and back, up and back, down and back. Tyner builds and builds with his blocks. Builds and builds; four and a half minutes building and building. You're in no state to ask what he's building to. You know he's building to something.

Coltrane returns with a fairly straight run-through of the 16-bar melody. And then he lets loose with six minutes of the most beautiful sounds you can possibly imagine. Trane soars, glides, dips, climbs, circles. Flurries of notes, "sheets of sound" (writer Ira Gitler's term): These come flying at you. Trane does some flat-out amazing interval jumps at triple speed. He plays so wildly, and so wonderfully, it is beyond my limited ability to describe these six minutes in words. I can call it a musical ecstasy. Only once during his solo does Trane restate the theme to remind you that this ecstasy is about "favorite things."

What favorite things? *His* favorite things. *Your* favorite things. The things you love. The things that have the most meaning in your life. Somehow Trane knows. And you know that he knows. How can he know? Elvin Jones, many years later, said Coltrane was "... like an angel on Earth. This is not just an ordinary person. I've been touched by something greater than... than life." It seems to me Trane knows that although our favorite things are different, we all have our favorite things. And this unites us to him and to each other. And realization of this unity of us all is Trane's ecstasy.

Finally he plays the entire 32-bar melody and ends it... slowly, beautifully. We come out of our trance and float lightly down to earth. What an experience—all 13 minutes of it. Now you know why "My Favorite Things" is one of my favorite things and how John Coltrane cured my headache.

CHAPTER 2
BIX BEIDERBECKE - FRANKIE TRUMBAUER
"SINGIN' THE BLUES"

https://www.youtube.com/watch?v=0Ue9igC7flI

"Singin' the Blues," as played by Bix Beiderbecke and Frankie Trumbauer, may well be the first song I ever heard. I can't say for sure because I would have been about a week old. Our house was always full of music and my old man had what passed for an album in the 1940s by Bix and Tram—several 78 rpm records collected under one cover. I do know that I could hum "Singin' the Blues" before I learned "Mary Had a Little Lamb."

"Singin the Blues," not to be confused with a 1956 Guy Mitchell song of the same title, has no vocals and is not really a traditional blues in the sense that Armstrong's "West End Blues" is blues. "Singin" follows a standard 32 bar AABA ballad format. It is a bluesy, bouncy, very hummable sort of song. And in its day—1927—it was extremely popular. It went on to become an influential jazz classic.

To understand why, we have to digress for a couple of paragraphs and go back to New Orleans. Jazz in the early years was characterized by collective improvisation. In very simple terms it worked like this: One instrument, usually a cornet, would play the melody or lead line; another, usually trombone, would lay down a second line underneath the lead; a third instrument, usually clarinet, would float a third line over the top. Meanwhile a rhythm section, which might consist of any combination of tuba/string bass, banjo/guitar, piano, and drums, would bounce along in two or four beats to the bar. Sometimes a violin, saxophones, an extra trumpet, a trombone, or a clarinet would play additional lines. All lines came out of the players' heads. There might be short breaks where an individual could really show his stuff for two bars, four bars, maybe even eight bars. But for the most part musicians had to make their separate lines blend. This was collective improvisation.

Two people were instrumental in changing that. Pianist Jelly Roll Morton formalized the "collective" and separated it from the "improvisation." Morton was first and foremost a composer/arranger, and he wanted his music played a certain way. He wrote out parts and he expected his groups to follow them. He left space for an individual to improvise during an extended break, but the main purpose was to present the composition. More to the point, Louis Armstrong turned jazz into a soloist's art. He had too much talent and too many musical ideas to be confined to a lead line with short breaks thrown in. He needed much more space to tell his story without a lot of distraction from second and third lines. His groups, small or large, had the job of supporting the soloist, whether Armstrong himself or another musician.

Bix and Tram followed Armstrong's lead on "Singin the Blues." Two of the three 32-bar choruses are solos with support; only one is collectively improvised and even that has an eight-bar break. While Bix and Tram followed Armstrong, they did not slavishly imitate him. They had their own style quite distinguishable from Armstrong's.

That Bix and Tram did "Singin the Blues" at all demonstrates an important lesson about jazz. They came from the wrong end of the river—Bix from Davenport, Iowa and Tram from Carbondale, Illinois. Neither was poor, neither was black, nor as far as I know neither had ever been anywhere near New Orleans. Beiderbecke, self-taught on cornet and piano, listened to jazz by the Original Dixieland Jass Band and the New Orleans Rhythm Kings. I don't know who Tram listened to. He came from a musical family and formed his first band in St. Louis while still a teenager. Well before they recorded "Singin the Blues," both Bix and Tram had their own styles, and both knew where Armstrong was coming from. The lesson: Jazz has room for anyone with a good story to tell and an interesting way to tell it. Or to quote trumpeter Clark Terry: "A note doesn't care who plays it."

"Singin the Blues" starts off with a four-bar ensemble introduction at medium tempo. The group drops out and Tram takes the first 32-bar chorus, supported by Eddie Lang doing some very tasty single string guitar work and Paul Mertz supplying rhythm on piano. If Chauncey Morehouse is drumming at all, he is so under-recorded you can't hear him until he hits one lick on the cymbal at the end of the chorus. In effect, you are listening to a trio. Tram sings the blues through a no-longer-made C-Melody sax, a hybrid horn lower in tone than an alto and higher than a tenor. Tram sings and swings so easy, it's like anyone could do it. I can state from experience you have to be really good to make it seem that easy: I played a C-Melody for three years. The group does a few stops where Tram blows some flashy double-time runs, but the overall mood stays very relaxed.

Tram finishes and Bix enters on cornet for his solo with guitar and piano behind him. He embellishes what Tram has laid out in the first chorus. Bix's playing is often described as lyrical and never was he more lyrical than on "Singin the Blues." What a beautiful tone. Jazzman Eddie Condon described Bix's playing as a girl saying "yes." "Singin' the

Blues" is around a three minute "Yes." If Bix lacked Armstrong's technical virtuosity, he had his own sense of delicacy and nuance.

The entire group collectively improvises during the final chorus. Bix, taking the lead, plays very tentatively the first four bars as if he is so overcome by his own solo that he needs a few moments to recover. So the group just has to hang back. However, by the fifth bar, everyone is going full out (not loud, just strong). Jimmy Dorsey on clarinet gets an eight-bar break. The group improvises some more, breaking again for Eddie Lang to execute a nifty little run on guitar. Then the entire ensemble takes it out and a Chauncey Morehouse flick of the cymbal ends it.

It wasn't really the end; it was just the beginning. Many musicians learned "Singin' the Blues" note for note. Lester Young carried the sheet music around in his sax case. Saxophonists Bud Freeman, Benny Carter, and Young all cite Trumbauer as a major influence. Cornet/trumpet players Red Nichols, Jimmy McPartland, Rex Stewart, and Bobby Hackett came under the musical spell of Bix. And these are but a few. Why?

Jazz, in its first twenty-five years, was called "hot music." Bix and Tram were the first "cool" jazz musicians. Both played "flat," with no vibrato (quaver) in their tone. Both played slightly behind the beat, creating that easy laid-back feel. Playing "flat" and behind the beat would eventually become a way of life for Lester Young and others. The legacy of "Singin' the Blues" is still with us in jazz today.

One question remains: Are Bix and Tram singing a happy blues or a sad blues? On the surface, the song sounds happy. Its easy-going swing and beautiful melody are indeed infectious. But maybe, in the words of an old blues line, they're laughin' just to keep from cryin'. Maybe not laughing so much but rather smiling a sad sort of smile. There's one note in Bix's solo that knocks my socks off—the first note of the "bridge" in bar 17. It's a leaping semi-growl, which in those days was called a "rip." Is that rip a happy, primitive Walt Whitman sort of yawp? Or is it a note of protest at Fate? Bix would be buried four years later in 1931, having drunk himself to death at the ripe old age of 28. Happy or sad? You have to draw your own conclusion.

One thing I believe: If you listen to the song a few times, you'll be "Singin' the Blues" for the rest of your life.

CHAPTER 3
KIPPIE MOEKETSI-DOLLAR BRAND
"MEMORIES OF YOU"

https://www.youtube.com/watch?v=xku-GR2bREA

have this recurring nightmare. The house is on fire. I get the kids out and rush back in to save my music. I'm staring at 2000 tapes and 700 CDs. Which to take? I can't make up my mind. First, I grab the Kippie Moeketsi with Dollar Brand and, as the flames engulf me, I wake up.

Kippie Moeketsi? Who is Kippie Moeketsi? Back in the 1980s I'd never heard of him either. A fellow had come down from Nairobi to help us out with a program design. Like me, he was a music freak who brought his Walkman to the office. I was checking out his tapes and saw one titled *Dollar Brand + 3 with Kippie Moeketsi.* (Brand has since changed his name to Abdullah Ibrahim, but I'll use the name on the album.) I asked to borrow it for a listen. The first track is "Rollin" and I'm rolling along with it while I go about my work. Then comes "Memories of You." Within seconds the hair on the back of my neck is standing up and I have goose bumps all over. I stop working. I'm frozen. The track ends. I rewind the tape and listen again. Then I'm out of my chair and down the hall, begging our visitor to let me have the tape for one night to make a copy.

I started consulting my books on music and every South African I met about Kippie Moeketsi. I have precious little to show for my effort. Even Wikipedia has a mere four short paragraphs. Briefly: Kippie Moeketsi played alto sax. He was in a group called the Jazz Epistles with Dollar Brand and Hugh Masekela in 1960-61. Brand and Masekela both cite Moeketsi as an influence. He died at the age of 58, broke and bitter. *African Rock,* a book by Chris Stapleton and Chris May, states that Kippie Moeketsi was South Africa's greatest alto sax player. I would go further. I would say Kippie is one of the finest saxophonists I've ever heard, though my evidence is scant. Forget which sax or which country. The man is just plain great. I guess the jazz fans in South Africa agree. They named a Johannesburg club "Kippie's"—like Birdland in New York, named after Charlie Parker.

I should urge everyone to run out and buy some Kippie Moeketsi right now. Good for your ears, good for your soul. Even after all these years of looking, I have very little Kippie Moeketsi on tape and CD (Abdullah Ibrahim's *Africa Sun* has four tracks from *Dollar Brand + 3* with Kippie Moeketsi. The same four tracks are on YouTube under Kippie Moeketsi.) I hope this little piece will be the start of a campaign —Moeketsi for the Masses!

Better still we need an African Jazz for All campaign. Most of the world is missing out on some great jazz from Africa—especially, but not limited to, South Africa. At the time the Jazz Epistles were playing, another group called the Blue Notes were also on the scene, made up of Chris McGregor on piano, trumpeter Mongezi Feza, Dudu Pumwani on alto sax, bassist Johnny Dyani, and drummer Louis Moholo. As a result of Apartheid government hassles because McGregor was white in an otherwise black group, they moved *en masse* to the United Kingdom and changed their name to Brotherhood of Breath. Check out the album *Country Cooking*—fine sounds. If singer Sibongile Khumalo lived in New York City, we would talk about her in the same sentence as Ella Fitzgerald and Sarah Vaughan. Tenorman Basil Coetzee earned the nickname "Manenberg" from his playing with Abdullah Ibrahim on that song. If you can find the Paul Simon *Graceland* concert in Zimbabwe with Miriam Makeba and Hugh Masekela, you will almost certainly be impressed with the backup band led by guitarist Ray Phiri. Saxophonist Barney Rachabane does a fine solo behind Hugh Masekela singing "Coal Train." The bass intro by Bakithi Kumalo to "Boy in the Bubble" is worth the whole video. I could write pages on jazz in Africa, but this is about "Memories."

The Moeketsi-Brand version of "Memories of You" froze me to my earphones because it came as an absolute shock. It was like plunging into a pool of ice cold water. In my mind "Memories of You" had always been associated with Benny Goodman and Lionel Hampton. Theirs was the definitive version to me and they have some very pleasant memories to relate at an easy-going swing tempo. Not Moeketsi and Brand. Moeketsi's *memories* are of anguish, torment, and pain. We get five minutes of exquisite misery. Exquisite because the playing is so beautiful, so intense, and because underlying it all, we find, much to our surprise, love. Only love can cause this much suffering.

Without doubt this is Moeketsi's song. These are his memories. But Dollar Brand supports him throughout in this duo performance. Brand is like your best friend, the one you pour your grief out to, the strong shoulder you lean on when you just can't make it on your own.

Brand introduces the number on piano. There is no set rhythm, rather a felt pulse to the song. It's as if Brand's piano is saying, "You look troubled, my friend. What's on your mind?" Kippie answers on alto sax, "Memories," by stating eight bars of the original melody, but after that he's creating his own lines with only brief references to the song as pianist Eubie Blake composed it.

In the second verse, Kippie breaks down moaning and sobbing. This turns to wails and screams in the bridge. He refers briefly to the melody again at the beginning of the final eight-bar verse but then is racked with agony. He plays a three-note phrase twelve times. This leads to an outpouring of grief.

Then Kippie goes back to the bridge so intensely gripped by pain you can barely listen to it... the sounds of distress, despair, misery. Brand rolls in on piano to support Kippie. The piano seems to call, "I'm here… take it easy." Moeketsi calms down, but only for a few bars. Then, unaccompanied, he builds up to a lonely, anguished scream. As he backs down, Brand catches him for the final note.

And it is not a note of resolution. No, it's just that this intensity can't go on. You are profoundly disturbed. What are these memories and when will they cease?

I can only guess. "Memories of You," as done by Moeketsi and Brand, is about South Africa. I repeat a quote by South African guitarist Kenny Mathaba contained in *African Rock*:

"The greatest difficulty is apartheid.... If you don't go along with it, you starve. Those that have resisted, they can't go on.... Kippie Moeketsi wouldn't take such jobs [poorly paid studio work]. He died penniless. Apartheid kills so much talent: people pass away unnoticed." The memories Moeketsi plays are about the nation he loves being torn apart by fear, hate, and racism. South Africa's apartheid system destroyed Kippie Moeketsi, as it did so many others, but it couldn't destroy his music.

When you hear "Memories of You," I believe you will agree that Kippie Moeketsi left an enduring monument of greatness. Fear and hatred cannot destroy that.

CHAPTER 4
THELONIOUS MONK
MISTERIOSO

https://www.youtube.com/watch?v=S8RDAjKYHC0

J azz musicians use their instruments as their voices. They can coax a whole range of sounds from their instruments. They growl, sob, moan, laugh, wail, scream. Some can make their instruments talk. Among them are Joe "Tricky Sam" Nanton (trombone); Cootie Williams (trumpet); and Johnny Hodges (sax). These are all with the Duke Ellington Orchestra. Guitarist Wes Montgomery, reedman Eric Dolphy, and many others can make their instruments "talk." They do this through a variety of techniques, one of which is bending notes. Either they start below or above the note and slide into it, or they hit the note straight on and slide off it. You can bend all horns, all strings; you can even bend drums, and harmonica players bend notes as a matter of course. You can bend notes on almost any instrument except the piano.

The piano is a "tempered" instrument. Each note is precisely tuned to half tones: A, B-flat, B, C, D-flat, D, E-flat, E, F, G-flat, G, A-flat, A.

Not a bloody thing the pianist can do about it. You simply can't mess with the notes on a piano, and no one ever tried. That is, no one tried until Thelonious Sphere Monk. Like every musician aspiring to greatness, he needed his own "voice." A listener should know this is Monk "talking." Monk wanted to bend notes on a piano. If he couldn't actually bend notes, he would imply bends. He would strike two keys simultaneously a half-tone apart to substitute for the bent note in between. This produces dissonance—an unharmonious, harsh sound. Classical composers had used dissonance. Duke Ellington employed it. But Monk made a habit of dissonance. People said, "This cat is weird," or "Monk plays funny." Some thought he was making mistakes. No doubt Monk did make mistakes. All musicians hit a "clam" now and then. But Monk knew exactly what he was doing. And he continued doing it until the world understood. Nowadays everyone does Monk, but nobody does Monk as well as Monk did Monk.

Monk not only invented a new approach to the piano, he also composed a number of songs that are now considered classics. The most classic of all his classics is "'Round Midnight," the most recorded song by a jazz composer. I must have 50 versions of it, including some vocal versions. That number is so rich, lends itself so well to individual creativity, that you can hear it again and again and never get tired of it. If Monk had done nothing but compose "Round Midnight," he would rank in the pantheon of jazz. But he also composed many other jazz classics. Had he only left us with his piano technique and compositions, it would have been enough.

But Monk also came up with a new concept of rhythm. Whereas other jazz musicians play ahead and behind the beat, Monk played so far ahead or behind he would create a rhythm within the rhythm. So many things are happening when Monk plays (even solo) that it's hard to keep up. John Coltrane said that working with Monk required complete concentration —if you let up, it was like walking into an empty elevator shaft. I bridle at the word genius; it has been overused into meaninglessness. But if Mozart was a genius, Monk was a genius.

We can hear an example of what Monk could do with rhythm on a 1957 album by Sonny Rollins titled *Sonny Rollins Volume 2* (but no Volume 1). It's an all-star line-up: JJ Johnson on trombone, Percy Heath of the Modern Jazz Quartet on bass, and Art Blakey on drums, with both Monk and the great Horace Silver on piano. They do Monk's composition "Misterioso." It begins with Monk stating the theme; then a repeat of the theme with the horns joining. Rollins wails for three choruses. Monk only plays for two. Then JJ Johnson starts his solo and something changes in the rhythm. You feel it immediately. Horace Silver has taken over at the piano now. Silver swings (Silver always swings) but it's less jagged, less quirky, no more elevator shaft.

I truly love "Misterioso," which is the reason I chose it over other Monk tunes I also love: "Round Midnight," "Evidence," "In Walked Bud," "Well, You Needn't," "Straight No Chaser," "Bemsha Swing," "Crepuscule for Nellie," "Blue Monk," "Rhythm-a-ning," "Brilliant Corners," "Bright Mississippi," "Friday the 13th," and a dozen or so others. "Misterioso" is simultaneously simple and quirky—a lot like its author.

Monk only composed 80 songs, but he recorded some of them many times, including "Misterioso." I've already mentioned the version with Sonny Rollins. The original "Misterioso" in 1948 had Milt Jackson on vibes. A solo version of "Misterioso" would be ideal. Monk did solo versions of some of his songs but not this one. I chose a live version from 1963 with tenor saxophonist Charlie Rouse, bassist Butch Warren, and drummer Frankie Dunlop, because Monk plays five choruses.

Monk starts off alone with the catchy little theme, seems nothing more than a finger exercise. He begins on the first note of the B-flat scale, jumps to the sixth, comes back to the second note and jumps to the seventh, and so on. The sort of piece you might assign a second-year piano student to work on. Having completed the first chorus solo, Monk does the theme again with Rouse and the rhythm section.

Then Rouse takes over on sax. You may realize for the first time "Misterioso" is a regular 12-bar, B-flat blues... sort of. Nothing is regular about Monk. Charlie Rouse plays seven choruses of some nice blues here but check out Monk on piano behind him. In the first chorus he does some strange comping (accompaniment), even quoting another of his compositions, "Blue Monk," and ending the chorus with a Monkish parody of hokey blues cliché. In Rouse's second chorus, he plays fewer notes. In the third he plays minimalist chords and drops out altogether by bar 7. What was he doing for the rest of the sax solo? Maybe Monk was doing a strange little Monk dance, not unusual for Monk. Maybe he was contemplating The Great Misterioso. Or maybe he was just giving Rouse some room to stretch out.

Now comes the really good part. Monk starts the first chorus of his solo with some double time tiptoeing, like a cartoon mouse out of his hole, looking for the cheese. Forget the bar lines. He's so far ahead of the bars and changes that the rhythm section has to block him out or they may fall into that empty elevator shaft Coltrane warned musicians about. Monk ends the chorus somewhere in the first bar of the second chorus—and I thought he was ahead. How did he get behind like that?

He takes what's left of the second chorus with mostly one hand. (The other readjusting his funny little hat?) He switches from right to left and winds up down at the bottom of the keyboard about two bars before the rhythm section gets there so he messes around on the low notes waiting for them to catch up. He becomes so impatient he starts the third chorus in the last bar of the second chorus.

What's he doing? The first chorus is twelve and a half, the second runs ten and a half, which means the third must be 13 bars. Is he making a mockery of 12-bar blues? Well, no, he's making a Monkery. It averages 12 bars, doesn't it?

His minimalist fourth chorus bespeaks a possible debt to Count Basie. (Maybe he picked up "less is more" from the Count; maybe it came to him in a dream. With Monk you never know.) We get some serious block chords in the fourth chorus ending on one of Monk's "wrong" notes.

I really love the fifth chorus that starts in the last bar of the fourth chorus, but we should be used to that by now. It's a veritable mini-concerto of "wrong" notes. Oh, but those wrong notes are so right. You can't say, "Right on, Monk"; you should say "Right off!" Many considered Monk a write-off. But he kept right on being right off until they caught on to his catch-up right-off far-out up-behind down-and-in under-over 100 percent Monk style music.

When you finish listening to Monk, you may find something has changed. You hear sound anew; you may even see differently. As Monk freed the piano from its tempered prison, so he has liberated you. And if we could somehow call Monk back from the grave and ask him what all this means, he might just say, "... ... ... Misteri-OO-so... ... ..."

CHAPTER 5
CHARLIE PARKER
"SALT PEANUTS"

https://www.youtube.com/watch?v=JcNkCG7A558

Hearing Charlie Parker blow alto saxophone the first time is like being hit by a brick between the ears. The particular brick that hit me was "Salt Peanuts," and it changed everything.

Until that day jazz for me meant Louis Armstrong, Duke Ellington, Count Basie, Benny Goodman, Bix and Tram, and Paul Desmond with the Dave Brubeck Quartet. "Salt Peanuts" was not Dixieland or swing or cool. Rather it is one of the early songs in a style that got tagged with a funny name—"bebop." Bebop in the mid-1940s caused the biggest fuss in jazz up to that time.

There was no hue and cry in 1900 when ragtime, brass band marches, blues, and church spirituals fused into a new style of music in New Orleans. Twenty-five years later when Louis Armstrong laid down the foundations for swing, no one was outraged. But when Charlie

Parker and Dizzy Gillespie released "Salt Peanuts" in 1945, it was like the sky was falling.

Bandleader Cab Calloway called it "Chinese music." Tommy Dorsey claimed, "Bebop has set music back twenty years." Critic Sigmund Spaeth said it was "the distortion of jazz." Writer Rudi Blesh went Spaeth one better by declaring, "Bebop is not jazz at all." Producer Norman Granz stated flatly, "Jazz in New York (i.e., bebop) stinks!"

What's all the hubbub, bub? Up until bebop came along, most jazz musicians considered themselves entertainers, part of the show business community. Armstrong mugged and rolled his eyes, Goodman played his latest hits for the jitterbug crowd, and Calloway sang "Minnie the Moocher" with the audience repeating "Hidee-Hidee-Hidee-Ho" every show. And back in Calloway's trumpet section was young John Birks Gillespie thinking there must be something more than Hidee-Ho five shows a night, six nights a week, 50 weeks a year. He wanted to play jazz, not Hidee-Ho. So Gillespie and like-minded young jazzmen, such as Thelonious Monk, guitarist Charlie Christian, and drummer Kenny Clarke, started getting together in a little joint up in Harlem called Minton's Playhouse, working out a new way to play jazz.

Enter Charlie Parker, who had his epiphany at 19 while playing the chord changes to a very popular swing piece titled "Cherokee" (so he claimed). Parker and Gillespie worked together for several years, defining, refining, expanding, demanding, destroying, creating. By 1945 they were ready to start a revolution.

The first thing most people think of bebop is that it's often played at ferocious tempos, I mean so fast it's almost impossible to count. But that wasn't new. A lot of swing musicians could also play really fast. Music writers may state that bebop expanded jazz's harmonic structure, which is true, but so did Duke Ellington even before bebop came along. Where bebop really changed jazz was at its most fundamental point—

the rhythm. We go back to New Orleans again. Jazz evolved from brass bands playing "When the Saints Go Marching In," two-beat syncopated marches. This degenerated into a kind of jerky doo-wacka-doo until Armstrong evened it out and made it swing. Basie took swing's four-to-the-bar to its ultimate chunk-chunk-chunk-chunk glory.

Kenny Clarke, the founding father of bebop rhythm, divided the four into a lightning eight played on his big cymbal, so smoothed out that it became more of a constant sizzle: szszszsz. He turned the steady four over to the bassist. That freed him to use the rest of his kit to place rhythmic accents wherever he chose: the occasional boom of his bass drum, the crack of his snare drum, the pop of his tom-toms—on the beat, off the beat, between beats. And bop pianists like Bud Powell, Al Haig, and Duke Jordan would also eschew a steady four. Instead, they would "feed" chords with the left hand (or sometimes with both hands) when they felt the music needed some extra oomph. To those used to doo-wacka-doo, chunk-chunk-chunk-chunk, and Hidee-Ho, it probably did seem like Chinese music. But in fact, all this random accenting lightened the rhythm, making it freer.

If you can accept my premise that jazz is about freedom, then bebop was a giant leap forward down the freedom road. And freest of them all was Bird. Charlie Parker did not acquire his nickname from the way he played. But his music soars. He swoops, he dives, he climbs, he glides. No one ever before flew as high and free as Bird.

He could play at blinding speed. He could play beautiful ballads. He could really get down on the blues. He could play anything. And even at Mach 2, he played with such lyricism, such feeling, it was at the time as far out as you could take music. Most ears weren't ready for Bird's trip in the mid-1940s. What most jazz listeners today take as given was a very radical departure from the standard of its day. But a few young dudes were ready. Parker showed them the route to follow and off they went, with Bird as their guide.

We encounter problems here when we try to separate the music, the man, and the myth. When some people discuss Charlie Parker, they move us out of music and into the realm of theology. Still, Bird was something of a musical deity. Some say that at the moment he died, aged 34 in March 1955, there was a clap of thunder. It is also said that the very next day, graffiti appeared on walls all over New York City as if by magic: BIRD LIVES!

For a while Bird had a disciple named Dean Benedetti who decided that his mission in life was to capture for posterity every note that came out of Charlie Parker's alto saxophone. Between March 1947 and July 1948 he recorded 461 Parker solos, one lasting a mere three seconds. But when I write that he recorded Parker solos, I mean he recorded *only* Parker solos; he never bothered to tape any of the other players, only the notes of his idol Bird mattered.

Nothing better illustrates the extreme reverence in which Bird was held than his 1946 recording of "Lover Man." Strung out from failing to get a fix, Parker's playing had some fairly horrible moments, yet producer Ross Russell released it anyhow. And Bird acolytes copied it note-for-note, including the squeaks. Whatever Bird did was IT.

Yet the man who did much to create modern jazz did not get off to a promising start. He begged his mother (who spoiled him rotten) to buy him a sax when he was 13. It sat gathering dust for two years till Charlie finally got interested in playing. But when he got interested, jazz became his obsession. He joined a school group called the Deans of Swing. Then he dropped out of school to go into the professional bands. Although he never had a formal music lesson in his life, he pestered anyone he felt had something to offer. He got practical and theory "lessons" from several Kansas City alto players including his band leader Tommy Douglas and the great Buster "Prof" Smith, whom he unashamedly copied.

At 18, Bird left Kansas City, first for Chicago then New York, where he took the only non-musical job in his life as a dishwasher in a club. That allowed him to hear pianist Art Tatum perform there every night for three months. It was during this time—1939—that the aforementioned epiphany occurred that eventually would lead to bebop. Yet even so, it would take another five years of exploring, developing, and practicing—alone and with others—before Parker was really ready to literally blow the world of jazz apart. In all, this "inspired genius" spent ten intensive years concentrating on almost nothing other than playing the alto saxophone... and shooting junk into his arm.

There are many great jazz musicians from all eras and all styles of jazz. A few are essential. Very select individuals might even be called indispensable. Louis Armstrong, Duke Ellington, and Charlie Parker are the holy trinity: without them, jazz would not sound the way it does.

I chose "Salt Peanuts" because it was that brick between my young impressionable ears: duh-dududuh-duh-dut-dah duh-Duh duh- Duh... Salt PEAnuts Salt PEAnuts. Every time I warm up on the sax, I go duh-dududuh-duh-dut-dah duh-Duh duh-Duh... Salt PEAnuts Salt PEAnuts. Dizzy Gillespie composed "Salt Peanuts," based on the chord changes to "I Got Rhythm." Coleman Hawkins originally recorded it as a swing piece in 1944. A year later Dizzy and Bird did it THEIR way—bebop. The version I first heard comes off the album *Historical Recordings*—a performance at the Royal Roost on December 12, 1948, with a young Miles Davis on trumpet. But in 2005 a CD of a June 1945 Town Hall Concert came out with Bird and Diz doing Salt Peanuts that is even better with pianist Al Haig, bassist Curley Russell, and bebop master-drummer Max Roach.

The introduction to "Salt Peanuts" is like the blasting cap that triggers an explosion. You're slammed back in your seat immediately, and this is just the beginning four bars. Hold on tight. It's faster than a speeding bullet, more powerful than a locomotive. Look up in the sky. It's Bird. It's Diz. It's BEBOP!

Drummer Max Roach begins at about 260 beats per minute. (Try counting from 1 to 15 in three seconds.) The group joins for four bars or so and then Parker and Gillespie hit the theme in unison: duh-dududuh-duh-dut-dah duh-Duh duh-Duh... Salt PEAnuts Salt PEAnuts. I can barely hum it as fast as they play it, and they do it together... for two full choruses. Bird plays it; Diz sings (?) it. The two do a few bars to introduce Al Haig's piano solo. Haig proves that white guys can bop with the best of them—his fingers fairly fly over the keys.

Diz plays a few notes, Bird repeats them note-for-note; Diz plays a few more, Bird repeats them. They get higher and wilder. It's like Irving Berlin's song, "Anything You Can Do, I Can Do Better." I'd say it's a toss-up.

Then Bird launches himself into the void. I can't begin to describe in words what Bird plays, so I won't. Bird's solo takes the music to the "edge." Great jazz is played on the edge, an almost indefinable place between what is possible and what is impossible. And the great jazz musicians go there to move the edge farther out. Bird plays rhythm beyond rhythm, technique beyond technique, sound beyond sound. Every jazz musician who picked up an instrument after 1945 would be affected by what Charlie Parker put down on "Salt Peanuts." Bird took jazz to the Edge and everyone else had to follow. Listening to it may move your edge, just as it did mine.

Then it's Dizzy's turn. He takes it right through the roof. Jazz has had so many great trumpet players that the list would run into the dozens but only three really changed the way jazz is played. First came Louis Armstrong, then Dizzy, and following right behind was Miles Davis.

And Gillespie had a tremendous influence on Miles because Davis knew he could never play virtuoso trumpet like Diz so he had to find another direction to go. When this version of "Salt Peanuts" was performed, Miles was still hangin' out, but he would shortly replace Dizzy when Diz decided to form a big band. Miles would play on many of Bird's most important recordings from 1946 to 1948.

When Gillespie finishes, Max Roach takes a chorus, managing somehow at the end to play a few phrases of the "Salt Peanuts" theme on his snare and bass drums. Then Parker and Gillespie do a short restatement of the intro to end it. You've just experienced the brick. How's your pulse? I can't begin to estimate how many hundreds of times I've listened to "Salt Peanuts." I use it as my ringtone. And every time it's WHAM! Right between the ears.

"Salt Peanuts" and bebop changed jazz forever. Rhythm became more complex. Chord structures became more complex. Notes that before had been considered "wrong" became "right." In addition, bebop changed jazz from dance music to art music. Boppers wanted their music taken seriously, despite the funny name "bebop," which most of the style's practitioners detested. No more jitterbugging, no more eye-rolling, no more Hidee-Ho. You sat and listened to bebop. These were virtuoso musicians playing very difficult pieces. And maybe even more than the music, the musicians (mainly black) wanted respect.

But me... all I want is duh-dududuh-duh-dut-dah duh-Duh duh-Duh... Salt PEAnuts Salt PEAnuts.

CHAPTER 6
LESTER YOUNG-COUNT BASIE
"LESTER LEAPS IN"

https://www.youtube.com/watch?v=f60JYoHdfVM

Lester Young played saxophone all wrong. He played all wrong because he didn't play like Coleman Hawkins. In the 1930s, you played tenor sax like Coleman Hawkins or you played wrong. Simple as that. Hawk was *the* man on tenor saxophone.

Before Coleman Hawkins, the tenor was a joke, used primarily to produce barnyard noises. From the time Hawkins came up with his style, the tenor sax began to dominate jazz. That's what sax players owe to Coleman Hawkins.

Hawkins played HOT. He jumped all over a song, right on top of the rhythm, blowing runs up and down the horn. His tone came out thick with vibrato (quaver). On slow numbers, it was like sliding in new socks over a freshly waxed floor. On fast numbers, he rumbled and boiled like an active volcano. Hawk played rococo saxophone. Hawk played HOT.

Young—or Prez, as he was sometimes called, short for "President," the nickname Billie Holiday gave him—played cooool. He used no vibrato. That produced a light delicate tone. Young laid so far off the beat, some thought he couldn't keep proper time or was lazy. He ran over bar lines with no apparent regard for where he was supposed to be. He played like he had all the time in the world to get to where he was going. And if he knew where he was going, no one else was quite sure. He certainly wasn't going to the same places as Coleman Hawkins. Prez was a gentle man who played a gentle horn. He was also stubborn. People told him he played all wrong. He didn't care. "To each his own," he would say, and kept on playing cooool.

Young joined the Count Basie band in 1936. Maybe Basie hired him because he heard the similarities between Young's style and his own. Basie also laid off the beat when he played solos. Basie used the minimal number of notes to express his musical ideas. Certainly, Basie's piano and Young's sax were not twins, but they were stylistic first cousins. Also, Basie heard the contrast between Young and Herschel Evans, his other tenor saxophonist who played Hawkins-style. Basie would show this contrast by giving each solos. So Evans and Young began to "battle." Evans would go: LA di DAH di DAH DAH DAH. Young would reply: ... laa... di daaaah, and not even bother about di dah dah dah. Evans blasted BOOM BO-BO-BO BOOOM. Young would answer... booo boo-booooooooom. Crowds loved those mock battles. Evans and Young started a tradition in the Basie band of battling tenors. It was carried on through the 1950s by the "Two Franks"—Frank Foster and Frank Wess.

In the late 1930s, Basie had the swingingest of swing bands. "Swing" has to do with timing and rhythm. The title of a 1932 Ellington composition, "It Don't Mean a Thing if it Ain't Got That Swing," enshrined swing as the *sine qua non*. In his turn, Basie got as close to defining swing as anyone has: "Four strong beats to the bar... and no cheatin'." Basie's band never cheated.

Basie had the strongest rhythm section in swing. Basie called it the All-American Rhythm Section: Jo Jones (drums), Walter Page (bass), Freddie Green (guitar), and William "Count" Basie (piano). These four would lock onto a beat like a pit bull and not let up for a second. The other three sections of trombones, trumpets, and reeds did not play like a dozen musicians in a band. They had the agility of a small combo. I mean, these gentlemen played tight. You didn't hear four men in a rhythm section; you heard *rhythm*. You didn't hear five saxophones; you heard one saxophone doing five-part harmony. The title of a 1950s Basie album sums it up: *Sixteen Men Swingin'*. The horn sections would riff behind a soloist. Then they would riff behind each other. They would build riff on top of riff; all the while the Jones-Page-Green-Basie engine room would go chunk-chunk-chunk-chunk—four to the bar... and no cheatin'. All the swing bands did it, but Basie's band DID IT. Check out Basie's signature tune, "One O'Clock Jump." I defy you not to jump. You hear those sections riffing and that rhythm—chunk-chunk-chunk-chunk—and you have got to jump.

"Lester Leaps In" was recorded in 1939 by a contingent of the Basie band under the name of the Kansas City Seven. (Basie, Green, Page, Jones, with Buck Clayton on trumpet, Dicky Wells on trombone, and Lester Young.) This song in all probability is what the Kansas City crowd called a "head" —somebody made up the tune in his head on the spot and everyone else picked up on it immediately. Heads were standard fare in K.C.

Basie and the rhythm section open with four bars at a brisk swing tempo. The group joins to state the simple bluesy eight-bar theme. Basie skips through an eight-bar bridge and the ensemble repeats the theme. Simple but swingin'.

Then Lester leaps in. Even though the tempo is brisk, Prez plays cool as a breeze rolling down 12th Street past the Reno Club in Kansas City. He'll let a whole bar pass without playing a note. He leaves plenty of space, even when he does, little runs up and down the horn. Prez makes it sound so effortless that you think maybe he could go on forever like this. No sweat, just cooool.

When Young completes his two choruses, he and Basie "trade fours." Basie plays a four-bar statement on piano; Young answers with four bars on tenor. "Check this out," plays Basie. "Nice," replies Young, "listen to this." "Here's another for you." "Okay, I got one for you."

Basie takes his solo. He plays lightly and politely. You can hear how well Basie and Young get along musically. Before going into the bridge, the rhythm section does a little stop-time reminiscent of the old New Orleans style breaks. Toward the end of Basie's solo we hear a perfect example of his "less is more" style. He has four bars to dazzle us with speed and technique. What does he do? He lets the first bar pass without playing a note. In the second bar, he plays just two notes— Doo-dup. Another bar of nothing but that chunk-chunk-chunk-chunk rhythm, and then the exact same two notes—Doo-dup. Blows me away every time.

The entire group comes back to state the theme once again and then they take it out with Dixie-style collective improvising. We experience a little piece of jazz history when "Lester Leaps In."

Hawkins was right, so was Young. It is hard, bordering on impossible, to overstate how important these two great musicians were to jazz saxophonists. Almost every sax player who came after initially copied one or the other or a combination of the two. The pair begot their lineages. Along with direct links to Herschel Evans, Ben Webster, and Don Byas, Dr. Hawkins has exerted indirect influence on most power players such as the Texas Tenors—Illinois Jacquet, Arnett Cobb—and to some lesser degree Buddy Tate. Prof. Young heavily affected a young Charlie Parker and an even younger John Coltrane. Paul Quinichette sounded so much like Lester, they called him the "Vice President." There was a whole group of young white tenor saxophonists in the

1940s collectively referred to as the Sons of Lester. Chief among them were Stan Getz and Zoot Sims. Dexter Gordon combined a bit of both Hawkins and Young. So did Sonny Rollins.

In the beginning the Hawk talked. Then Lester leapt in; and we all caught him.

CHAPTER 7
MILES DAVIS
"SO WHAT"

https://www.youtube.com/watch?v=ylXk1LBvIqU

f you've read this far and want to blame someone, the culprit is the late Richard Finley. Dick loved jazz and golf and his wife, not necessarily in that order. But he didn't just love jazz, he wanted everyone to love jazz. So he decided to have a "jazz evening" at his house here in Dar, Tanzania. He would invite a few friends who would invite a few friends, and they would all sit around and listen to jazz for two or three hours. So, he says, "Professor, I need your help." (He called me "Professor" because he considered me knowledgeable about jazz... for a white guy.) We had our jazz evening and around 50 people showed up. Africans, Asians, and Europeans were crammed into every corner of Finley's sitting room while he and I talked about jazz and played selections. It went down so well that we did three more, the last in an auditorium because there were too many people to fit in his house.

Dick Finley loved jazz, but most of all he loved Miles Davis. He told me he wanted to collect every track Miles ever cut. He never got the chance. In 1989, an earthquake in the Philippines took Dick Finley away from us. And I think if I were to write about jazz without some attention to Miles Davis, my man Finley's *kivuli* (spirit) would be on my case forever.

Ah, but which Miles Davis? There are so many to choose from: Bebop Miles with Charlie Parker, Cool Miles, Symphonic Miles with Gil Evans, Modal Miles, or Fusion Miles. In short Miles is styles, many styles. Miles *is* much of jazz history from 1945 on.

Now, Davis didn't "invent" any of these styles. But he took all these styles and molded them with his own unique musical character.

When Davis plays, you immediately know it is Miles, so individual is his "voice," whether on open trumpet, with Harmon mute, or on flugelhorn, the trumpet's lower-range brother. Davis employs "less is more" to stunning effect, creating so much space that even the silence becomes part of his song. He is cool yet intense, strong yet tender. I've read that Davis doesn't have the facility on his horn of a Gillespie, or a Clifford Brown, or that he can't play in the trumpet's upper register. True, he's not a roof-raiser. That written, Miles has been more influential on trumpet than anyone, save maybe Armstrong and Gillespie. And I emphasize "maybe."

How can I choose a Miles tune? Anything off *Birth of the Cool,* those early '50s albums with Sonny Rollins and Jackie McLean, everything with John Coltrane, the three arranged by Gil Evans (I owe my college degree to *Sketches of Spain*), the '60s albums with Wayne Shorter, *Bitches Brew,* and on they go. The only solution to this dilemma of what to choose is to slaughter a pure white cockerel and hope the *kivuli* of Dick Finley will whisper an answer.

Kind of Blue, with John Coltrane, Cannonball Adderley, Bill Evans, Paul Chambers, and Jimmy Cobb. The late Ian Carr, trumpeter and writer, said *Kind of Blue* is "… probably the most influential LP in jazz history." All five tracks are about as close to perfect as music by humans can get. We'll go with Side One, Track 1... "So What." Hey, don't blame me. Take it up with Dick Finley's *kivuli*.

To preface "So What," I want to go back to a statement I made at the beginning of this book: Freedom underlines all jazz. *Kind of Blue* was so influential because it represented another step (a big step) on the road to freedom. It "freed" musicians from chord changes. Instead of following chord changes, Miles and his group play scales (do re mi, etc.) on "So What." This is called "modal," and it allows musicians to greatly expand their creativity, to develop melodic lines. I might add that Davis Miles claimed that all the tracks on *Kind of Blue* were first takes, except "Flamenco Sketches." However it was done, five musical masterpieces were the result.

Paul Chambers and Bill Evans begin "So What" with a rather dark folk-like introduction. The way Chambers' bass leads, follows, and plays along with Evans' piano—if there was no rehearsal—is uncanny. Then Chambers states the eight-bar theme. Chambers "calls," Evans "responds" with two notes that sound like "so what." Jimmy Cobb taps lightly on the big cymbal. In the second verse, Chambers calls, and the three horns join Evans in the response, "so what." Except, and this is important, the horns drop out the last bar of the verse, leaving only Evans to respond, "so what." This creates surprise and tension. You expect a full "so what"; you only get Evans on piano. To push the intensity, drummer Cobb has added a second cymbal. Up they go a half-step into the bridge, Chambers calling and the group responding, "so what," except for the last bar when Evans plays alone. Then back down a half-step for the last eight bars. Cobb is really pushing that cymbal now.

Chambers calls: I really got the lonesome blues.... Group responds: So what

Chambers: I really got the lonesome blues now.... Group: So what

Chambers: I really got the lonesome blues... ... ... Group: So what

Chambers: They're killin' me now... ... ... Evans: So what

(I wrote my lousy lyrics before hearing the words that Eddie Jefferson put to "So What.")

Cobb finally lets loose on the drum kit to introduce Miles' two chorus solo, and Paul Chambers starts walking the bass. He doesn't walk straight up and down; he makes harmonic side-steps that enhance the melody line. Evans lays out a carpet of rich tone textures for Miles to move around on.

And what does Davis play while this is happening? Davis plays himself. He is not jive. Miles does not play jive music. Every note, every space, every tone, every silence is meant, is honest, is Miles Davis. Miles could rock a baby to sleep with one hand while punching out the Devil with the other. He starts ahead of the first bar with some very subdued blowing. Before long he's laying back behind the beat creating tension and moving up the horn for intensity. But he backs off, lets a bar pass in silence, bends notes for bluesy effect. He really hits a note up, falls off it, plays down at the bottom, hits another high note loud and holds it this time, only to run back down, but then he's back up. Tension-release. Tension-release. Finally, he moves down the horn, not even bothering with the obvious last note. Which perfectly sets up Coltrane's entrance.

Coltrane takes three steps back (lets the first three beats of the bar pass) and then BAM on four, he kicks out the jams. Miles used Coltrane for contrast the way Charlie Parker used Miles. Miles is quietly intense. Trane is just plain intense, as if his entire existence depends on every note he plays. And the man *plays*. Modal jazz and Coltrane were meant for each other. Freed from chord changes, he can explore new musical territory. He restricts himself to the middle register of his tenor sax and only lets out a few short flurries of notes until the bridge. Then those "sheets of sound" come flying at you. The first one falls. Then he's skipping up the horn and... Dweedy dwee-dee on high notes that tenor saxes aren't supposed to produce. He tumbles down toward the bottom and then... dweee. Run up. Roll Off. Tension-release. Splits. Sheets. Tension-release. Trane glides down one last time, echoing Miles' final bars, to open a new door for Cannonball Adderley.

Cannonball rolls in on his alto sax. He waits even less time than Coltrane to let it rip. Julian "Cannonball" Adderley played in Davis' group from 1957 to 1959. *Kind of Blue* was his last album before forming a new quintet with his brother Nat. And what a way to exit. To the earlier influence of Charlie Parker, Cannonball picked up some elements of Coltrane's style and added his own approach to the blues. Give Cannonball Adderley some blues, and he can really whip it on you, light yet funky, sometimes even FONky. And this he proceeds to do in his solo. At one point during his second chorus, he repeats practically note-for-note a statement Miles played in his solo. "Hey, dig this, Miles." Cannonball rolls out. And... ...

All three horns take up the two notes, "so what." Only now it's not a response; it's a call, played at the beginning of the line. The horns call, and Bill Evans responds on the piano with light, lush block chords. Cobb backs off the snare, which he's been using to great effect throughout the three horn solos, to only a light tap every fourth beat. "So what," call the horns; Evans comments. I can't hear any blues at all in what he plays. But he uses harmonic voicings that other pianists would immediately pick up after "Kind of Blue." Evans plays his one chorus solo using very few single notes from the right hand; rather block chords or Monk-like combinations—"wrong" notes that are oh-so right. All the while, the horns call to him, "so what."

Then Chambers improvises for eight bars while Evans, on his own, responds with "so what." Chambers has his little story to tell on bass and, as always, he tells it well. Then he returns to the theme.

They finish the chorus this way—Chambers calling, the group

responding, "so what." And the song fades out. A nine-minute master-piece on a landmark album.

Davis would go on to make other landmark albums. Coltrane would also make some landmarks of his own, as would Evans and Adderley. Chambers set new standards for bass players. And Jimmy Cobb is still tap-ta-ta-tapping.

After 65 years on the planet and 45 years in the limelight, Miles Davis left this earth to play with Gabriel in 1991. His last recording began to explore a fusion of jazz and hip-hop. He was playing as coolly and intensely as ever, rocking babies and punching out Devils. And wherever Dick Finley currently hangs out, I hope this piece meets with his approval and his *kivuli* leaves me to sleep easy at night.

CHAPTER 8
BILLIE HOLIDAY
"FINE AND MELLOW"

https://www.youtube.com/watch?v=YKqxG09wlIA

began *The 101 Best Jazz Albums* by Len Lyons with more than a few reservations. Here we go again with ranking. I definitely have no use for *the* best, *the* greatest, *the* Number One, and I'm about to read the "101 Best." Why not 100? Why not 1001 like Dave Marsh ranks rock and soul? What would have been 102? No, I probably wasn't going to like this book.

Had I checked out the subtitle, *A History of Jazz on Records,* I might have felt somewhat less mistrustful. In fact, Lyons does a bang-up job, and even this Missouri-native skeptic has to admit that he can't find much fault with the 101 selections. Lyons even includes one of my favorite singers, Mose Allison, who hardly ever gets a mention. But then Lyons omits another favorite, Joe Williams. Lyons has given us an excellent jazz primer. If you own a selection of these 101 albums, you have a pretty fair sample of jazz from the beginning to the end of the 1970s.

One interesting feature is his inclusion of nine women: Bessie Smith, Billie Holiday, Ella Fitzgerald, Sarah Vaughan, Carmen McRae, Betty Carter, Annie Ross, Toshiko Akiyoshi, and Flora Purim. Granted, Bessie Smith could just have easily been labeled a blues artist instead of jazz; and Ross, Akiyoshi, and Purim are all included as members of groups. Nine out of 101 is not a great representation, to be sure. But part of the issue may be that men far outnumbered women players over the years. So nine out of 101 may not be so bad. I have read plenty of other writers on jazz, including some women, who don't even come close to Lyons' female-male ratio in their compilations. I could fault him for excluding Mary Lou Williams... but hey, that's just me.

Equally interesting, I think, is that eight of the nine women are vocalists and Akiyoshi is a pianist. If I estimate that 90 percent of the women in jazz are either vocalists, pianists, or both, I am probably on the low side. Of course, there are some outstanding exceptions. To name a few: guitarists Emily Remler and Mimi Fox; saxophonists Jane Ira Bloom, Melissa Aldana, and Lakecia Benjamin; trumpeter Ingrid Jensen; trombonist Melba Liston; bassist Esperanza Spalding (who also sings); drummers Terri Lyne Carrington and Allison Miller. I've left out many others but most women in jazz are either singers or keyboard players.

No doubt there's a reason why most female jazz artists are vocalists, pianists, or both, and it probably has to do in part with wrong-headed male perceptions of what a woman's role in music ought to be. It's one thing for a man to get outplayed by a woman pianist—and Mary Lou Williams could outplay just about anyone. It is quite another to be outdone in a sax duel with Melissa Aldana. I will leave that discussion to others better qualified than I am while I do a little dealing on Lady Day—Billie Holiday.

Most people have their ups and downs in life. Billie Holiday had mostly downs, mostly caused by men. She may have been a victim of child rape, she was a prostitute before most girls learn the facts of life, and was used and abused by more men than you can shake half a dozen large sticks at. She was a heroin addict and an alcoholic. And if that wasn't enough misery for any dozen humans, she suffered the outrageous indignity of getting arrested on her deathbed in 1959 at the age of 44. Billie Holiday was also one of the greatest jazz vocalists of all time—some would insist the greatest.

If you haven't heard Lady Day (the name given to her by Lester Young who called everyone—female or male—"Lady" something), you may not agree with this assessment on a first listening. For many, she, like fine whiskey, is an acquired taste. By pop standards, Holiday possessed almost no tools of the trade. She had a very limited vocal range, was unable to sustain pitch, and her tone was, shall we say, unusual. But pop singing is not jazz singing. Some jazz singers can do pop; very few pop singers can hope to do jazz. Jazz singers bring to their craft all the skills jazz instrumentalist have: an ability to improvise, an acute sense of timing and rhythm labeled "swing," and most of all the fine art of telling a story in an interesting way. These Billie Holiday had in abundance. Her vocals were the equivalent of Louis Armstrong's trumpet (with less range). In fact, she claimed she learned to sing from listening to Satchmo.

At her best, Holiday was about as good as jazz singing gets. Not surprisingly given a life full of abuse, she didn't always perform at her best. "Fine and Mellow," from a December 1957 television program on jazz, is definitely not her best and not even indicative of the material she normally sang. She took—or was given—most of her material from pop songs and standards. Some of it was fairly lightweight stuff, but Lady Day could turn such pabulum into milk of the gods. If I were to select Holiday at her best, I would go for the desperation of "Don't Explain," or the powerful "Strange Fruit," or that most Lady-like number, "God Bless the Child":

Them that's got shall get, them that's not
    shall lose
So the Bible says and it still is news
Papa may have, Mama may have
God bless the Child that's got his own...
That's got his own

All three of the above are nothing less than masterpieces. They illustrate a consummate jazz artist at the peak of perfection. I find it beyond my power to imagine anyone, and I mean anyone, doing "Explain," "Fruit," or "Child" at that level... and many have tried. They made the mold with Billie Holiday and then they broke it. Others may be as superb in their ways as she was in hers. But her way was hers alone; there's only one Lady Day.

Billie Holiday went on television in December 1957 a shattered, battered woman. Her voice was shot, her body was shot, and her life would soon be over. She had been selected along with other jazz giants —and some of lesser stature—to do their music on what would be the finest presentation of jazz on television up to that point. Her "backing group" consisted of, among others, Coleman Hawkins, Roy Eldridge on trumpet, and most especially Lester Young, Lady's long-time friend and musical colleague. Although many thought they were lovers, Prez maintained that their relationship was platonic. Anyone with ears and a sense of jazz can tell that Holiday sang the way Lester played, without vibrato and by laying off the beat. The critical similarity was that both understated their stories, maybe Billie even more than Lester. "Hush now, don't explain/You are my joy and pain." Is she singing joyfully or painfully? Not on the outside. It all comes from inside. And Holiday's understated stories scream louder, contain more power, than those of any shouters.

Holiday couldn't shout if she wanted; she didn't have the pipes.

And that sets her apart from most jazz greats. She did more with less than any of them did. Young could have done more, Miles Davis could have done more, and even the self-deprecating Count Basie could have done more. All made conscious decisions to understate, to play less and get more. Holiday didn't have the natural vocal skills of Ella Fitzgerald or Sarah Vaughan, but she had so much music in her, the natural vocal business hardly counts.

So here we have a Lady Day in serious decline doing "Fine and Mellow" on national television. It's a simple blues, as if blues done properly is ever simple. (We'll get to more blues later.) I was a young teenager when the program aired but already a budding jazz freak, son of a father who was certifiable on the subject of jazz. I was not about to miss this this opportunity of a short lifetime.

The song begins with the saxes playing a little blues introduction. And then Lady Day explains why "Fine and Mellow" is a blues:

> My man don't love me
> Treats me oh so mean...
> He's the meanest man
> That I've ever seen.

The way she sings, "oh so mean," is pure Lady Day. Listen to her phrasing, her timing, the way she slides up to or down from the note.

Then up steps Ben Webster to whip some serious tenor sax gut bucket blues on us. Contrast that solo with the following one by Lester Young—very laid back, very fine and mellow. Which leads Billie to explain what this blues is all about:

> He wears high drape pants
> Stripes are really yellow...
> But when he starts in to love me

He is so fine and mellow.

Only she sings: "he IS so FIIINE and mellllow." That's Billie Holiday and no one else. I would wager any amount at whatever odds that if you gave 100 singers who'd never heard Billie Holiday the sheet music to "Fine and Mellow," none would even come close to singing it the way Lady Day does it.

Next in the song, Vic Dickenson and Gerry Mulligan get lowdown, literally, on trombone and baritone sax.

Billie then continues her dissertation on love:

> Love will make you drink and gamble
> Stay out all night long...
> Love will make you do things
> That you know is wrong.

(That "do" in the third line is pure Lady Day.)

Coleman Hawkins decides to explain how wrong "wrong" can get. Note how much he sounds like Ben Webster, his most ardent disciple, and how different he sounds to Lester Young. Roy Eldridge follows with a trumpet chorus that's so nice he does it twice.

Then we get to the crux of the song and Billie Holiday's life:

> Treat me right baby
> I'll stay home every day...
> But you're so mean to me baby,
> I know you're gonna drive me away.

Does Billie Holiday have a broken heart? You *know* she does. She's bleeding all over this song. But the bleeding is internal. Another singer might scream or moan. Not Lady Day. She sits there on her stool and delivers her song, her life, up to the world with such understatement and stoicism. And what's that? I believe she's smiling. She turns toward her old friend and soulmate, Lester Young, and I detect a smile. Not a happy smile, to be sure. Scarcely a smile at all. It's a sad hint of a smile at the corners of her mouth. How can that be? All that pain and misery and she's smiling. That's the blues—the strength of the human spirit to overcome adversity. Billie said, "Anything I do sing, it's part of my life."

And this abused child, teenage prostitute, dopoholic, she conquered all her troubles and sorrow with music. She sang it, and in the singing, she was free from it. And that is how I wish to deal on Lady Day.

CHAPTER 9
DUKE ELLINGTON-PAUL GONSALVES
"DIMINUENDO AND CRESCENDO IN BLUE"

https://www.youtube.com/watch?v=MemoebN05yM

Once in a while all the parts come together in a magic moment of music. Anything can strike the spark. It may start with someone in the band playing a phrase that flips out everybody else. It may come from the drummer giving the rhythm a little extra oomph. Maybe the audience is especially appreciative of what the group is producing that night. Maybe a dancer with particularly fine moves turns everyone on. Whatever kicks it off, such moments are to be treasured. And if perchance those moments get recorded, then we all can share them. Such magic occurred on July 7, 1956 at the Newport Jazz Festival during the Duke Ellington set. Fortunately, the set was recorded. It was the night Paul Gonsalves blew 27 choruses on "Diminuendo and Crescendo in Blue."

To write about Duke Ellington is to write about more than just jazz. He has been called America's greatest composer. Some would go further and submit that Duke Ellington is one of the greatest composers of all time. (I might agree.) His group was not a band but an orchestra doing what the New York Philharmonic or the London Symphony Orchestra do, only more. The "more" is the fact that the men in Duke Ellington's orchestra not only presented music by one of the world's greatest composers, they could create their own music through improvisation. And they could swing like nobody's business. I've written that Count Basie's band epitomized Swing. Duke Ellington's Orchestra epitomized Music.

One of the most often quoted comments on the Duke comes from his long-time collaborator and alter ego Billy Strayhorn: "Ellington plays the piano, but his real instrument is his band." Duke composed pieces for specific members of his orchestra. That was neither new nor particularly remarkable. But when Ellington wrote "Concerto for Cootie," the music was Cootie Williams. "Black, Brown and Beige" is not about "the history of the American negro," it is that history in music. Ellington could turn a 12-bar blues into a symphony. He seemed to bring out the best in every musician who played with him. Duke Ellington, in my thinking, ranks among the greatest musicians of all time. Permit me to label him a genius.

Like other geniuses, Duke had his ups and downs. The early 1950s were particularly down. Drummer Sonny Greer, who had been with Ellington since the beginning, left the group, as did star alto saxophonist Johnny Hodges and trombone mainstay Lawrence Brown. In compensation, tenor saxophonist Paul Gonsalves joined up, having played with the Basie band for three years and Dizzy Gillespie for several months. Gonsalves secured his place in the orchestra with his knowledge of former Ellington great Ben Webster's work. He could definitely deal on "Cottontail" and "Chelsea Bridge." But Gonsalves could also wail on his own. Duke kept his orchestra together in the '50s by the royalties he received from many of his classic pieces. (He wrote around 3000 in, say, 50 years—not all classics to be sure—but enough so that he could have retired any time he wanted without a financial worry. He didn't because, in his own words, "They get all the money; I have all the fun.")

To quote from a "sermon" by Stanley Crouch on the Wynton Marsalis album *The Majesty of the Blues,* Ellington was so consumed by jazz "... this noble sound, this thing of majesty..." that he "... never NEVER came off the road." Duke began performing in clubs back in the early 1920s. His music was for dancers and then cabaret acts. The idea of sitting in a concert hall and just listening to jazz didn't come until much later. But even before then, Ellington, always ahead of his time, was composing "extended pieces." The first of these was "Creole Rhapsody" in 1931. It ran six minutes and filled both sides of a 78 rpm record. Still, most jazz including Duke's material was pop music through the mid-1940s and the advent of bebop. We may marvel at the Ellington Carnegie Hall performance in January 1943, but much more typical was *Duke Ellington at Fargo, 1940: Live!* It was another night on the road. Duke continued on the road until 1973, a year before his death.

Newport, however, was not just another gig. In 1956 Newport was *the* jazz festival. To play Newport was akin to performing in Carnegie Hall. You played your best because you played against the best. The Ellington orchestra was about to show the folks its stuff; Paul Gonsalves was about to blow the solo of a lifetime.

The Ellington set began with "Newport Jazz Festival Suite," an extended composition in three parts that Ellington and Strayhorn wrote especially for the occasion. After the suite, the Ellington orchestra cracked open an old chestnut, "Diminuendo and Crescendo in Blue." For reasons best known to the record's producer, the number ended up last on the record. "Diminuendo and Crescendo in Blue" was first recorded in 1937 as two sides of a 78. Since then, Ellington would pull out one part or the other or sometimes both for live performances.

When Gonsalves was still a relative newcomer, he'd played it once, adding a tenor sax solo connecting the Diminuendo part to the Crescendo part. It had been well received, but the orchestra hadn't played it in five years. When Ellington resurrected it for Newport, he told Gonsalves to play the connecting solo and to play as long as he liked. That little addendum—"play as long as you like"—assured Paul Gonsalves a place among the legends of jazz.

The "Diminuendo," at medium but driving tempo, begins with Ellington on piano backed by James Woode (bass) and Sam Woodyard (drums). After three choruses, the whole orchestra joins with some rather complicated ensemble playing, the lead switching among the sections. Then the saxes call and trumpeter Ray Nance responds. The trombones take over with baritone saxophonist Harry Carney playing a chorus under-mic-ed. I read a comment somewhere that Ellington had two reed sections: the first was five saxophones; the second was Harry Carney all by himself. The orchestra drops out, leaving Ellington and the rhythm section alone for two choruses. On the second chorus, Ellington does a little parody of Count Basie style piano.

And then Gonsalves takes over. His first two choruses sound like he's playing tenor sax in the wrong key; actually, he's messing around with the top intervals in the chord changes which Charlie Parker did as a matter of course. By the sixth chorus, the crowd is beginning to sense something special is happening. And it is.

By the ninth chorus, Gonsalves has stopped playing the music. Music is now playing Gonsalves. This may seem like Zen but it happens. It's happened to me. You go into a trance-like state. You don't know where you are, what time it is, or who's around you. All you hear are sounds coming from somewhere. They're coming from you, but you aren't making them. Something else is making those sounds from inside you. You have become the instrument. Later, Gonsalves told swing chronicler Stanley Dance that he thought he played only a few minutes. I believe he was in a trance of Music.

By the 10th chorus, a young woman named Elaine Anderson can't hold back. She jumps up and starts dancing. By the 18th chorus, the crowd sounds like it is going crazy. By the 22nd chorus, it sounds like sheer pandemonium. But a transported Paul Gonsalves doesn't know about this. Gonsalves isn't at Newport. Music, in the form of Paul Gonsalves, is at Newport. At the end of Chorus 26 and the beginning of Chorus 27, Music holds Gonsalves on one note for over five bars then lets him go.

What happens after that is good but rather anticlimactic. Ellington and the rhythm section run through several modulations or key changes. The orchestra comes back in for the "Crescendo," doing its complex section switches. In the last three choruses, Cat Anderson does his roof-raising trumpet bit. And that's it.

Only it wasn't over. After Newport, Ellington's picture was on the cover of *Time* magazine. The album *Ellington at Newport* became his all-time best seller. And Paul Gonsalves was hounded for the rest of his life to repeat his Newport performance. Gonsalves could fire at will— one night he blew 66 choruses on "Diminuendo and Crescendo in Blue." However, I believe that only that once, on July 7, 1956, did he become Music. Gonsalves died on May 14, 1974. Ellington, the man who freed Gonsalves to "play as long as you like," died 10 days later. But the music didn't die. I'm listening to it right now, the night Paul Gonsalves blew 27 choruses on Duke Ellington's "Diminuendo and Crescendo in Blue."

CHAPTER 10
LOUIS ARMSTRONG
"WEST END BLUES"

https://www.youtube.com/watch?v=4WPCBieSESI

When I was growing up, every kid I knew tried doing Satchmo imitations. Holding an invisible trumpet, they'd open their eyes as wide as possible, get a big smile going, wipe the sweat off their brow with an imaginary handkerchief, and in the lowest, most gravelly voice they could muster sing, "de-bo deedle-la-BOM." One day I asked my younger daughter what she knew about Louis Armstrong. She replied, "de-bo deedle-la-BOM," in the lowest, most gravelly voice she could muster.

By loving consensus, Louis Armstrong was one of the greatest entertainers of our time. He brought happiness and pleasure to millions. And with it he brought jazz to millions. I think that more people in more places have been turned on to jazz by Armstrong than all other musicians combined. The respect held for Satchmo is reserved for few other Americans. I met a fellow here in Tanzania who, learning I was

American, said, "Did you know Louis Armstrong played a concert here? It is one of the high points of my life."

Armstrong was born, not as legend has it on the Fourth of July, 1900, but as a birth certificate proves on August 4, 1901. He grew up in the roughest section of New Orleans. At an early age he was singing for loose change on the streets. He was arrested for disturbing the peace in 1913 and was sent to the Colored Waifs Home for Boys. This may rank as among the most fortuitous arrests in history, for it was at the Waifs Home that Armstrong was given a cornet. Within a short period, he was leading the Waifs band. He began picking up professional jobs at 16, and in 1919 replaced Joe "King" Oliver in Kid Ory's band. A few years later, Oliver asked Louis to join his Creole Band in Chicago on second cornet, where he cut his first records in 1923. He did a stint in New York with the Fletcher Henderson band and backing various blues singers including the great Bessie Smith, then returned to Chicago. During this time—late 1925 through most of 1928—Armstrong recorded 66 sides collectively referred to as the Hot Fives and Hot Sevens. On one of these, "Heebie Jeebies," he sang his first scat vocal using sounds rather than words, the aforementioned "de-bo deedle-la-BOM." The Hot Fives and Hot Sevens changed the way jazz was played.

Not all 66 numbers were classics, but jazz would certainly be poorer without such songs as "Cornet Chop Suey," "Wild Man Blues," "Twelfth Street Rag," "Potato Head Blues," "Struttin' With Some Barbeque," "S.O.L. Blues," "Hotter Than That," "Basin Street Blues," "St. James Infirmary," "Weather Bird," and above all "West End Blues," just to name a few. The danger in listing any Hot Five or Hot Seven cut is that some Satchmo freak may want to wring my neck for omitting his personal favorite. For some, Louis Armstrong has about the same status as Moses, and various Hot Five and Hot Seven numbers are like the Ten Commandments of jazz. Some tributes:

"... Louis was simply the greatest trumpeter ever..." (Digby Fair-weather—a pretty fair jazz trumpeter himself).

"Armstrong towers above twentieth century music..." (John Swenson—critic).

"The first and still perhaps the greatest solo star in jazz; the most influential musician of the century..." (Donald Clarke—editor).

Miles Davis was a man of few words: when asked about the influence of Louis Armstrong, he said, "no him, no me."

And finally, in case you haven't fallen to your knees yet, "... we must insist that any who are unaware of these records [the Hot Fives and Hot Sevens] make their acquaintance as soon as possible." (Richard Cook-Brian Morton—Penguin Guides).

I wouldn't go so far as "insist," but would advise that the more you listen to Armstrong's best numbers the more you hear and the more amazing they become. For example, there's a bar in Armstrong's solo on "Ory's Creole Trombone," where he goes totally outside the song's melodic and harmonic structure. He's playing free jazz in 1926! No one else would try for another 30 years. He also does some octave jumps on that number not unlike the playing of Eric Dolphy in the 1960s (discussed ahead). To say that Satchmo was ahead of his time is a gross understatement. Folks are still trying to catch up with Satchmo in this 21st century.

Louis Armstrong was the first great jazz soloist—unless you want to give that honor to Satch's homeboy, Sidney Bechet. Armstrong was also the first great jazz singer. But more influential than either his playing or his singing was his innovation. For Armstrong very definitely did affect the way jazz is played. And if it is true that jazz influenced the way all musicians play their instruments and the way all music is approached, then maybe John Swenson is not off base to state that Louis Armstrong towers over 20th century music.

Probably no song better illustrates the musical greatness of Louis

Armstrong than his version of King Oliver's composition, "West End Blues." From the first few bars (a bit of flash called a cadenza by musicians), Satchmo proclaims to the world that jazz has come of age and risen to a level of magnificent and glorious sound almost unimaginable before. In short, DIG THIS MUSIC!

We should remember that "West End Blues" was recorded in 1928. For two decades, jazz had stood for collective improvisation: one musician taking the melody or lead line while several others played countermelodies or harmonies above or below that line. Usually three lines, but sometimes five or more, all happening simultaneously, extemporized out of the players' heads.

Unaccompanied, Armstrong introduces "West End Blues" with "the most celebrated cadenza in jazz history," according to John Fordham. These few bars gave people a taste of the new thing. That taste would have been more than a mouthful for most trumpeters of the day. The purity and strength of tone had no equal. In the second bar, Armstrong hits a high C, considered at that time nearly impossible on a trumpet, and holds it just so listeners know it's not only possible but easy... for Satchmo. Then he runs a few more arpeggios to end on that golden Armstrong tone, thick as honey and quivering with vibrato. And this is just the introduction.

The first chorus starts with Armstrong's statement of King Oliver's theme. The rest of the band accompanies him with chords and rhythm, no counter-melodies. Armstrong plays the melody, oozing blues, with such style and grace, we have more than one King at work here.

Trombonist Fred Robinson takes the second chorus solo—only accompaniment, no counter-lines. Jimmy Strong on clarinet takes the third solo with Armstrong singing "responses" to his calls. This isn't the gravel-voiced Satchmo of de-bo deedle-la-BOM. No, here he croons the blues in falsetto, throwing in a bit of harmony. Pianist Earl Hines plays the fourth chorus unaccompanied, with Mancy Carr on banjo and drummer Zutty Singleton dropping out to change the mood and give Hines more room to move around on the keys.

Armstrong begins his improvised solo with THAT NOTE. I met a tipsy Norwegian in Somalia. Let's call him Jon for that was his name. In the fullness of time, our conversation turned to Satchmo.

"You know THAT NOTE in 'West End Blues'?" queried Jon.

"What note is that?" I asked, question for question.

"THAT NOTE he holds for 16 bars," Jon informed me.

"He holds one note for 16 BARS?" said I, doubtfully.

"Suuuuure," he answered, turning a one-syllable word into Norwegian.

Back at home with my tape collection, I dug the recording out and began to listen. And to count. Twice. Sorry, Jon. THAT NOTE only stretched to 16 *beats*, but a very long 16 it was. THAT NOTE. No running up to it. Just two pick-up notes and waaaaaaaaaah. No strain. Absolutely crystal clear. Steady—not a single decibel weaker at the end than at the beginning, a bravura performance that suggests he probably could hold it a full 16 bars. He only stops THAT NOTE because he wants to play a few more, including another high C and an even higher D. The piano drops down alone, and with a final bit of quivering honey, the group harmonizes out.

You have just heard a classic. Armstrong's biographer James Lincoln Collier calls "West End Blues," "... one of the masterworks of 20th century music..." (Note that he said "music," not "jazz.") Armstrong's solo is for Collier "almost certainly the most nearly perfect statement in recorded jazz." Gunther Schuller, head of the New England Conservatory of Music, has done a note-by-note analysis. He uses over 100 words to describe the first four notes!

Impressive enough, but what really blew me away was a video I saw of jazz trumpeter Freddie Hubbard making a new recording of Armstrong songs including "West End Blues." Trumpeter-jazz writer

Ian Carr writes of Hubbard, "Virtuosity and versatility are hallmarks of his individual style." Hubbard states on the video that when friends asked why he was wasting his time on Armstrong and "this old music," his answer was, "you have no idea how great this man was and how hard that stuff was." He said "hard," this versatile virtuoso! And he was right. On the opening cadenza, Hubbard cracks trying to hit that high C. He cracks again on THAT NOTE and runs out of breath on the twelfth beat. "West End Blues," simple though it may seem, is more than hard—it's DAMNED HARD!

The experts will tell you that the Hot Five and Hot Seven recordings synthesized all of New Orleans jazz, brought it to the peak of perfection, and blazed a new trail for the music to take. True, but wildly inadequate. Freddie Hubbard demonstrates how difficult a "simple" blues is and what a technical master Armstrong was. Again true, but that also doesn't do it justice. The only thing that matters is the impact "West End Blues" has on YOU when you listen to it. It may make your ears smile. The West End is a place I go to when I need my spirits lifted. And you can go there too.

CHAPTER 11
ART BLAKEY AND THE JAZZ MESSENGERS
"A NIGHT IN TUNISIA"

https://www.youtube.com/watch?v=FHKyVJ5YfNU

Ask any band musician who is the most essential person in the group, and I bet you the most common answer will be the "drummer." How important is the drummer? How important is the motor to a car, or the foundation to a house? Yet, few drummers ever become stars. Mention the Rolling Stones and everyone immediately thinks "Mick Jagger." Nobody thinks "Charlie Watts." But about half of the Rolling Stones gutbucket feel is the drumming of Charlie Watts. (Most of the other half is the guitar riffs of Keith Richards.) At parties, people ask a pianist for a few tunes or a guitarist to lead a sing-along. They don't ask a drummer to do a few licks on the snare drum and add a cymbal crash or two. I can pack up my gear after a performance in maybe five minutes. The drummer has only begun to dismantle his musical kit of many pieces. I might get good if I practice. I run some scales, play some tunes, strum some chords, and bend some notes. When a drummer practices, it's Boom-bah-Boom... tap-ta-ta-

tap... r-r-r-r-r-o-o-o-l-l-l-l. Must drive them crazy. Most drummers I know are a bit wacky. That may be why we never hear someone say, "he marches to a different trombonist."

Almost no group in jazz became famous without a great drummer. We have Baby Dodds and Big Sid Catlett with Louis Armstrong, Gene Krupa with Benny Goodman, Sonny Greer with Duke Ellington, Jo Jones with Count Basie, Max Roach with Charlie Parker, Philly Joe Jones and Tony Williams with Miles Davis, Elvin Jones with John Coltrane. The list could go on. I submit that Paul Desmond would not have written "Take Five," nor the Dave Brubeck Quartet ever produced the album *Time Out,* if they hadn't had the phenomenal Joe Morello to beat out those odd time signatures.

And then there's Art Blakey. Blakey was more than a great drummer. He was leader of the Jazz Messengers. For over 35 years The Jazz Messengers were the foremost proponents of a style labeled hard bop—the offspring of bebop. But Art Blakey was more than the leader and the Jazz Messengers was more than a band. The Messengers was a graduate school for jazz musicians and Art Blakey was its chancellor. (Miles Davis led another graduate school, but the difference lay in its purpose—Miles made his sidemen famous and then they formed their own groups. Blakey's purpose with the Jazz Messengers was to "educate" talented young musicians.)

Why did a man who could, and did, drum with the best players in jazz choose to work with young, virtually unknown, musicians? Here's what Blakey had to say: "I'm gonna stay with the youngsters. When these get too old, I'll get some younger ones. Keeps the mind active." This was 1954 and Blakey at 35 was the "old man" in the group, having been on the national scene for 12 years already. He continued bringing various Messengers into his particular college of musical knowledge until his death in 1990. I'll only mention 10 alumni: Jackie McLean, Wayne Shorter, Johnny Griffin, Lee Morgan, Freddie Hubbard,

Wynton Marsalis, Bobby Timmons, Cedar Walton, Keith Jarrett, Curtis Fuller. We could triple that list. Each group had its own character because many wrote, and Blakey appointed various "musical directors." But there was a unifying sense of adventure, and of course Blakey's drumming. Some of the Jazz Messengers' albums are a bit rough around the edges—after all, these musicians were polishing and perfecting their skills—but there's an atmosphere of excitement in listening to these groups working things out and developing their talent. And some Messengers played better than others. Most had interesting music, and all had the Art Blakey rhythm.

"A Night in Tunisia" was recorded in 1960 with Wayne Shorter (tenor sax), Lee Morgan (trumpet), Bobby Timmons (piano), and Jymie Merritt (bass). The song is a jazz classic, with enough versions extant to fill a few CDs. Dizzy Gillespie composed the song in 1942, reportedly using a garbage can lid as a writing surface. Blakey and these Messengers more than do justice to the piece. That is true for several reasons. First, this is a particularly fine arrangement of "Tunisia." Second, Shorter and Morgan were fairly advanced Messengers in 1960. Third, and most important, Art Blakey was the drummer.

"Tunisia" kicks off with percussion—Blakey on drums, Shorter tapping claves (two sticks), and Morgan shaking maracas. Merritt soon joins on bass. What we hear is a fairly good facsimile of an African drum choir, most appropriate considering the title. This goes on for a full minute before Timmons enters with block chords on piano. Shorter abandons the claves and lays out a tenor sax riff for Morgan's statement of the eight-bar theme, which he plays twice. Shorter takes the bridge on tenor and Morgan once again does his 8 bars. Then Morgan and Shorter play in unison before Shorter takes his solo with Morgan giving him a high-note send-off.

Shorter rips. If you listen and have an "educated" ear, you will know immediately who Shorter is taking "lessons" from. You are listening to

John Coltrane Jr. Shorter would go on to develop his own distinctive style and become one of the top saxophonists in the world. But in 1960, Shorter was very definitely a Trane disciple. Still if you imitate, go for the best. (In fact. almost all jazz greats, including Louis Armstrong, started out imitating someone.) You hear Shorter, in 1960 with the talent, with the tone, with a story to tell. He lacks only his own individual voice to tell it.

Morgan is very much in command during his solo, which isn't surprising. He had ample opportunity to get acquainted with both the song and its composer as a member of the Dizzy Gillespie band before joining Blakey. Morgan has Dizzy's technique and speed coupled with a broad tone derived from Clifford Brown. And he really shows both to great effect, at the ripe old age of 22.

Merritt then adds his bit. Blakey with Shorter and Morgan back on clave and maracas and Timmons on piano provide accent and comment. Then we get some serious percussion discussion.

This is about as close to African drumming as non-Africans can get. I've lived on the continent most of my adult life and heard plenty of the real thing. Blakey was, I believe, the first jazz drummer to make a serious study of African percussion, and it shows. The cross-rhythms come at you constantly, belying the fact that only three men are percussing. That's because Blakey was capable of playing four different rhythms simultaneously. Joe Morello could do it too.

The group returns to the eight-bar theme—this time no "bridge." Blakey gets in a few more licks, then they take the theme again with Morgan playing an octave higher on trumpet. And it's over. No, it isn't.

Morgan takes off again—alone. He really struts his stuff. After his first bluesy phrase, someone (probably Blakey) comments, "Not bad." So he does it again even better. Blakey and group return for the dramatic finish. No, it's not finished.

Shorter can't let Morgan get away with the last word. He takes off.

Now he's Trane Jr. with some Sonny Rollins thrown in to boot. (Sonny Rollins by himself could outdo most groups.) Shorter turns it on to full thrust with afterburners.

Then they do finish it, slowly building climax after exquisite climax until you don't think you can handle it anymore. But all good things do come to an end. One more and it really is over. You anticipate that maybe they'll sneak another one in on you.

They don't, but I will.

Go back and start all over again, only this time, forget about the horns and the solos. Listen instead to what Blakey does while the horns play. Drummers know how to keep time or they shouldn't be drummers. Most drummers can bash—witness the heavy metal crew. But only good drummers know when to lay it on and when to lay off. And great drummers know how to enhance another musician's solo by turning it on and/or toning it down.

Having set the "African" mood in the intro, Blakey backs off during the theme, letting his cymbals carry the rhythm with snare accents at the end of the verse. During the unison part, he begins using the snare in earnest. And for Shorter's solo send-off he really lets fly. Then he immediately gets out of Shorter's way, knowing he only needs to roll along behind the sax. He and Timmons add some tasty accents, and toward the end they turn those into a rhythmic pattern. Blakey gets louder and lets loose again to bring on Morgan's trumpet.

A trumpet makes more noise than a sax and Blakey plays accordingly, plus adding more complex rhythms to build intensity and excitement. You may have thought Morgan's solo was "better" than Shorter's. Well, maybe so and maybe not. Shorter "sets up" Morgan. I can only imagine what Shorter's playing does to Morgan's adrenal glands. And just in case Shorter hasn't pumped Morgan up enough, Blakey is going to make sure he plays all out. So what Blakey does behind Morgan is partly for the listeners but mostly for Morgan, which again is for the listeners.

A good drummer thinks first of the group, second of the soloist; the last thing he worries about is his own solos. (This applies equally to bassists.) Of course, great drummers can do it all. When you listen to Blakey on "A Night in Tunisia," you will understand why he was a great drummer. And you will also understand why musicians think the drummer is the most essential member of their group.

CHAPTER 12
WES MONTGOMERY
"IMPRESSIONS"

https://www.youtube.com/watch?v=8Vai7lTj4aI

Contrary to what you hear from the heavy metal gunslingers blasting megawatts out of stacks of Marshall Amps loud enough to bring Central American dictators to their knees, the guitar is a rather gentle instrument. Without the aid of electricity, the guitar cannot boom like a bass, ring like a banjo, or wail like a horn. There were several good guitarists in jazz before George Barnes recorded the first electric guitar jazz solo—Eddie Lang and Django Reinhardt immediately come to mind. But say "jazz guitar" to fanatics and toward the top of the list will be Charlie Christian and Wes Montgomery.

Charlie Christian is the father of modern jazz guitar. This is somewhat amazing considering that this Okie from Muskogee was only on the national scene for three years with Benny Goodman before dying of tuberculosis in 1942. According to the *Rolling Stone Jazz Record Guide*, Christian left a recorded legacy of two albums, one of which is an amateur taping of jam sessions in a New York club. Christian's rhythmic approach pushed the transition from swing to bebop, and his extended melody lines further developed Lester Young's musical ideas. Charlie Christian defined *the* way to play jazz guitar for 15 years.

It was Charlie Christian to whom a 19-year-old, already married, Wes Montgomery listened when learning to play guitar. He copied Charlie Christian note-for-note, going over a number again and again and again until he got it. He also developed a facility for playing in octaves. Django Reinhardt played in octaves. To this he added soloing in chords rather than single notes—a technique used by Barney Kessel. It's difficult. But Montgomery practiced it and practiced it. Wes Montgomery got headaches perfecting his octave technique. He literally made himself sick learning to play guitar. For what? To work a day job in order to support a wife and family, then play a regular club date for five hours, then jam sessions until the morning. All of this in the musical backwater of Indianapolis, Indiana. He went out on the road. Nothing happened. Back to Indianapolis. Work, play, jam. Work, play, jam. Wes Montgomery in 1959 was 34 years old, father of seven, and exactly nowhere.

And then, ZAP! Cannonball Adderley heard Montgomery jamming and told his record producer, Orrin Keepnews, about this amazing guitarist in Indianapolis. Montgomery's impact was immediate and permanent. No jazz guitar freak can possibly discuss his/her favorite instrument without a long, long lecture on the wonders of Wes. That is not too surprising. However, even people who don't generally listen to jazz may have Montgomery music they are very fond of.

What is special about Wes Montgomery? His techniques—single lines, octaves, and chords— were all derived from others. Wes synthesized these elements and then added that which is uniquely Montgomery. Once you've heard him, you will never mistake Wes for any other guitarist. (Unless you confuse him with his funky disciple, George Benson, when Benson isn't singing like Stevie Wonder.)

I think Wes Montgomery's uniqueness stems from his isolation. He had for many years no one to go up against other than himself. Armstrong played behind King Oliver; Ellington bounced ideas off his orchestra; Parker and Gillespie were at it with each other; Coltrane had to contend with Sonny Rolllins and vice versa. But Wes had only himself to deal with.

All alone in Indianapolis, Wes Montgomery fashioned a style that was simultaneously soft and soulful, mellow and earthy, able to create musical tension while remaining completely laid back. A Montgomery solo is both subtle and dramatic, as if every note has been carefully selected for maximum impact even at tempos almost too fast to count. For jazz guitar freaks, the albums Wes made for Orrin Keepnews between 1960 and 1964 are nothing short of exquisite. For non-jazz fans, the attraction to Montgomery is even simpler: The man plays so damn pretty. And that's what he did for producer Creed Taylor from 1965 on.

Jazz fans disown Wes' easy listening albums. Creed Taylor is the villain, the greedy businessman who turned Montgomery into a musical whore. While not a great Creed Taylor apologist, I believe we ought to keep things in perspective. Like most sensible people, Wes preferred wealth to poverty. Orrin Keepnews made him famous; Creed Taylor made him rich. He didn't use a gun to force Wes to record *Goin' Out of My Head*, which won a Grammy in 1966, or *A Day in the Life*, one of the all-time best selling jazz albums. Creed Taylor talked money and Wes Montgomery listened.

I selected "Impressions" off the album *Smokin' at the Half Note Vol 2* for two reasons. First, Montgomery really cooks, displaying the full array of technique and style that brought him all that much-deserved praise from jazz fans. Second, this album was produced by none other than Creed Taylor. It shows that Montgomery had lost none of his amazing musical power, even when he wasn't called upon to use it very often. Granted, Taylor tried to mess things up by adding orchestrations later in the studio (the original non-orchestrated master was re-issued as *The Small Group Recordings*), but "Impressions" was so good on its own that even Creed Taylor wouldn't mess with it. So, we get Montgomery uncluttered, backed by the Wynton Kelly Trio (Kelly on piano, Paul Chambers on bass, and Jimmy Cobb on drums). The trio had formerly comprised the rhythm section of the Miles Davis Quintet on the album *Kind of Blue*. It's no surprise these three gentlemen knew how to support a soloist, enhancing his lines instead of getting in the way. (I wish the same could be said of the producer.)

"Impressions" is a John Coltrane number; Montgomery worked briefly with Trane in 1962. The structure of the piece is identical to "So What," which we've already listened to. "Impressions" is a 32-bar modal blues. (I've got a live cut of "So What" and "Impressions" combined as a medley. It takes careful listening to hear when the group switches from one song to the other.) The Montgomery style—single notes, octaves, chords—lent itself marvelously to lush ballads and also worked well on bouncy numbers. Although as mellow as they come, Montgomery really enjoyed "smoking," which he did at the Half Note. You're about to hear how he applies his style while zipping along at 3 beats per second.

The group takes off with Wes stating the theme somewhat faster than Coltrane usually did it. He plays the first 16 bars on single strings, switches to octaves for the eight-bar bridge, then returns to single strings for the final eight bars. Off he goes on single strings, thumb flying. (He never used a guitar pick.) After several choruses, he gives us just a taste of chords. Then he moves to some scintillating octave work. Is what he does possible? You can only shake your head in wonder. But don't shake your head too much because Wes has laid only two-thirds of his style on you. Next, he goes into soloing with chords for several choruses. Having quite possibly blown your mind altogether, he restates the theme playing the bridge in chords rather than octaves. Then for good measure, he ends alternating between octaves and chords. It is a five-minute guitar *tour de force.*

On "Impressions," Wes Montgomery demonstrates far more than his mastery of six thin strands of wire. Even at a speed most musicians find difficult to handle at all, Wes plays as melodically and as mellow as if it were a romantic ballad. Furthermore, he restructures the original "bridge" (the third eight-bar section) as Coltrane did it into a complementary line, which then becomes a second theme when he gets into octaves and chord solos. Even when Wes did pop schlock for Creed Taylor, he could find something fresh and interesting to play.

So for you guitar maniacs out there getting a bit tired of all that distortion-whammy bar-feedback, and beginning to feel those fuzz tone riffs are growing stale, why not do your ears a favor and taste the ever-light, fully refreshing sounds of Wes Montgomery? No, please, you don't have to thank me for it. Just pass this on to a friend.

There's an old joke about a tourist in New York stopping a jazz musician: "Can you tell me how to get to Carnegie Hall?" the tourist asks. The musician gives him a knowing look: "Practice, man, practice."

I don't know if Wes Montgomery ever got to Carnegie Hall, but he is definitely in the pantheon of great jazz stylists. Not bad for an old man from Indianapolis.

CHAPTER 13
BRANFORD MARSALIS
"LONELY WOMAN"

https://www.youtube.com/watch?v=hIAJ9JvOo_g

When I was scuffling to stay alive as a guitar instructor at the Nairobi Conservatoire (that's how they spelled it), I crossed paths with George Medoe, a South African refugee and fellow scuffler who taught drama at Nairobi University just across the street. Medoe loved jazz so we hit it off immediately. He particularly liked modern players and we had no trouble at all regarding Coltrane. But George was heavily into Ornette Coleman, and I couldn't stand him. So George began a crusade to convert me.

We'd go to his place to listen to music—I didn't have any at that time. He'd soften me up with some Coltrane, Miles Davis, and a few beers, but eventually out would come Ornette. I would listen. After all, George was my host. It was his beer, his Hi-Fi, his music. And George was the only person I knew in Nairobi who liked jazz. I would cringe inside while Medoe sang Coleman's praises: Ornette played the only really new and creative, truly free music; Ornette was the heaviest of the heavies, the greatest of the greats; Ornette was an inspiration to all those who wished to liberate themselves. And on and on.

Intellectually I could understand where George—and Ornette, too, for that matter—was coming from. But my ears recoiled. I just couldn't enjoy the music of Ornette Coleman, no matter how true, creative, and free it was. But on another occasion when Medoe was subjecting me to the marvels of Ornette, I heard something. I sat up. I really listened hard. Medoe was grinning like a Cheshire cat. His crusade had paid off. I had finally seen the light—Saul on the road to Damascus.

"A-HA!" said George.

"What was that cut?" I asked.

"That's 'Lonely Woman.' Marvelous, no?"

"A fantastic piece of music. I hope someone other than Ornette does it."

Now, I'm not knocking Ornette Coleman. In fact, I would urge everyone to give him a long hard listen with an open mind and open ears. If you can get into what he plays, you are so much the richer for it. I just can't dig Ornette and that's *my* loss. I've known people who think Louis Armstrong plays old fuddy-duddy stuff. I've had people tell me Charlie Parker plays chaotic rubbish, that Coltrane is unlistenable, that all jazz stinks. That's *their* loss.

While I ought to give you "Lonely Woman" by Ornette Coleman, I can't because I wrote in the introduction I would present music I like and hoped you would like it too. And I don't like, although I appreciate, Ornette Coleman. So here's the wonderful Ornette Coleman song "Lonely Woman" by Branford Marsalis.

Branford Marsalis plays beautifully. Branford Marsalis, I expect, can play anything. He has played hard bop with the Jazz Messengers, done fusion with Miles Davis, recorded European classical music, elevated pop-rock a couple of notches with Sting, sat in with the very avant-gardish World Saxophone Quartet, led the extremely show-biz

"Tonight Show" band. Branford Marsalis is one of a number of saxophone MONSTERS who came up in the 1980s and '90s. And his younger brother Wynton is an all-time trumpet MONSTROSITY. These brothers play jazz so well, you'd think it's in their genes, which it might be since their father Ellis is not only a pretty fair pianist but also a highly respected jazz educator. With the Marsalis brothers came a tremendous surge in jazz talent through the 1980s and into the '90s. There are so many fine players in jazz from that period that I would not even know where to begin... except the Marsalis brothers came first.

And maybe because they came first, or because they became very successful very young, or because Branford "sold out," or because Wynton tends to make papal-like pronouncements, they have been both praised and pilloried by jazz writers. A huge (by jazz standards) debate has arisen concerning the Marsalis brothers and their legions. Some term them "classicists"; I call them the "Retros." Those involved on both sides are really *serious.* I find it all really silly. About 90 percent of the argument can be dismissed as righteous hogwash. You either enjoy what the Retros play or you don't. My only question regarding any music from Bach to Blues is this: Can YOU dig it? Not very erudite, but we're the ones who buy the albums. I concur with one point in the argument, though. A trumpet playing friend of mine summed it up quite well: "There ought to be a law against anyone playing as perfect as Wynton Marsalis."

That's my problem with almost all the young lions today—there is no note too high, no tempo too fast, and no rhythm too complex. They've gone beyond playing like humans—they're bionic jazzmen. And many lack what Miles Davis called, "That THING."

Ornette Coleman, on the other hand, is completely human and definitely has That THING. And with "Lonely Woman" he has done something I find amazing. In this blues ballad, which does not follow the rules for blues or ballads, Coleman has delved into the very essence of "woman." He has not presented his interpretation; he *is* woman. Most men deny their feminine side. Coleman does more than acknowledge his femininity, he celebrates it. He praises his isolation, his beauty, his love. He loves his femininity because he loves his whole self. And he has the creativity and talent to honor his woman in music. Which just goes to prove that my friend George Medoe was right all along: Ornette Coleman is liberating, creative and, most of all, free.

Ornette played "Lonely Woman" on his famous plastic alto sax. Marsalis plays it on tenor sax, employing the horn's full range. There is no set rhythm here. Instead we have what is called "rubato," freedom to speed up or slow down the piece. Branford leads and the group follows. And what following. Kenny Kirkland's piano work, in and of itself, could stand as a valid track. I had never heard of either bassist Delbert Felix or drummer Lewis Nash when I bought Marsalis' album *Random Abstract*. These days Nash is all over, drumming with just about everyone. His playing on "Lonely Woman," quiet yet powerful, was a perfect job application for as much work as he could handle. Kirkland, Felix, and Nash perform their role—to support and enhance—with consummate style and grace.

And Branford does what Branford always does. To write that he plays superbly seems pitifully inadequate. Holy mother of Adolphe! It's as if the inventor of the saxophone said to himself in 1846, "Someday a young man from New Orleans will come along and play my creation the way I dream it should sound."

Try listening to Marsalis' "Lonely Woman" with your eyes shut. Let the sounds roll over you. Kirkland's intro conjures up leaves falling. Felix and Nash join in. It's late afternoon. Branford's sax is Woman looking out the window... waiting. He starts the theme—her thoughts. Woman waiting... alone... alone as the wind blows (Nash's drums) and the leaves swirl (Kirkland's piano). Branford runs into the upper register of his horn, Woman cries out—a protest against this isolation.

Kirkland, Felix, and Nash are really agitated. The music ebbs and flows, flows and ebbs, as Branford's exquisite sax tells us about Woman's (and Ornette's) truth and beauty. Then Kirkland gives us a lyrical weather report. Branford returns for the bridge and then back to the theme one more time... lonely but with conviction and strength. That's how I hear it.

You may hear something else, but for sure this song will get to you, I guarantee it. I hear a super saxophonist playing a beautiful song. And I also hear something a great jazzman once said: "When I realized I could make mistakes, I knew I was on to something." And that great jazzman was... you want three guesses?... Ornette Coleman. And good night, George Medoe, wherever you are.

CHAPTER 14
MOSE ALLISON
"EVERYBODY CRYIN' MERCY"

https://www.youtube.com/watch?v=7puTwi_r3JU&t=6s

This little piece concerns HIP. According to the dictionary, hip (sometimes spelled "hep" but as Henry "the Hipster" Gibson sang: "Don't you ever say hep, it ain't hip…") means aware, cognizant, wise, particularly regarding the latest styles and attitudes. When it comes to jazz, almost all the hip (or hep) cats have been African-Americans. Louis Armstrong was hip, Dizzy Gillespie was hip, and the hippest of the hip was no doubt Lester Young.

I should state right off that hip does not necessarily equate with good. Bix Beiderbecke and Frank Trumbauer, Jack Teagarden, Benny Goodman, Bunny Berrigan, Red Nichols, Red Norvo, Red Rodney, Al Haig, Al Cohn, Stan Getz, Zoot Sims, Gerry Mulligan, Pepper Adams, Dave Brubeck, Paul Desmond, Kai Winding, George Shearing, Louie Prima, Louie Bellson, Barney Kessel, Jim Hall, Joe Pass, Joe Morello, Gene Krupa, Buddy Rich, etc., are all good and all white. Some are/were a bit hip, some fairly hip, and some not even a little hip.

In my opinion, Mose Allison ranks up there with the really hip. What does Mose Allison have in common with Lester Young? He is totally cool, he has a rather wry sense of humor and, most important of all, he makes not the slightest effort to be hip. The only way to be truly hip is not to try. If you have to work at being hip, you'll wind up being only pathetically pretentious and foolish.

Maybe Mose was born hip in Tippo, Mississippi. Maybe his parents bestowed hip on him when they named him Mose. Maybe he acquired hip when he learned to play piano and got into bebop. He started out as a pianist in 1956 backing Stan Getz, Gerry Mulligan, and others. Maybe hip suddenly came upon him when he opened his mouth to sing.

And on that point, "sing" does not accurately describe a Mose Allison vocal. The sounds coming out of his throat hardly qualify as singing the way most people think of it. Mose doesn't exactly speak or chant the words, but he doesn't exactly sing either. His vocals are flat in the sense that he uses no vibrato and in the sense that he is often lower than true pitch. He is also, like Lester Young, almost allergic to staying on the beat. It's like his voice box is full of glue and when the words finally work free, they stick wherever they land. In truth, Mose Allison has a fantastic sense of rhythm. You can't possibly sing (sort of) the way he does unless there's a strong internal metronome at work.

Some people probably call Mose Allison's singing awful; some might call it weird; some might call it different. I call it unique. Mose's treatment of "You are My Sunshine" could have given its composer, country singer-politician Jimmy Davis, apoplexy, but then maybe the Ray Charles version did also. Or how about the Duke Ellington classic, "Do Nothing Till You Hear from Me"? Those used to the standard versions may hate the way Allison sings it. But I expect Duke, the hippest genius America ever produced, probably thought: "Cool." I know the first time I heard Mose Allison sing "Parchman Farm" in the late 1950s, I thought, "This cat is hip."

Everything Mose Allison sings comes out blues, even if the songs weren't written that way. When Mose composes numbers, they're blues up and down. In a 1986 interview, Allison grouped his songs into three categories: slapstick, social comment, and personal crisis. "Parchman Farm" and "Your Mind is on Vacation" (and your mouth is working overtime) are two examples of what he calls slapstick. "I Don't Worry 'Bout a Thing" ('cause nothin's gonna be all right) and "Ever Since the World Ended" are satirical social comment. "Perfect Moment" and "You Can Count on Me" may fit the personal crisis category. Finally, I will add that Allison usually keeps it short and to the point. Most of his own songs run between two and a half and three minutes. So, emulating the hip Mose Allison, let's get it on.

"Everybody Cryin' Mercy," from the 1968 album *I've Been Doin' Some Thinkin'*, is considered one of his best songs by jazz critics, and I agree. Dozens have covered the song from Bonnie Raitt to Elvis Costello. It definitely fits into satirical social comment with a large helping of irony. No intro. Allison jumps right in to tell us what this song is about:

I can't believe the things I'm seein'
   I wonder 'bout some things I've heard
   Everybody Cryin' Mercy
   When they don't know the meaning of the word

This is not a three-chord, twelve-bar blues. The song follows a jazz chord progression but Allison's vocal saturates it with blues.

. . .

A bad enough situation
    Is sure enough getting' worse
    Everybody cryin' justice
    Just as long as it's business first

You will note how Mose heavily emphasizes certain words and syllables: "a BAD eNOUGH situation…" for example, and especially "every-BODY cryin' MERCY… "

Here comes the bridge, chock full of irony—life as a spectator sport:

Toe to toe
    Touch and go
    Give a cheer
    Get your souvenir

People runnin' 'round in circles
    Don't know what they're headed for
    Everybody cryin' peace on earth
    Just as soon as we win this war

This song was released in June 1968, six months after the Vietnam War Tet Offensive began.

And now we get to a second bridge and the underlying message of the song:

. . .

Straight ahead
    Knock 'em dead
    Pack your kit
    Choose your hypocrite

Mose Allison concludes:

Well you don't have to go to off-Broadway
    To see something plain absurd
    Everybody's Cryin' Mercy
    When they don't know the meaning of the word
    Nobody knows the meaning of the word

"Choose your hypocrite"—lots to choose from. Something plain absurd isn't confined to off-Broadway. Look around—it's everywhere.

Some months after "Everybody Cryin Mercy," Roberta Flack came out with the Gene McDaniels song "Compared to What":

Possession is the motivation
    Hangin' up the whole damn nation
    Looks like we always end up in a rut
    Tryin' to make it real but compared to what?

The song enumerates a number of societal ills and exhorts the listener to try to make it real. Then comes the rhetorical question: In an absurd world, "real" compared to what?

Marvin Gaye followed with the hit song "What's Goin' On":

You know we've got to find a way
    To bring some lovin' here today…
    Talk to me, so you can see
    What's goin' on

All three songs fall into Mose Allison's social comment category. All three lay out issues of the day. "Compared to What" was a hit for Roberta Flack. "What's Goin On" sold over two million copies. "Everybody's Cryin' Mercy"? Well, let's just note that it didn't make the Billboard Top 40. But Allison has what very few others do: A wry satirical and often skeptical point of view, with a very subtle and cool delivery.

Mose Allison is singing to us about us. Pay attention: This cat is hip.

CHAPTER 15
DON BYAS-SLAM STEWART
"I GOT RHYTHM"

https://www.youtube.com/watch?v=1y9dZk-GMiM

f someone—maybe you—were to say, "Okay, you've sold me; I'll give jazz a try. Just tell me, where do I start?" Start anywhere you like, would be my reply. But on second thought, I might suggest the *Smithsonian Collection of Classic Jazz.* Assembled and annotated by the great jazz writer Martin Williams, it starts with Scott Joplin and ends with Coltrane doing "Alabama" in 1963. Williams takes you from ragtime to the 1960s, and he knows how to pick 'em. There are very good tunes on this set. From there, you're on your own.

Part of the fun of jazz, or any music I suppose, is discovery. You hear something new, something you didn't expect. Thanks to the Smithsonian and Martin Williams, I discovered the Don Byas-Slam Stewart version of George Gershwin's "I Got Rhythm." Now, anything less won't do.

The Byas-Stewart record was made at an all-star jam session at Town Hall in New York City on June 9, 1945. Jam sessions are generally play-it-by-ear affairs. And I mean this literally, because good musicians are supposed to listen carefully. One of the best compliments one jazz musician can bestow on another is "you have big ears" or "huge ears" or, best of all, "elephant ears." Nowhere is listening more important than at a jam session because often musicians are not playing set pieces. Everything from start to finish is made up on the spot. Thus, it helps to do songs everyone already knows. Forget fancy numbers. Let's get down to basics. You don't get much more basic than "I Got Rhythm." Every jazzman worthy of the name can play "I Got Rhythm" forwards, backwards, or upside down. That number is as essential to the jazzman's musical vocabulary as "Row Row Row Your Boat" is to a nursery schoolteacher. If you want in on a jam session and someone calls out "I Got Rhythm," your only question had better be, "What key?"

This explains how "I Got Rhythm" wound up being played at that 1945 Town Hall gig. It doesn't explain why the Don Byas-Slam Stewart version wound up in the Smithsonian Collection, which included Jelly Roll Morton, Louis Armstrong, Bix Beiderbecke, Bessie Smith, Coleman Hawkins, Charlie Christian, Lester Young, Art Tatum, Billie Holiday, Count Basie, Duke Ellington, Dizzy Gillespie, Charlie Parker, Charles Mingus, Miles Davis, John Coltrane, Sonny Rollins, Ornette Coleman, and others. Don Byas and Slam Steward are good, but do they really belong in that exalted company? We'll get to that later.

Don Byas was a prominent Coleman Hawkins disciple. He began playing tenor sax in swing bands in the 1930s. He came to national attention in 1941 in the Count Basie Band. Unlike many swing players, he got heavily involved in the experimental music that would come to be called bebop and was part of the first bebop combo with Dizzy Gillespie. In 1946 Byas moved to Europe where he remained until his death in 1972. One writer described his playing as "ferocious." He had, as my friend Henry Gordon says, "monsta chops" (excellent facility), in part derived from pianist Art Tatum's technique. In short, the cat could blow. Byas is less well-known than he ought to be because he took himself out of the main scene by migrating to Europe.

Bassist Slam Stewart was a conservatory-trained musician who is best known for his novel approach to bass solos. Typically, jazz bassists pluck the strings. On solos, Stewart would bow the strings and hum along an octave higher. He got fairly famous bowing and humming, especially as half the novelty duo with guitarist/singer Slim Gaillard. Calling themselves "Slim and Slam," the pair had a big hit in 1938 with a marvelous piece of nonsense titled "Flat Foot Floogie with the Floy Floy." Bowing and humming aside, Stewart was a fine bassist who worked off and on with the Art Tatum Trio for over 15 years.

So here we have the ferocious Don Byas and bower-hummer Slam Stewart in 1945 about to get down on "I Got Rhythm," a number they could probably play in their sleep. Do they sleepwalk through it? Most certainly not. They rip. They smoke. They play as if they're possessed by the Holy Spirit of Rhythm.

Byas and Stewart faced a fairly daunting task that night. Most jazz is played by trios, quartets, and larger groups for a reason. Each musician has a role to fill. The bassist provides the musical foundation, the drummer provides the momentum, the pianist provides the chordal filler (sometimes a guitarist has this function), and the horns provide melody and/or harmony. Byas and Stewart must do all these things between the two of them. Stewart in particular takes on the burden of supplying not only the foundation but also the momentum of the drummer, the filler of the pianist or guitarist, and to some extent the harmony of a second horn. Having Byas in tandem was an advantage, for Byas had an innate sense of swing and could play all over his tenor sax. He also employed the Coleman Hawkins *full* tone and that was important: "I Got Rhythm" never seems thin or empty, even though only two musicians are playing.

Slam slams out of the gate at 290 beats per minute. Byas follows two bars later with a 32-bar chorus pretty much the way George Gershwin composed the song. If you've listened to a lot of Coleman Hawkins, or even a little, you might think this is Hawkins himself. Byas had Hawk's style *down*. Byas then takes off on his own. All that buzzy vibrato sounds like a jet-propelled bee. He's down in the lower register, runs it up; he's all over the horn. Less is not more here. More is more here. He tears through bar lines as if they don't exist. He runs chorus into chorus. All you can do as a listener is fasten your safety belt and enjoy the ride. Then, after four choruses, he turns it over to Slam Stewart.

Stewart whips out his bow and hums his way through eight bars of the "I Got Rhythm" theme. Then, like Byas, he goes off on his own, bowing and humming and stomping his foot. They say possession is nine-tenths of the law. The question here is whether Stewart possesses Rhythm or Rhythm possesses Stewart. It seems to me as though both things are not just possible but damned near certain. He plays like a man possessed. Having bowed and hummed through two lightning choruses, Stewart goes back to plucking with hardly a pause. What did he do with the bow? Drop it? Throw it over his shoulder? I wish I'd been there... although in 1945, it was well past my bedtime in Joplin, Missouri.

Now Byas is at it again, not even bothering with the Gershwin theme. Whereas his first four choruses were fairly straight, fast swing, he now explores the new territory of bebop. He plays more "outside" the normal melodic structure with an intensity level of nine-point-something on the Richter scale. Words can't capture this sort of play-ing; you have to hear it for yourself. Byas and Stewart eventually end it, a bit ragged but somehow right.

How to explain such a performance? It is absolutely true to say that Don Byas played a ferocious tenor, that Slam Stewart was a fine bassist even when he didn't bow and hum. But as an explanation, it falls short. That these two fellows had probably played "I Got Rhythm" so many times that they had all their licks down pat doesn't quite do it, either. There is more at work here than two highly competent musicians going through their bag of tricks. I listen to Byas and Stewart doing "I Got Rhythm" that particular night and I hear an inspired performance. It goes well beyond "a whole lot of notes played extremely fast." "Inspired" is like pornography. I can't define it, but I know it when I hear it.

Can we call it a great performance? Maybe "great" ought to be reserved for those who achieve excellence consistently. I frankly haven't heard enough Byas or Stewart to call them great. But this performance of "I Got Rhythm" qualifies as something special, and "great" is the best I can come up with. I suppose Martin Williams agreed or he wouldn't have included it in the Smithsonian Collection. In the end, it doesn't matter what Williams, acknowledged expert, or I, the jazz fan, think. When you listen to Don Byas and Slam Stewart run through "I Got Rhythm," you will render the only verdict that matters—yours.

CHAPTER 16
BOBBY HUTCHERSON
"BOUQUET"

https://www.youtube.com/watch?v=0k9yvgezdbc

L et's try something totally different. With Bobby Hutcherson's "Bouquet," you have to throw away any preconceptions of jazz. It doesn't have the raucous good time feel of traditional New Orleans jazz or the toe-tapping swing of big band jazz or the astounding technique of bebop. Some might not even call this jazz. That's fine by me. Let's dump the labels. Let's just say we're going to listen to a piece of music—a bouquet of sounds created by three master musicians.

Actually, I came close to missing this grand listening experience altogether. I happened upon "Bouquet" by sheer luck. I needed a gift to take an old friend of mine in Denmark, the famous Njugu Kijabe. Njugu at one time in his checkered career had considered becoming a jazz bassist. The obvious present for a jazz fan is some music. I was browsing through a store in Boston when I came across a four-volume set titled *One Night with Blue Note*. Blue Note is one of the premier jazz labels and the musicians contributing to this three-hour tribute are indeed impressive. The Njugu was duly impressed as we listened to it in his Copenhagen apartment. After hearing "Bouquet," Njugu and I just sat there looking at each other. Finally, Njugu gave it his highest rating with a sound only he can make, "HoLAA!"

Bobby Hutcherson plays vibraphone. Some people like vibes; some don't. Frankly, I'm a "don't." Though I've got some Milt Jackson, a bit of Lionel Hampton, and the sumptuous Gary Burton-Chic Corea collaboration, *Crystal Silence*, vibes as a rule do not do a number on me.

"Bouquet," though, is a piece I find hard to imagine being played as well on any other instrument. Maybe it's because Hutcherson composed it or because I haven't heard it done by another musician. Still, "Bouquet" needs that quivering tone of the vibes to give it the right feel.

While Bobby Hutcherson very definitely has the spotlight on "Bouquet," which first appeared on his 1966 album *Happenings*, he gets outstanding support from start to finish by pianist Herbie Hancock (who played on the original version) and bassist Ron Carter. Neither takes a solo. But the more I've played that number, the more I appreciate what these two musicians do. Both are masters of their instruments. They came to prominence in the 1960s as two-fifths of the second great Miles Davis Quintet. Both have gone on to make a lot of wonderful music on their own. But neither Hancock nor Carter is averse to giving some strong backing to a colleague. And lord have mercy, how they do it on "Bouquet."

In 1798, the English poet Wordsworth wrote, "We murder to dissect." Music, when done properly, embodies gestalt. Musicians strive to present the listener with a song greater than the sum of its parts. You do not hear sounds, rather SOUND. Then music critics come along and tear that sound to pieces. I do not want to murder "Bouquet," but what follows might get me tossed into jazz jail for felonious assault.

Hancock and Carter begin "Bouquet" with a three-beat pulse. This is definitely not a waltz, but something much more subtle. Carter slides into his third note (in effect making it a four-note phrase) well before the third beat. Hancock can't slide on the piano; instead, he plays two notes and a chord, similar to what a guitar might do. The changes, flowing from major to minor chords and back, convey a back-to-nature, folk song quality. Hutcherson enters with a bluesy line, but he's not following blues form or using blue notes. Hutcherson's playing throughout contrasts and yet blends with Hancock's piano and Carter's bass. They keep the three-beat pulse while the vibes run all over the place, sometimes double or even triple time. Hutcherson creates tension; Hancock and Carter release it.

But Hancock and Carter have their own tension-release thing going. One jumps ahead of the first beat while the other holds it down. One, usually Carter but sometimes Hancock, will delay that third note or chord. The three dip down into a minor mode with Hancock adding dissonance to really build the tension for 12 beats. Then they release it by returning to the primary major mode. Carter moves off his three beats and goes into what might be a solo if Hutcherson wasn't playing on top of it. Carter does a few short runs, executes a roll with two fingers on strings instead of sticks on a drum, and then leaps into harmonics, with Hancock holding down the pulse. Meanwhile, Hutcherson colors the flowers in this bouquet with a rainbow of notes, rhythmically swaying, swirling, quivering, vibrating; all in glorious SOUND, not sounds.

They achieve this glory first because, to quote Morton and Cook in *The Penguin Guide to Jazz*: "'Bouquet' is one of the most underrated jazz compositions of the 1960s..." Second, these gentlemen listen to each other—those "big ears" I mentioned. Immediately Hutcherson does something, Hancock and Carter are right there. Third, underlying this apparently simple little pastoral piece, a lot is going on.

You may not be aware of it. You're not supposed to be. A bouquet is a selection of different flowers collected to create a single beautiful arrangement. Hutcherson, Hancock, and Carter want you to appreciate the song as a whole, just like the audience did that One Night with Blue Note back in 1985. And if you really dig it the most, why not try a… HoLAA!

CHAPTER 17
BENNY GOODMAN
"SING SING SING"

https://www.youtube.com/watch?v=0NigiwMtWE0

n the 1950s as a kid in southwest Missouri, I only wanted two little things out of life: to hit baseballs like Stan Musial and play clarinet like Benny Goodman. Not much to ask, I thought. Life had several strange things in store for me, none of which entailed hitting baseballs or playing clarinet. But it seems proper in a book of this sort to pay respects to a boyhood hero.

Benny Goodman has taken his fair share of knocks over the years, which I doubt concerned him too much; he was very famous and very rich. Many of his equally talented colleagues in jazz achieved neither wealth nor fame. That is scarcely Goodman's fault. Some say he only got where he got because he was white. Goodman was born very poor and very Jewish, much poorer than, for example, Miles Davis, whose father was a well-to-do dentist in East St. Louis. Davis' father sent Miles to Julliard, the finest, and most expensive music school in the U.S.

Goodman was doing gigs at 13 for money to help his family, and was a session musician by the age of 17 in New York City.

It is said that Goodman was egotistical and hard to work with. More than a few other great artists—jazz and otherwise—had similar characteristics. That's why we sometimes speak of "an artistic temperament," isn't it? Yes, he was the center of attention in his band; it was HIS band. Who was the center of attention in Cab Calloway's band? While he was not the first to integrate a group of black and white musicians, Goodman was the first to make a public display of it. Goodman was instrumental in breaking down the color bar. But let's talk about Benny Goodman as a musician.

Goodman gets knocked because he copied his early licks from New Orleans great Jimmie Noone. And Lester Young copied the approach of Frankie Trumbauer. He stole musical ideas from his sidemen. So did Basie and Ellington. Other clarinetists were just as good, if not better. Well, that's debatable. Claiming that Goodman was a great clarinetist detracts not one bit from the legacies of Noone or Johnny Dodds or Buster Baily or Barney Bigard or Artie Shaw. I wouldn't crown Goodman king of anything. I wouldn't crown anyone else king, queen, or prince of anything, but then I believe we ought to forget this royalty nonsense. I submit that Benny Goodman was a clarinet virtuoso who played some great jazz. If anyone wants to challenge that statement, let's get out the music and listen.

I really wanted to select something other than "Sing Sing Sing." It's the number I wish to avoid exactly because it's so famous. I checked out my tapes with the Trio (Gene Krupa and Teddy Wilson) and the Quartet (add Lionel Hampton). I went over everything I had with guitarist Charlie Christian. Yet I kept coming back to "Sing." Why? "Sing x 3" shows the best band Goodman ever had at its peak on one of the finest performances ever recorded. And I have to confess I also really like it.

Louie Prima composed "Sing Sing Sing." (Prima later became the voice of King Louie the orangutan in Disney's *The Jungle Book*.) Goodman's arranger, Jimmy Mundy, essentially created a new song by combining Prima's song with Chu Berry's song, "Christopher Columbus." Goodman used "Sing" as the climax to his shows, leaving the crowd shouting for more. And that's just what he did on a January night in 1938. And he did it at Carnegie Hall, no less.

"Sing" begins with Krupa on the tom-toms, followed by growling trumpets. We might think we're back in Duke Ellington's "jungle" territory. "Sing" is a series of eight-bar phrases, sometimes repeated, sometimes not. The band takes the first 32 bars and is four bars into the next section when Goodman's clarinet comes sailing in over the top. He only gives a bluesy preview of what will follow. Krupa oscillates between four-to-the-bar swing drumming and that jungle beat on the toms. The band builds to a climax, then comes in with a new section and builds to another climax, and then another section and climax, all connected by Krupa's drumming. Krupa takes a 24-bar solo then back comes the band with trumpets blasting. (Harry James was not only a star soloist but also led the trumpet section.) And it's over. At least, the audience in Carnegie Hall thought it was over. But no, it's just the end of the first movement.

Krupa begins again to introduce the trumpet solo of Harry James. Listen to that solo and you'll understand why critics and fans were wild about Harry. (So, eventually if not permanently, was Betty Grable.) James could play and, like Krupa, he could put on a show. (James started out playing in a circus orchestra with his father.) Blowing straight doesn't turn you on? How about some triple tongue? In the middle of his solo, the trumpet section returns. James leads them <u>and</u> solos at the same time. Why not build up some runs and hit a few blasts at the top? The group joins again for a finish. Applause.

Krupa keeps drumming to introduce Goodman with Jess Stacy

behind on piano. Krupa shifts the accent to the third beat while Benny warms up. Then he shifts again to the second and fourth beats as Goodman goes into a workout that would have made his classical instructor, Franz Schoeppe, proud. Krupa backs way off, just four-to-the-bar on bass drum. Benny hits a high A, so far up on the register you need oxygen, holds it for seven bars, only to end it on an even higher C. Lord, have mercy! That's great jazz by any standard.

But it's not over yet, for the most amazing thing in this amazing performance is about to occur. Whether it was planned or an accident I don't know. Goodman has hit that high C to climax his solo. Krupa pounds his tom-toms to take Benny out. The audience is clapping its approval, but as it fades out so does Krupa's drumming. We're about to have a dreaded silence. Now, all musicians have drilled into their brains from the day they start performing: NEVER EVER STOP... DO SOMETHING even if it's wrong.

So into the void ventures pianist Jess Stacy to play the solo of his career. He knocks on the door of immortality with three hesitant notes... oops! Goodman says, "Yes, Jess." Everyone has a good laugh, and Stacy is off doing what he called an "A minor thing." He starts his five chorus solo with some heavy two-handed stride a la Fats Waller, moves into an Earl Hines-Teddy Wilson groove, then it's all Stacy. He explores the never-never land between classical music and blues. He runs up to finish, like Benny, at the high end of the keyboard. (That is much easier on a piano than on a clarinet.)

Krupa calls the whole band on his cow bell, and they come wailing back for the real 16-bar climax. Trumpets lead. Goodman is over the top and Krupa is letting loose with everything he has. The Carnegie listeners can't contain themselves. They put up a mighty roar. One critic called that performance "bombastic." If that's bombastic, I say... bombs away!

I have written of inspired performances by Paul Gonsalves with the

Duke Ellington Orchestra at Newport and by Don Byas and Slam Stewart doing "I Got Rhythm." Benny Goodman's 1938 Carnegie Hall Concert had many magic moments, not only by the soloists in Goodman's groups, but "guests" from the Count Basie and Duke Ellington bands. Along with Goodman, Krupa, Teddy Wilson, Lionel Hampton, and Harry James, we hear the Count, Lester Young, and Buck Clayton from Basie's contingent, and Johnny Hodges, Cootie Williams, and Harry Carney from the Ellington Orchestra. And it says something to me about the nature of jazz that on this night of nights, after all those jazz immortals blew their best, culminating in the solo of Benny Goodman on "Sing Sing Sing," the not-quite-great Jess Stacy gains immortality with his inspired performance. Goodman and the others would have many more great moments during their musical careers. But let the record show on that night in 1938 at Carnegie Hall in New York City, Jess Stacy had the final word.

CHAPTER 18
ERIC DOLPHY-CHARLES MINGUS
"WHAT LOVE"

https://www.youtube.com/watch?v=JB6zApFJFRc&t=4s

J azz has a way of fostering strange partnerships. The most famous of these is probably Charlie Parker and Dizzy Gillespie. Gillespie was an extrovert and a cut-up. He acted dizzy but planned everything. A friend said he was dizzy like a fox. Parker was quiet and screwed up—a man of superior intelligence who killed himself by overindulgence—with food, booze and drugs: pick your poison. These two men loved each other. Gillespie called Parker "the other half of my heartbeat." But there was an intense rivalry between them. In the end, due to Bird's excesses, Diz pretty much gave up on ever being able to work with the other half of his heartbeat.

Less famous, but perhaps even stranger, was the relationship between Eric Dolphy and Charles Mingus. Dolphy played with Mingus' Jazz Composers Workshop from 1960 to 1961 and then again in 1964. You cannot find more contrasting personalities than Dolphy and Mingus. One of Dolphy's best compositions is titled "Serene." That single word describes Dolphy. Mingus, on the other hand, was a keg of gunpowder with the fuse lit. Dolphy got along well with everyone. Mingus couldn't get along with anyone. He goes down in jazz history as the only man Duke Ellington ever fired. Dolphy was at peace with the world. Mingus was at war with the world. He got so angry at his trombonist, Jimmy Knepper, one night that he punched him out on stage. Mingus was haunted by inner demons. He once admitted himself into the Bellevue Hospital psych ward. If you want to know about Charles Mingus, read his book, *Beneath the Underdog.* It's billed as an autobiography, but most people who knew Mingus would say he was "improvising." In any case it's a very interesting read.

Gauging by personality, Dolphy and Mingus were like water and fire. Musically, they got along just fine. Once the serene Dolphy picked up his horns—he played alto sax, bass clarinet, and flute—he blew with great intensity and passion, which is exactly how Charles Mingus played the double bass. And as chaotically as Mingus lived, he composed music with discipline and logic. Gary Giddins writes about "… the diversity and courage of his music, its relentless honesty and prophetic impact…" Mingus strove to create music like his two models, Jelly Roll Morton and Duke Ellington. (One of his compositions is a tribute called "My Jelly Roll Soul." Another is "Duke's Sounds of Love.") The three had in common great musicianship and an itch to innovate that had to be scratched.

Mingus grew up in Los Angeles and started playing music on the trombone, switched to cello, then switched again to double bass. He also studied piano. One of his first professional gigs was as bassist with no less than Louis Armstrong. It has been written that Mingus and Dolphy, a Los Angeles native, played a high school dance together. Maybe, but when Mingus left high school, Dolphy would have been a boy of 12.

Dolphy started playing clarinet at the age of six or seven (depending on the source). He also studied oboe. At 13, he began playing alto saxo-phone. He was so serious about music that his parents converted their garage into a studio for little Eric. He took lessons from reedman-flutist Buddy Collette, a friend of Charles Mingus. Dolphy worked in the Los Angeles area playing for a time in drummer Roy Porter's big band. (Porter had recorded with Charlie Parker in 1946.) After getting out of the military in 1953, Dolphy continued playing in various L.A. groups until at age 30 he joined the nationally known Chico Hamilton Quintet in 1958. Hamilton played a laid-back, cool sort of music, which one critic called "cocktail jazz."

After two years of cocktails with Chico, Dolphy was ready to break loose. He took up residence in New York and in the single year of 1960, he participated in 15 or 16 recording sessions including three that have become classics: Oliver Nelson's *Blues and the Abstract Truth*, George Russell's *Outer Thoughts*, and Ornette Coleman's landmark double quartet album *Free Jazz*. He also began a musical relationship with John Coltrane, who had just left Miles Davis to start his own group. Dolphy recorded with Coltrane twice in 1961. But most impor-tant, he joined Charles Mingus' Jazz Composers Workshop for some of the best music that group ever produced.

I find it difficult to describe how Eric Dolphy played. His style was highly "vocalized," meaning he made his horns talk. Blues harmonica players do this all the time. Trumpeter Buber Miley and trombonist Tricky Sam Nanton used to carry on conversations in the Ellington orchestra. But Dolphy talked a different language altogether. Writers have used phrases to describe Dolphy's playing like "urgent," "emotion-al," "rare," "elegant," "ornamental," "angry," "fiery," "collage," "sponta-neous," and "free association." Even with the contradictions, I'll go along with all except "angry," because Dolphy has been described as "a saint" by Mingus, and "one of the sweetest people I ever met" by L.A. saxophonist Harold Land. Some labeled Dolphy's playing Free jazz, some "advanced bebop" (whatever that means). My own self, I call it "ZIGZAG."

The Maasai of East Africa have a proverb: "Zigzag is the way to success." No one in jazz could zigzag better than Eric Dolphy. Jazz writers use phrases like horizontal for improvising off the melody and vertical for improvising off chord patterns. They write of "inside" players who stick to a song's harmonic structures and "outside" players who go beyond those structures. Eric Dolphy played vertically and horizontally, inside and outside, all at the same time. What's all that? Zigzag.

I selected not a Mingus composition but rather a Mingus reworking of a Cole Porter classic, "What is This Thing Called Love?" which Mingus called "What Love?" It is based on the harmonic structure of the Porter composition, but with a totally different melody. It also demonstrates what Dolphy could do on the bass clarinet. Although several jazzmen had played bass clarinet occasionally—most especially Harry Carney with the Ellington orchestra—as far as I know Dolphy was the first to *feature* bass clarinet. Additionally, "What Love?" is an excellent example of a Dolphy-Mingus musical dialogue. When Dolphy and Mingus start talking, it is intensely interesting—interestingly intense too.

This version of "What Love?" is from a concert in France at the Antibes Jazz Festival in 1960 with Ted Curson on trumpet and Dannie Richmond on drums. We are listening to what some call a "pianoless" quartet—generally two horns, bass, and drums. Omission of the piano means no audible chord structure for the horns to work from. On the other hand, there is a lot more space to play with. The absence of a piano (or a guitar) puts a heavy responsibility on the bassist. And what better bassist than Charles Mingus?

The group begins a rather foreboding theme in F minor—every note composed by Mingus—with Curson on trumpet and Dolphy on bass clarinet playing in unison. Bassist Mingus and drummer Rich-mond do not "keep time." There is no set rhythm. Anyone can lead—usually the soloist—and it is up to the other three musicians to feel the pulse and blend in. This may be why Mingus chose the virtually unknown Richmond as his drummer in 1956. It is erroneously reported that Dannie auditioned for the Mingus group as a saxophon-ist, but that Mingus told him, "You look like a drummer." Richmond did indeed play sax but had switched to drums before he met Mingus. Mingus, I am guessing, wanted a "musical" drummer (like his former partner Max Roach) who knew how to listen and respond... especially to Mingus. There is a special bond between bassists and drummers—they need to have something akin to rhythmic ESP. If you listen care-fully, you will hear how Richmond "plays off" Mingus and the others throughout "What Love?"

Although in stating the theme, Curson and Dolphy play in unison, they do not necessarily play the same notes. They start together with Dolphy in the bass clarinet's upper register but then Dolphy drops an octave lower, adding tension to what is a fairly dark melody. After the equivalent of something like eight bars, Curson drops down to his lower register but only for about four bars, when they both jump up an octave. Sometimes they play exactly the same notes together, but some-times they are together without being completely together. What love?

After the theme, Curson takes a three-minute solo with Dolphy occasionally adding comments and lending support. At one point, Curson leads Mingus and Richmond into a short blues passage played in strict 4/4 swing, but this quickly dissipates. Curson continues on his way—some might decide that he loses it. His solo doesn't so much end as wind down. Mingus steps in for two minutes with Richmond throwing in some sugar and spice. What love?

Dolphy returns and what follows is a four-minute dissertation on what love is. He starts his solo by stating two bars of the original composition, "What is this Thing Called Love?" Then he plunges into the lowest register of the bass clarinet. After a minute and a half, Dolphy begins to vocalize. (Were Antibes a sanctified church, I might say "testify.") This sort of playing was startlingly new, especially in Europe where proper citizens don't usually testify. A mere ten seconds of vocalizing and the crowd is applauding and Mingus is urging Dolphy on. But Eric has still more passionate views he needs to express and he soars into his higher register. We are now nine minutes into this number and Dolphy, always a sensitive listener, wants to exchange ideas with someone. So begins a musical dialogue between bass clarinet and double bass on the subject of love. Frankly, I don't know if they're laughing, crying, arguing, or what. Richmond joins in briefly but then decides this is between Dolphy and Mingus and moves to the sidelines. It's an amazing four minutes, especially the last two.

But it's not over. Curson returns, and with Dolphy, they play the opening theme in unison. A lot of jazz ends with a restatement of the theme, but not when Eric Dolphy is involved. Not content to just end it, Dolphy adds a harmony. This is the first harmony we've heard in 12 minutes. It's not a simple harmony, either. He expands it with Bach-like counterpoint. Mingus moves in underneath with Richmond contributing accents. And it fades into a subdued but beautiful sunset on the Riviera.

Both Mingus and Dolphy also faded into the sunset prematurely. Eric Dolphy would zigzag for a mere four more years after this performance at Antibes. Nine days past his 36th birthday in 1964, he died of a heart attack brought on by diabetes. At around the same time and maybe not just coincidentally, Mingus hit a creative block—between 1964 and 1974 he issued only two albums. He contracted ALS, Lou Gehrig's disease, and spent the last few years of his life in a wheelchair. And yet shortly before his death in 1979, on a collaborative album with singer Joni Mitchell, Mingus said, "I been lucky all my life. I've been blessed by God… God blessed me."

Both the volatile Mingus and serene Dolphy left lasting legacies for us. One of the best large ensembles in jazz today is the Mingus Big Band, a loose grouping of musicians devoted to reworking the compositions of Charles Mingus. Some of its members weren't even born in 1979. And we can still listen to the marvelous zigzagging of Eric Dolphy. It will clean all the garbage and goo out of your system. You'll feel fresh and ready to take on the world. A little zig here, a bit of zag there, and sooner or later, like the Maasai proverb goes, you're a success. A success at what? At living. With Eric Dolphy talking to you, you can zigzag right on through.

CHAPTER 19
ELLA FITZGERALD
"HOW HIGH THE MOON"

https://www.youtube.com/watch?v=iR1__k-BxhY

Some say the most perfect musical instrument is the human voice. If that is so, then the most perfect instrumentalist may be Ella Fitzgerald. Perfect pitch, perfect intonation, perfect diction. Every sound that came out of her mouth was crystal clear. She even laughed in tune. The only knock against Ella is that she was too good to be true. But almost every song she ever sang confirms that she was indeed that good. "Almost" because I don't think she could do Bessie Smith songs as well as Bessie Smith, or Billie Holiday as well as Billie Holiday. She did an album of soul music produced by Richard Perry and it was embarrassing. But give Ella some George Gershwin, Cole Porter, or Duke Ellington material and it's as good as it gets.

How good is that? Well, in 1966 she was recorded live with the Duke Ellington Orchestra (*Ella and Duke at the Cote D'Azur*). They went into a Force 10 rendition of "Cottontail" with Ella scatting (singing syllables rather than words) like someone who has overdosed on aviation fuel. Full thrust with afterburners. Up came Paul Gonsalves to engage Ella in a little cutting contest. Gonsalves was one of the champion blowers of all time on tenor sax and "Cottontail" was *his* song. I doubt that even Ben Webster, who first did "Cottontail" with the Ellington band, would want to go head to head against Gonsalves on that number. Ella scats a chorus; Paul blows a chorus. They start trading fours; they get down to twos. And Ella smokes him. Gonsalves gives up. Surrenders! Paul Gonsalves! On "Cottontail"! I would have thought it impossible, but Ella blew Gonsalves off the stage. That's how good Ella Fitzgerald was.

Calling Ella perfect may be stretching it. How much can an Ozark hillbilly know? So, I consulted some acknowledged experts:

Stephen Holden writes that Ella "has the most perfect pop-jazz voice on record."

British jazz critic Benny Green describes her "perfect intonation, natural ear for harmony, vast vocal range and purity of tone."

Swing chronicler Stanley Dance claims Ella is "one of the greatest singers jazz has ever produced."

Well, these fellows are writers. What do musicians think?

Jazz trumpeter Digby Fairweather called Ella "America's finest female interpreter of popular songs."

Count Basie has this in his autobiography: "So what can I say? The only thing Ella knows how to do is go out there and be wonderful."

Jazz authority Joachim Berendt stated that Ella was "not only a great Swing vocalist but also one of the great voices in all of modern jazz. No other female singer—and hardly any other jazz musician— commands a wider range of music."

The Encyclopedia of Popular Music, edited by Donald Clarke, maybe puts it best: Ella "transcends category."

Ella Fitzgerald was born in 1918. She began singing professionally at age 16. She was soon featured with Chick Webb's band, which dominated the Savoy Ballroom in New York City until Webb's death in 1939. She had her first hit jazzing up the nursery rhyme "A-Tisket A-Tasket" in 1938. For close to 60 years she gave the world her perfect gift.

I do not mean to detract from other great jazz vocalists such as Carmen McRae, Betty Carter, Joe Williams, Johnny Hartman, Annie Ross, Billy Eckstine, Anita O'Day, and especially Sarah Vaughan. I admire them all. But along with Donald Clarke I believe that Ella Fitzgerald transcends category.

Morgan Lewis wrote the music and Nancy Hamilton the lyrics of "How High the Moon" for a 1939 Broadway show. Jazz musicians love the song because it gives them a challenge and room to stretch out. Ella recorded it several times. This version comes off the 1960 album *Ella in Berlin*. She is backed by Paul Smith, piano; Wilfred Middlebrooks, bass; Jim Hall, guitar; and Gus Johnson, drums. Ella takes the two 16-bar verses fairly straight with only a few melodic embellishments at a medium swing tempo. Gus Johnson knew a thing or two about swing tempos, having propelled the Count Basie band among others. Ella makes the obligatory gesture to the song's composers then gives Johnson a nod. He kicks the tempo into overdrive, and she improvises both the melody and lyrics for two more verses.

Now it's scat time. I mean the lady GOES. She's not only as high as the moon, she's between the Devil and the deep blue sea. She's out of nowhere. She's swinging on a star. She takes the song places it's never been before and probably couldn't get to without her. After a 32-bar chorus of improvising off "How High the Moon," she switches to Little Benny Harris' tribute to Charlie Parker titled "Ornithology." Both songs have the same chord changes. After a chorus of "Ornithology" she's on her own with the band swinging like oscillators gone amok.

During the next several choruses she quotes an Irish jig, a Hawaiian war chant, a Latin samba, and throws in a bit of "Stormy Weather,"

"Heat Wave," and "Donkey Serenade." The group drops out except for Johnson on the drum kit while Ella does some operatic exercises and imitates a muted trumpet complete with Cootie Williams growls. After a few quasi-oriental bars, she calls the rest of the band back to help on a verse of "Smoke Gets in Your Eyes," which she changes to "sweat gets in your eyes." I can believe it. Then she ends it by running up to a note so high in falsetto you need a ladder to hear it.

Writer Len Lyons calls this seven-minute performance a *tour de force*. I'd call Lyons a master of understatement if I could come up with something better. I challenge anyone to name a singer living, dead, or yet to be born who can top Ella Fitzgerald on "How High the Moon." No one has ever done what Ella does as well as Ella does it. She's in a class of one.

I'll leave the last word to another class of one, Louis Armstrong. On their album *Ella and Louis,* Satchmo sings:

You took the chops
    Away from Pops
    So tenderly

CHAPTER 20
WEATHER REPORT
"BIRDLAND"

https://www.youtube.com/watch?v=vz7nMBLUnDc

I discovered fusion in the mid-1970s. It had already been around for five years or so, but it was new to me. Actually, I got in on the ground floor with Miles Davis' *Bitches Brew*. I just didn't know it at the time and so I missed everything that came after.

Fusion meant jazz with a rock beat, in its simplest form. Miles Davis said he wanted to form the "best damn rock and roll band in the world." As usual with Davis, it wasn't anywhere near that clear cut. And fusion wasn't that clear cut either. To begin with, fusion is a misnomer. Jazz has always been a fusion of various styles. The problem, as I see it, comes when people insist on labels. Some jazz people don't even like the label jazz. They might call it improvised music. But that wouldn't be accurate either because some jazz is almost entirely composed. Anyway, certain styles (not a single style) of music dating from the late 1960s get labeled as fusion. I say "styles" because the music of Miles Davis in that period was different from, say, the music of the Crusaders, from the Mahavishnu Orchestra, from Chick Corea's band Return to Forever, from Chuck Mangione, from Herbie Hancock's Headhunters, from Grover Washington, Jr., etc. What all these people had in common was a desire to make music accessible to a wider audience and, as a result, make more money.

Fusion was to some extent a reaction to the Free jazz movement of the 1960s. Many found Free jazz simply un-listenable—chaotic noise filled with squeaks and squalls. Free jazz, at its best, was not chaotic noise, but certainly it had only a small audience. Fusion attempted to do what Free jazz claimed to do. Free jazz was trying to express the joy, oppression, and rage of the masses. Fusion wanted to make music the masses would listen to and buy.

Fusion came in many varieties. It sometimes was little more than a funky groove or simple elevator music. It could also get extremely complex. But at its best, fusion offered up some really fine music and more expansive horizons. It did, to a lesser degree than it desired, bring jazz to new audiences. But just as important, in my opinion, it pushed jazz beyond the continental United States and into becoming World Music. That is not to imply that jazz had been strictly American music until fusion came along. From its earliest period, Jelly Roll Morton did music with "the Spanish tinge." Jazz had always made room for anything it could use from anywhere on the planet. Sun Ra took his inspiration from outer space. But with fusion, jazz really opened up to Latin, African, Asian, and even (even) European music. And some of its best practitioners were not "made in America." Up to the 1970s, non-Americans primarily (but not always) imitated American-made jazz. During the fusion era, they incorporated their own music cultures into jazz and enriched jazz in the process.

A good example of this new internationalism can be found in the original lineup of Weather Report: saxophonist Wayne Shorter and drummer Alphonse Mouzon, Americans; keyboardist Joe Zawinul,

Austrian; bassist Miroslav Vitous, Czechoslovakian; and percussionist Airto Moreira, Brazilian. Weather Report began as an offshoot of the Miles Davis group that recorded *Bitches Brew* in 1969. Both Shorter and Zawinul had been members; and their first album in 1971 was like Bitches Brew Part V. But over time, the music (and personnel) changed. It became less "jazzy" and more "funky," more structured, and more highly produced, especially as Zawinul added more technologically advanced synthesizers to his keyboard arsenal. Their development reached its stylistic and commercial zenith in 1977 with the album *Heavy Weather*, which rose to No. 30 on the Billboard album chart. The big "hit" on this hit album was "Birdland." The number typifies the best of fusion and also hints at what might be its worst.

On its most fundamental level, "Birdland" is a great tune. Zawinul could knock out tunes before breakfast. He wrote "Mercy Mercy Mercy" and "Country Preacher" while with the Cannonball Adderley group. He contributed the title track to Miles Davis' *In a Silent Way.* "Birdland" has an infectious groove provided by drummer Alejandro Acuna and percussionist Manolo Badrena. In short, the song is hummable and danceable. It's got voices and handclaps (to help you hum and dance in case you miss the point).

Zawinul uses his synthesizer the way the swing bands used horn sections. In fact, "Birdland" was inspired by a Count Basie performance that Zawinul attended at the Birdland club in New York. Rather than riffs, Zawinul, who is classically trained, goes for counterpoint. "Bird-land" is a veritable potpourri of sound. A whole lot of music comes at you underpinned by a funky beat. But... well, we'll get to the "but" shortly (or more specifically, Shorter).

"Birdland" begins backwards (as I hear it). It is common in jazz for the bass to kick things off. Then another instrument states the melody line. On this song, Zawinul takes the bass intro on the synthesizer. Electric bassist Jaco Pastorius plays the melody, using string bends and harmonics (high overtones). It doesn't sound anything like an ordinary bass, but then Pastorius wasn't your ordinary bass player. He, along with Eberhard Weber in Europe, revolutionized players' approach to the instrument. Pastorius, through harmonics, makes his fretless electric bass sound like a guitar, sort of. Zawinul provides the bass on one synthesizer and harmony on another. Acuna and Badrena lay down the groove and they're off for 16 bars. Then Shorter comes in on soprano sax for what we might, in another song, call the bridge. Zawinul harmonizes on synthesizers and Pastorius takes up something that is similar to a bass line but is actually a bottom harmony. Zawinul and the percussionists take 24 bars of groove. Shorter blows about eight bars on soprano. Then we get some more groove until they all hit the main four-bar vamp with Shorter on soprano in the lead, Pastorius below, and Zawinul and his synthesizers everywhere. As the four bars are repeated, Zawinul keeps adding layers of sound—24 bars' worth. Zawinul and the percussionists groove some more. Finally Shorter takes maybe the only improvised piece in the entire song—a whole 14 bars wailing on tenor sax *behind* the synthesizers. If you don't pay attention, you might miss it.

Then they start all over again with Pastorius on lead bass and Shorter making some funky comments on tenor for a few bars. Shorter switches to soprano and harmonizes with Pastorius until they get to the sort-of bridge. Again, Shorter plays lead on soprano, with Zawinul harmonizing and Pastorius underneath. Some more groove and they hit the hummable, danceable vamp with voices to encourage humming and hands clapping to inspire happy feet. Zawinul builds his layers and adds counterpoint with everything in his tool kit. These four bars are repeated over and over for almost two minutes, the clappers getting so excited toward the fade-out that they go into double-time.

It would be difficult for anyone not to like "Birdland." As my daughters and I listened to the song in the process of my writing about it, they were humming along and we all had to get up and boogie a bit. Zawinul has accomplished the ultimate goal of fusion on "Birdland": He's written a piece of music the masses will listen to and buy. He and the group bring it off beautifully.

But.... Now we get to the "but." In fact, two "buts." I consider synthesizers very dangerous because they can do so much. They can effectively disguise weak musicianship on the one hand. On the other, the huge array of sounds and effects begs to be used by a master such as Zawinul, Herbie Hancock, or Stevie Wonder. Sadly, it is too often the case that the electronic marvels are simply overused. Overuse produces musical mush, an unfortunately apt description of much fusion. Zawinul fortunately does not overdo it on "Birdland." He takes it to the limit but stops just short of the sonic cesspool.

Wayne Shorter is without question one of the master saxophonists in jazz but he gets short shrift here. When John Coltrane died in 1967, Shorter assumed the role of chief "egg scrambler" (his term). On "Birdland" he hardly gets an opportunity to crack the shell. Other than tooting a few lead lines and adding a bit of harmony, Wayne has 14 bars to do any blowing, barely a warm-up. (For a contrast, check out his tenor playing on the Art Blakey selection "Night in Tunisia.") Shorter got some room to move in Weather Report concerts, but in the studio it's mostly Zawinul and his synthesizers.

Zawinul wrote this number to pay respect to Count Basie and the swing era, but there may be another connection between the song "Birdland" and the New York club named in honor of Charlie Parker. Parker and the beboppers came along and gave jazz a new twist; a quarter-century later, fusion did the same thing. They were all after broadening horizons and making good music. Weather Report did just that between 1971 and 1977. Enjoy!

CHAPTER 21
SONNY ROLLINS
"THERE'S NO BUSINESS LIKE SHOW BUSINESS"

https://www.youtube.com/watch?v=dUou9UlZnz0

magine: You're in a taxi driving from Manhattan to Brooklyn over the Williamsburg Bridge at about 3 a.m. in 1959. You see a man walking slowly towards you. A man walking on the bridge at 3 a.m.? And he seems to be holding something like... could it be... a saxophone?! You roll down the window to get a better look and you hear the sound. He's playing it. And good too. "You know who that is?" you ask the taxi driver. "Oh, that's Sonny Rollins. He's out here every night. Crazy jazz musician."

Right and wrong. Sonny Rollins is a jazz musician but he's not crazy. He's practicing on the bridge so he won't disturb his neighbors late at night. The question is not why he's on the bridge, but rather why he's practicing at all. For in 1959 many considered Sonny Rollins among the finest tenor men in jazz, if not the finest.

Sonny Rollins dropped out of the jazz scene in 1959 amidst considerable speculation. Some said John Coltrane was making him nervous (not even close). Some said he couldn't deal with all the adulation and analysis by critics. (Rollins wrote: "I really didn't understand what I was doing until I read Gunther Schuller...") Rollins himself claimed he wanted to work on his chops. Chops, slang for technique, are fundamental to all musicians. Classical musicians are judged by how well they can execute and the depth of feeling with which they can infuse a piece of composed music. A jazz musician also spends years working on execution, but that is just the beginning. When jazz musicians start to play, they are both interpreters *and* composers, judged on how well they can improvise.

Sonny Rollins has always been noted for his ability to improvise. Francis Davis proclaimed Rollins "the greatest living jazz improviser." He also called Rollins "the least predictable of jazz artists" and "the most perverse." (These are compliments.) Gary Giddins, one of the most literate and perceptive jazz writers today, praised a particular Rollins solo for its "unpremeditated intentionality." (Say what?) On almost any Sonny Rollins album done between 1955 and 1959, you will hear the art of improvising at its best.

I find it interesting that Rollins decided to hibernate in 1959. That year marked two highly significant jazz events. First came the Miles Davis album *Kind of Blue*, which popularized modal jazz with minimal chord changes. Then out of the West came a Texan with a plastic alto sax whose quartet sent shock waves through the jazz community. Ornette Coleman, *The Shape of Jazz to Come,* had arrived with his "harmolodics," which used tone centers rather than notes and pulse rather than rhythm. In short, Free jazz. Perhaps Rollins needed some time on his own to delve into these new styles and get himself sorted out. His first album back on the scene in 1961 was titled *The Bridge*.

Maybe the bridge is where Sonny Rollins went to get beyond what he already could do, to learn, to develop, to move on. Francis Davis writes: "The image of the quintessential jazzman—heroic, inspired, mystical, obsessed..." fits Rollins for he "... epitomizes the lonely tightrope walk between spontaneity and organization implicit in taking an improvised solo." I can understand that. For a while I walked that tightrope three nights a week, usually falling off. Every time you improvise on your horn (or in your life), you run the risk of making a fool of yourself. For those who improvise at anything, the bridge beckons.

Rollins will improvise off anything, even songs no one else would touch. Who but Sonny Rollins would bother with such musical junk as "I'm an Old Cowhand"? I expect he looks upon this rubbish as a challenge to his skills as an improviser. And maybe he hears something in these tunes that others don't. He certainly transforms them, much as a fairy godmother waving her wand, with a chorus from his magic tenor. Rollins has also composed some fine numbers, such as "St. Thomas," "Oleo," "Doxy," and "Airegin" (Nigeria spelled backwards). To give you Rollins at his best, I ought to choose one of these or a song like "Blue 7." For sheer musical excitement, you can't do better than *Tenor Madness,* the sole recorded encounter between Rollins and Coltrane. The two of them just plain smoke. For virtuoso playing, check out "Autumn Nocturne" off the album *Don't Stop the Carnival.* But I personally love Rollins the Alchemist.

Which brings us to "There's No Business like Show Business." Now I expect some, possibly many, might dispute my assessment that this song is musical fluff. If you like Irving Berlin, Ethel Merman, *Annie Get Your Gun,* and all that show biz glitz, fine by me. I remember that when I taped the 1955 album *Worktime,* I figured I wouldn't bother with this track. One listen made me change my mind in a hurry. And as with most good jazz, the more you listen the more you hear. I thought I was alone in finding "No Business" appealing. Then I read Gary Giddins describing it as an example of Rollins' "unprecedented ability to sustain lengthy improvisations with authority, coherence and wit." Francis Davis and Len Lyons also note the delights of this as Rollins puts it together. And Barry Kernfeld, editor of the *New Grove Dictionary of Jazz*, wrote of Rollins' "a penchant for unlikely, at times bizarre, popular melodies."

The number begins with Max Roach doing a four-bar intro on drums. Almost the entire song is played at double time. I mean it rips. Roach calls in the rest of the group and Rollins on tenor takes up the hokey theme. He doesn't play it exactly straight. He adds notes here, omits notes there. Mostly, though, the group varies the rhythm. That is not surprising with Max Roach on drums. Rollins jumps out in front of the beat then falls behind only to dash back ahead and let it pass him by. The only straight four bars you get is from Roach's cymbal. George Morrow's bass is galloping along in double time. Still the group, and in particular Rollins, leaves no doubt that "there's no business like show business."

With a drumroll from Roach, Rollins and Morrow do a chorus of tenor-bass duet, with Morrow starting at double time, slowing it down to a regular four, going back to double time, then down to four, then doubling again where Roach and pianist Ray Bryant join in at the end of the chorus.

Rollins does another chorus fairly straight with Roach adding some off-beat accents, then Sonny lets loose. He effectively creates a new song during the following two choruses, yet if you listen closely, you'll hear little references along the way to the original theme. You will also note that Rollins does more than improvise notes. He and Roach rearrange rhythmic accents. Yet it is all of a piece; it all holds together.

Ray Bryant then takes over to show his stuff. Bryant's fingers fly over the keys. His left hand especially puts me in mind of Teddy

Wilson, a very influential pianist of the 1930s who played with, among others, the Benny Goodman Trio. Bryant's left-hand rhythm is so strong that Roach backs way off on the drum kit, giving plenty of space to Bryant. Morrow continues his double time gallop, but his bass is much more subdued than when Rollins was blowing.

Then Roach has some choice remarks to make on his drum kit. You'll know why Max became one of the all-time great drummers in jazz. This is no flash crash-banging. Roach, the most musical of drummers, builds his solo so that you can practically hum along. Bryant does a bit of accompaniment to help you hum in tune. Or if humming isn't your bag, how about tap dancing?

Rollins goes through the theme, principally embellishing the melody; once again Roach adds all sorts of rhythmic quirks. Rollins adds a little solo flourish at the end and it's over.

This is six-plus minutes of first-rate musicians playing a third-rate tune. I expect Rollins picks this schlock, at least partially, to show off. But there is also something else involved. I wrote that jazz has always taken music composed in another style and "jazzed it up." If we go back to the early days, most of the pieces used were modified spirituals, marches, work songs, and proto-blues. I think it is no accident that it was African Americans who created jazz. The slaves had their freedom, languages, and cultures taken from them. They were not allowed to even play their drums. (Plantation owners thought the slaves might be sending messages of insurrection via drumming.) The music they were allowed belonged to Massa and, perhaps for precisely that reason, the slaves felt the need to change it so it would become *their* music. If they couldn't be physically free, they could seek musical freedom. Freedom underpins all jazz. That may offer a clue as to why Sonny Rollins does a number like "No Business." It is equally possible that I am full of baloney. I take solace in the fact that there is no right or wrong in jazz.

Sonny Rollins has pulmonary fibrosis and will likely never again play in public. But I was fortunate to hear him in person in May 2005. Incredible. Some years ago, I read an interview with Branford Marsalis, a fairly prodigious improviser himself. He said that after playing on the same stage with Sonny Rollins, he wanted to pack up his horn and quit. Well, lemme tell ya, Bran-baby, and I mean it sincerely: There's no business like show business. Let's go on with the show.

CHAPTER 22
PAUL DESMOND & DAVE BRUBECK
"STARDUST"

https://www.youtube.com/watch?v=PM2WcgR3rtw

will never forget my twelfth birthday. I got a 45rpm record player. (We had no turntables or sound systems back then.) In addition, the folks gave me a whole dollar to buy the record of my choice. My mother expected I'd get one of the 3 B's—Bach, Beethoven, or Brahms. The old man also expected I'd get one of the 3 B's—Benny, Bix, or Basie. I did get a B alright, only it was Bill as in Haley and the Comets. To their shame, horror, and disappointment, my folks discovered that the son they hoped would be a musical genius had for some time been a closet rock and roller. I didn't know then—and wouldn't realize until I became a father myself—that the main occupation of teenagers is annoying their parents.

The first jazz I brought home was an EP—"extended play" or half an album. It was *Jazz Goes to College* by the Dave Brubeck Quartet. And the reason I got that particular group reduces itself to two words—Paul Desmond. I will readily admit that I am an incurable Paul

Desmond nut—just as I am a Charlie Parker-John Coltrane-Kippie Moeketsi nut. All musicians on all instruments strive for an individual sound. Individual sound on alto sax, without debate, would include Johnny Hodges, Charlie Parker, and Paul Desmond. After those three, you can debate all you like. (I might include Kippie Moeketsi if more people had heard of him.)

Before we go any further, I have to warn you: Liking Paul Desmond is not cool. The only thing less cool is liking Dave Brubeck. The Dave Brubeck Quartet was the ultimate cool West Coast group. It became very un-cool among the arbiters of jazz taste. But if you are willing to be scoffed at by those who not only "know" but want you to know that THEY know, read on.

Paul Desmond was not a technical wizard. He claimed to have won several prizes for being the world's slowest alto player. He could not bowl you over with power. He said he had also won a special award for quietness. He would not take you to The Edge. He knew his limitations and played within them. Desmond is one of the most consistent musicians in jazz. Buy any album with Paul Desmond and you know what you will get.

First, you will get the lightest alto sax tone in jazz. This is the first thing almost everyone digs about Desmond. He got his tone straight from Lester Young's tenor sound. Ironically many accused Lester of playing the tenor like it was an alto, which may not be far from the truth because Young used C-melody saxophonist Frankie Trumbauer as his model. Desmond said he wanted to make his alto sax sound like a dry martini.

Second, Paul Desmond is a master of the altissimo register—that territory on the saxophone above high C. Many other alto players can hit those high notes; some can go even higher than Desmond, but nobody plays altissimo with such ease. And he never makes a big deal of it. He'll be soloing and all of a sudden—TWEE—E above high C. But then he'll go right back to the middle. You might think your ears were fooling you, then up he'll go again, maybe a three or four note cluster. And those three or four notes will never sound like squeaks. They'll be just as mellow and light as notes in the middle. Paul Desmond owns the territory above high C; the others are merely visiting.

Third, Desmond has a very individual approach to improvisation. Jazzmen talk about horizontal improvisers, who play off the melody line, and vertical improvisers, who base their solos on the harmonic structure—the chord changes. Asked whether he was a horizontal or vertical improviser, Desmond replied he was more of a diagonal improviser. There is more than a grain of truth in that witty response. I have a Paul Desmond solo on "Body and Soul" where he starts horizontally for two bars, then vertically improvises for two bars, then goes back to horizontal but only for a bar, then he mixes it up so much that you really can't follow it, so you just lean back and enjoy. Enjoy what? Diagonal improvisation. Free jazz saxophonist Anthony Braxton cites Desmond as a major influence and calls him "a profound thinker... what you heard had been edited completely, only the essence remained." Braxton also supplies the best description I've come across of Paul Desmond's style: "... because he understood his craft so well his music has this air of easiness about it, as if it's kind of floating."

Dave Brubeck's piano does not float. His style is often described as percussive, and that is more or less accurate. It's less accurate in that he isn't always percussive but when he gets into it, he percusses like mad. I rather think of Brubeck's style as intense. Even when he is playing quietly, he's quietly intense. Then he immerses himself more and more into the music and starts on the two-handed block chords, and soon enough the poor piano gets pounded into submission. He does a solo on "This Can't Be Love" that is painful to listen to. The only pianist I can think of more percussive than Brubeck is Cecil Taylor. We are not surprised to learn that Taylor, a pioneer of Free jazz, greatly admired Brubeck.

Brubeck and Desmond first met in 1944. Desmond said that when they started to jam on a blues, Brubeck's approach "almost scared me to death." However, once they understood each other, they connected beautifully. Desmond was in Brubeck's octet in 1946-47, but Brubeck cut down to a trio until 1951 when Desmond returned to make it a quartet. Brubeck and Desmond continued together for 16 years, not counting various reunions thereafter.

I am once again confronted with the problem of selection. As I wrote above, Desmond is the most consistent musician you are likely to come across. I have five albums he made in the '60s with Jim Hall on guitar; each is a gem. Or Desmond returning the compliment and playing on Hall's 1975 album *Concierto*. Great. Or his guest performance with the Modern Jazz Quartet in 1971. Super. And then there are all those albums with Brubeck. I might go for Brubeck's classic composition, "In Your Own Sweet Way." Even Miles Davis, who had no use for the Brubeck Quartet, recorded "Sweet Way" (and another Brubeck composition, "The Duke," a tribute to Ellington). Or the most famous of all Brubeck Quartet tunes, "Take Five" (from the album *Time Out*), which made it into the Top 40. (*Time Out* does not have a bad cut on it.)

"Take Five" is a classic study of musical *gestalt*—how four jazz men can produce art greater than the sum of its parts. Desmond wrote the catchy little 24-bar tune. He does the lead and takes a two-chorus solo. Brubeck does nothing but a two-bar vamp for most of the song, establishing the odd time signature of 5/4—he plays 1AND-2AND 4-5/1AND-2AND 4-5 for about five minutes. That's all. To keep everyone together and make it swing in 5/4, somebody has to let everybody know where "one" is—to emphasize that first beat. Bassist Eugene Wright's nickname was "The Senator"—he made the rhythmic law of the Quartet. So, to let the band know where "one" is and to make it swing, he played 4-5-**1**... pause... 4-5-**1**. That ONE is very heavy. Then he pauses for two beats, then plays a light four and five and ONE. Like telling everyone, "We're (4) at (5) ONE. We're at ONE." And finally, we hear Joe Morello's drum solo in 5/4 time, which is not all that hard with Brubeck playing 1AND-2AND 4-5/1AND-2AND 4-5and Wright going 4-5-**1**.

However, the recorded solo is a mere shadow of what I heard when I was lucky enough to catch the Brubeck Quartet in concert in the early '60s. Morello played the drums, then he got up from the kit and played both Brubeck's piano and Wright's bass with his sticks. Then he played the FLOOR. Then he got really serious; he put down the sticks, and played the drums—and cymbals—with his fingers! Not a couple of little flicks and thumps, he played for perhaps five minutes with just his hands... and an occasional elbow just for fun. Then he picked up the sticks again and let go with a barrage, a world war of drum sounds. It was a 20 minute drum solo to end all drum solos. And I don't generally like drum solos.

"Take Five" kept Desmond in what he called "slot machine change" the rest of his life and became a staple of lounge combos. Yet, it is in no way an example of great alto sax playing. If not "Take Five," why not choose my first love "Le Souk" off *Jazz Goes to College*, or "Blues for Fun" (which could be renamed "Blues for Prez"), or the ultimate Brubeck contribution to jazz, "In Your Own Sweet Way"? In the end I just couldn't choose, so I let someone else choose for me.

The late Emil Katona was by vocation a professor of economics; he taught at the University of Dar es Salaam in the 1980s. By avocation, Emil was an extraordinarily gifted reed player. Classically trained, he had two clarinets—your ordinary B-flat garden variety and a special clarinet for playing Mozart. Though I would scarcely call it dabbling, Katona said he "dabbled" in flute. Ah, but when he picked up a saxophone, SHAZAAM! He was so good that he could find no one to play with. He was left putting on tapes and playing duets with Stan Getz, Sonny Rollins, Sonny Stitt, Gerry Mulligan, and Paul Desmond. And to my ear, Emil held his own, even in that fast company. He presented me with a tape of some of his favorite numbers, one of which was the Brubeck Quartet doing the Hoagy Carmichael composition "Stardust" from the 1953 album *Jazz at Oberlin College.* When in doubt, go with the professor. On "Stardust," it's all there: that "dry martini" tone, the Lester Young phrasing, the diagonal improvising, and above all (literally) lots and lots of altissimo.

Brubeck starts things off with a simple but lyrical four-bar intro at medium tempo. Desmond comes in with the rhythm section, repeating exactly the first four notes of Brubeck's intro, but now it's the first four notes of the tune. Only it's not the melody of "Stardust" as Carmichael composed it. We get no hint what song the quartet is doing until Desmond plays a snippet of the melody in the seventh and eighth bars. He is improvising vertically to the chord changes. Then he goes horizontal along the melody through bar 16. After that it's pretty much diagonal until the end of the first chorus. Desmond, self-proclaimed slowest alto in jazz, begins his second chorus doubling the time. It does not sound flashy because he is totally relaxed going twice as fast as everyone else. And there is not a note out of place. Every note, as Braxton said, was completely edited. He packs so much into what he plays that I was surprised to discover he had only done two choruses, a mere 64 bars. And note how he winds it down toward the end so that Brubeck can build it back up again.

Let me begin by saying I like most of what Brubeck plays in his two choruses. However, he commits every sin his critics accuse him of. There is no reference whatsoever to the melody. Listening to what Brubeck plays, you would not know this is "Stardust." In fact, if you took away the bass and drums, you would not know this is jazz. There is no syncopation, no swing. It sounds to me like a battle between a Debussy etude and a Tchaikovsky concerto. That's not necessarily bad. Brubeck likes contrast. Sometimes he plays l-i-g-h-t; sometimes **H-E-A-V-Y.** Once in a while he gets pretty ham-fisted. But on the whole, it's a nice piece of work. And most important, after his 64 bars, he sets up the finale with Desmond.

Desmond repeats Brubeck's final phrase—a single note cluster— then we get a 50-second lesson on cool jazz. We get a lesson, too, on playing in the alto's altissimo register. By the 10th bar, you may think you're listening to a clarinet. We also hear how Dave Brubeck could accompany others as he does here in enhancing Desmond's solo. We hear the Desmond-Brubeck interplay in the six-bar ending, or outro. It sounds as if they had ESP. But most outstanding to me is that Paul Desmond exhibits in that final 50 seconds the two qualities that were the foundation of everything I ever heard him play: modesty and confidence. I have listened to those last 50 seconds again and again and again, and I never cease to be impressed by Desmond's quiet certitude. These are the notes played; they are the ONLY notes that can be played. Each note is perfect. And the next time Paul Desmond played that final half chorus and outro to "Stardust," I am guessing the notes would all be different. But they would still each be perfect. And that is why— cool or un-cool—I love to float with Paul Desmond.

CHAPTER 23
LEON THOMAS
— "UM UM UM"

https://www.youtube.com/watch?v=UtbgB4CE02U

L et us take a few paragraphs to consider the jazz artists who didn't make it big. Jazz for most of its history has been minority music... in several senses of the word. To be tops in jazz is not the same as being tops in pop music. Jazz superstar Wynton Marsalis is not a household name. If a jazz album sells 100,000 units, it's a mega-hit. If Beyoncé sold "only" 100,000 units, she'd get dropped by her company. No doubt jazz musicians would love to sell in gold and platinum figures but, except for bean-counting executives, jazz is not judged by sales.

Read books on jazz or listen to jazz request programs, and the same names pop up again and again: Armstrong, Ellington, Basie, Holiday, Parker, Davis, Monk, Coltrane.... These (and several dozen more) are the giants of jazz. What about the thousands of other great jazz musicians? One of the really fun things about jazz—more so than any other kind of music I've come across—is the endless debating. Every serious jazz fan has a comment (informed or not) on almost every topic remotely related to jazz. You put two jazz fans in a room together and you will have at least three opinions. My friend Kevin and I go around and around about the merits of Dexter Gordon. Another very knowledgeable friend has no use whatsoever for one of my main men, Paul Desmond. Jazz fans can spend truly exorbitant amounts of time discussing the pros and cons of almost any musician who ever blew, strummed, stroked, banged, or sang.

Just about every serious jazz fan champions certain musicians who aren't in the "Top Ten" or haven't made the Downbeat Hall of Fame or aren't voted "the best" in the Playboy poll. Most of the people I've written about here are among the best of the best by almost any measure you care to apply. But a few are not up there in the front line. That brings us to Leon Thomas.

Leon Thomas? Yes indeed. I love Leon Thomas. Leon never made it big... even by jazz standards. Maybe he came close. I don't know, having spent most of the years since 1965 out here in Africa. But I can guess why he didn't make it.

Leon Thomas is unique. People either love him or hate him. I don't believe there's a middle ground. Obviously, I love him, and just as obviously most people don't. What makes Leon Thomas unique? He, uh, yodels. Yes, he yodels. The 19th century field hollers, called arhoolies, invariably involved yodeling. Yodeling is common throughout Africa. Where I live, no important ceremony is complete without the women giving out a high pitched ululations—lulululululululululu. When Africans came to the Americas, they brought their yodeling along. It turned up in the arhoolies.

Thomas didn't start out his musical career as a yodeler. In the late 1950s he was a straight-ahead jazz singer—if you can call any good jazz singing straight. In fact, he had the honor of replacing the great Joe

Williams in the Count Basie band. I doubt that he yodeled with Basie. When or how he picked up yodeling, or voice shaking as he called it, I don't know. I might speculate he got it from the arhoolies or he listened to recordings by ethnomusicologists of traditional African singing or maybe from the Lomax field work in the South. In the end it doesn't matter much. For those of us who like it, we're just happy Leon learned to yodel. In the process he picked up the title "the John Coltrane of jazz singers."

I was introduced to the marvels of Leon Thomas in 1969 on a horse ranch in the Rocky Mountains at about 2 a.m. A late-night jazz DJ on a Denver FM station was playing Leon's *piece de resistance,* "Um Um Um." It knocked my socks off.

Thomas is backed on "Um Um Um" by James Spaulding on flute, pianist Art Sterling, Bob Cunningham on bass, drummer Roy Haynes, and percussionist Pablo Landrum. Haynes and Landrum begin immediately laying down a complex base of cross-rhythms. Bassist Cunningham enters to firmly anchor what is about to happen. In comes Sterling on piano and from the way he's playing, you feel you have another percussion instrument in the group. James Spaulding joins on flute, giving you just a taste.

Thomas prefaces his singing with a spoken explanation. "Um Um Um," he tells us, "is a common denominator." It's part of a universal language. If he heard his arthritic grandma going "Um Um Um," he knew it would rain. The fellows on the street corner would see a beautiful lady walk by and say, "Um Um Um." You hear the U.S. Government has spent $100 billion on a space program to bring back some moon rocks. What can you do but go "Um Um Um?"

Then he sings:

Blues ever get you till you didn't know what to do

Have you ever cried the whole night and all the morning too
Um Um Um/Um Um Um/ Um Um Um

So, this is blues he's dealing with here. Not the 3 chord/12-bar variety. Not simple four beats to the bar either. But it's blues, nonetheless.

Thomas sings another verse about how messed up the world is—Um Um Um. Then out come those amazing sounds from somewhere deep inside. What the hell is that? He does it again. Holy Moly! Yodeling. He mixes the yodels with scat singing. This is just an appetizer.

Spaulding is into blowing some very intense Um Um Um flute now. He starts with a sound bubbling out. He toots. He runs. He trills. He's all over the place. Sure sounds good! Um Um Um!

Then it's just Thomas and the percussionists. Thomas gets into some extremely serious yodeling mixed with scat. I can't describe it. To call it a baritone Tarzan sound out of the savanna of Africa doing modal blues doesn't even come close.

After one and half minutes of this wild and wonderful sound, the percussionists pound out cross-rhythms like crazy. Thomas re-enters with more yodeling and scat. The rest of the group joins in. Thomas sings three verses. They finish with some more Um Um Um. Strange and exhilarating music.

If your idea of good music is Lawrence Welk, Abba, or Madonna, you probably won't like "Um Um Um." Maybe you have to be a little bit bent around the edges to appreciate what Thomas offers. Or I can lay it out another way. Jazz, I believe, is the most open-ended, open-minded music on Earth. It is always changing, always coming up with new stories to be told in new ways. Obviously not everyone is going to like every story or every storyteller. But one of the things that jazz provides you is a wide range of choices and the freedom to choose. If you are ready for a new listening experience, something you won't hear anyone else do, I highly recommend Leon Thomas.

I believe excellence should be treasured, and to my ears and soul, Leon Thomas is nothing less than excellent. There is only one rap song I can really dig. The title? "Things that Make You Go Um!" Leon, you left a legacy!

CHAPTER 24
TERRI LYNE CARRINGTON
"LOVE AND PASSION"

(no link on You Tube)

When I was a kid, my father would get me to eat vegetables by mixing them in with mashed potatoes. I loved mashed potatoes, didn't like vegetables. The spinach and peas would get conglomerated with starchy tuber and down the hatch. Dad called these combinations, depending on which vegetables, "Mish-Mash No. 42" or "Mish-Mash No. 67." Anyway, I got the proper amounts of vitamin A, niacin, and iron.

It seems to me that in the 1980s jazz became something like Mish-Mash. It incorporated everything from ragtime to free, with New Orleans, swing, bebop, and rock thrown in. And for someone who detests labels, this was great. I particularly enjoy the so-called experts desperately trying to come up with labels. Wynton Marsalis plays classicism. Steve Coleman plays neoclassicism. And how does neoclassicism differ from classicism, Mr. Expert? Wellll, you see, classicism is based on bop (sort of) and neoclassicism is based on Free jazz (sort of), only both have a lot of elements of each and other styles too and... blah blah blah blah. As I have written, forget what the so-called experts say. Wynton Marsalis and Steve Coleman play music you may or may not like. Since the experts feel compelled to stick labels on them, let's call it all Mish-Mash in honor of a man who could get down on Bix Beider-becke *and* Fats Domino. This will probably not win me an honorary degree from Experts U, but since you and I are the ones who buy the music, we have the right to call it anything we like.

By some convoluted logic I haven't quite worked out yet, this brings us to the subject of one Terri Lyne Carrington (or Terry as I've seen it spelled). I know exactly two important facts about Terri Lyne Carrington: 1) Carrington is a drummer; 2) Carrington is a woman. I intentionally put drummer first. This is not a tract on women's libera-tion. First and foremost, Terri Lyne Carrington is a drummer. I mean she's a terrific drummer. I am sure she is thrilled to be a woman; I am thrilled that she's a drummer. I also know she's American, born in 1965 (or maybe 1962, depending on your source), and played drums with Wayne Shorter after he split from Weather Report. But the central point here is that the lady is a very fine drummer.

I expect she started out banging on pots and pans when she was little. Her father was a musician. He may have decided that as long as she liked to bang on things, she may as well do it on a proper drum kit. And that was that. She's been banging on drums ever since. I have no way of knowing whether she was encouraged or discouraged in this interest. Was she told, cruelly and unfairly, to stick to more traditional female pursuits? I don't know, but if she was, I am glad she ignored the guidance. Breaking stereotypes rates very high on my scale. Witness this writing. But good musicians rate even higher. And I consider Terri Lyne Carrington to be very good indeed.

If it weren't for my friend, the famous Njugu Kijabe, I wouldn't be writing about Terri Lyne Carrington at all. On one of his visits to

Africa, he brought along an album ~~entitled~~ *The Truth*. It's from a live 1988 performance in Copenhagen with pianist Niels Lan Doky as nominal leader. I know very little about Niels Lan Doky. He's a fine pianist and he's Danish. The bassist is Bo Stief, also Danish, also fine. And on tenor sax is Bob Berg who I do know a little about because he played with the Miles Davis group, 1984-87.

There are four cuts on *The Truth*, and each is a gem. I was seriously astounded by the song "Panduro." Bob Berg and Terri Lyne Carrington do a sax-drum duet reminiscent of John Coltrane and Elvin Jones working their musical magic together. Berg and Carrington do go at it. "Love and Passion" is the last number of the set. I wonder what the experts would label this. Latin-Rock-Funk-Bop-Free-for-all. Or why not Mish-Mash? Or we can follow the Ellington maxim of two (and only two) kinds of music. If so, this is the good kind.

Niels Lan Doky introduces "Love and Passion" with a two-bar, riff-like phrase on piano. (Riff is just a technical word meaning a repeated musical phrase. I'll call it a riff and let the experts call me a moron.) Carrington and Stief join in after eight bars, laying down a Latin kick and the three move it into fourth gear for another eight bars. Berg states an eight-bar theme on tenor sax with Lan Doky playing along. Then Lan Doky returns to his riff while Berg restates the theme. So far we've heard an arranged piece. Then they move into the solos when Berg plays "Take It!" on his sax.

Lan Doky responds with a vengeance to Berg's "take it." Carrington and Stief switch from their Latin kick to a funky crisscross groove. Listen to Carrington push Lan Doky—not that he needs much pushing—to keep the intensity level way up there. This is power drumming, but what touch. I usually check out a drummer's touch by listening to the cymbal work. I'm very cymbal-minded. When Carrington hits her cymbals, they never sound like inverted pie pans. She knows where to hit to get the sound she wants and just how much force to use. Touch is the difference between good and really good. (Creativity raises it to great.)

Stief takes over from Lan Doky. He attacks the strings in much the same way a funk bassist plays an electric, only he does it on upright acoustic, which is fairly awkward to solo on at fast tempos. Carrington gets into some serious funk rhythm making. The funkier her drumming, the funkier Stief plays. While I shouldn't generalize, I can testify that Danes are not as a rule the funkiest folks around, having worked with a bunch of them for three years. Stief, with Carrington pushing, proves to be an exception and gets on down to Funkytown.

Carrington starts her solo with some Steve Gadd "50 Ways to Leave Your Lover" marching band snare and heavily syncopated bass drum interplay. (Her bass drum could stand as a solo on its own.) She throws in some Elvin Jones and Billy Cobham crisscross and a whole lot of Terri Lyne Carrington. As good as this solo is, I'm more impressed by what she plays with the others. However, I've already done my little solo on that when discussing Art Blakey, so enough said.

Berg returns with his eight-bar theme twice and then launches into orbit. It's Coltrane modal, Rollins linear, King Curtis R&B, inside-outside, up-and-down, let it roll Mish-Mash. Lan Doky is riffing, Stief is free-bassing, and Carrington somehow surrounds the whole lot with her massive rhythm. She's pushing, pulling, behind, in front, raising the intensity level, raising it again, and then another again. Berg is blowing so intensely he's just this side of the Twilight Zone.

Finally, the group hits the two-bar riff. Berg falters the second time through (possibly as a result of the previous two minutes of *in extremis* wailing) and they then lay into one hell of a dramatic finish. Lan Doky rumbles the keys, Stief rolls the bass strings, Berg runs some funky blues arpeggios, and Carrington detonates/explodes/erupts/you name it. Maybe Stief's fingers fall off and Bob passes out right there on the stage, leaving Niels and Terri Lyne to battle it out for who is going to get the last word in. Eventually they call it a draw and end together.

How to summarize this Mish-Mash music? Let's go to the title: These four play with passion and I love it. But I believe the key to this really outstanding performance is Carrington's drumming. I cannot comment on Lan Doky and Stief. I haven't listened to much Bob Berg. What I have indicates the man can blow. But nothing I have takes it to this level of blowing. They all play on the edge because Carrington drives them there.

The experts are forever posing the question: Is Jazz Dead? Let Terri Lyne Carrington beat some sense into them. And learn to spell her name correctly.

Sorry, I couldn't find a link but if you're a member of Spotify, here you go:

https://open.spotify.com/album/1jHpV4SLU7NSAB6jgCWxNo

CHAPTER 25
RAHSAAN ROLAND KIRK
"ONE TON"

https://www.youtube.com/watch?v=2tIYLpp5o2s

The word "fan," as in jazz fan, derives from fanatic. Some jazz fans get pretty fanatical. They can also get pretty defensive. They will tell you jazz is just as serious as European symphonic music. They will tell you Keith Jarrett plays piano just as well as Vladimir Horowitz. Or that Charles Mingus studied classical cello as well as being a premiere jazz bassist. Or that Wynton Marsalis is the only musician to win a Grammy for best classical album and best jazz album in the same year. You never hear classical fans say Mozart is just as good a composer as Duke Ellington. Or that Luciano Pavarotti sings as well as Ella Fitzgerald.

Jazz fans also sometimes feel like an oppressed minority. MTV blasts synthesized schlock at viewers 24/7. How much jazz is featured on television—a few hours a year? Madonna makes millions. Most jazz musicians scuffle just to put food on the table. Jazz represents less than 1.1 percent of total music sales in the U.S. Jazz has to be one of America's greatest cultural contributions to mankind and most Americans ignore it. Do I sound like a fanatic?

American jazz fans can't hold a candle to their European counterparts. For some Europeans, jazz borders on religion. The true believer in traditional jazz must sometime during his life go on a pilgrimage to New Orleans to worship at the holy of holies, Preservation Hall.

But let's face it, jazz has produced some fairly weird characters. Thelonious Monk wore funny little hats and would stop playing in the middle of a song to get up and do a strange little dance. Lester Young had his own language; you needed an interpreter to understand what he was saying most of the time. And Charlie Parker: Freudians could have a field day studying his life.

Sometimes jazz is produced on instruments you wouldn't normally associate with jazz. Julius Watkins plays jazz on a French horn. Illinois Jacquet blows jazz on a bassoon. Yusuf Lateef wails blues on the oboe. Howard Johnson has an ensemble called Gravity that plays jazz on six tubas. And Rufus Harley maybe tops them all—jazz bagpipes!

But for pure weirdness, I would nominate Rahsaan Roland Kirk. Kirk could play three saxophones at the same time. He used a regular tenor sax and two antique saxes he called the "stritch" and the "manzello." He also played various whistles, a nose flute, and a kazoo. He could sing and play a regular flute simultaneously. It's not that Rahsaan couldn't play straight jazz, but I just love his strange stuff. When you listen to Coltrane, you hear a man searching for the Love Supreme. When you listen to Kirk's "One Ton," you hear a man running full speed toward the Weird Sublime.

Kirk, blinded in a childhood accident, takes the stage with enough instruments attached to various parts of his body to open a hardware store. He recorded the album *Volunteered Slavery* at the 1968 Newport Jazz Festival with Ron Burton, piano; Vernon Martin, bass; Jimmy Hopps, drums; Kirk on everything else. "One Ton" rips the stuffing out of a conventional 12-bar blues. The tempo is so fast, in effect, this is a six-bar blues.

Kirk blasts forth on three saxes. Don't ask how he does it. Who cares how he does it? He's doing it! The melody line is fairly simple stuff. Still, who cares? Three saxes at the same time. Then he's on to the flute. I mean he's on to it. He's playing it. He's singing into it. He's spitting into it. He's doing harmonies with it. He does everything but eat it. Then he throws in some nose flute. Why not—it sounds gooood. Now he goes back to regular flute for a serious workout. A friend said it sounds like he's having sex with it. I'll buy that. I'll buy any idea anyone has on Kirk. He ends his solo with a blast on the whistle. Orgasm?

Ron Burton takes over on piano with some faster-than-a-speeding-bullet honky-tonk boogie-woogie. Rahsaan jumps back in on three saxes. Go. GO. GOOO! In a burst of sound, "One Ton" crashes to a close.

Jazz is serious music. Jazz writers have some serious things to say about Rahsaan Roland Kirk. His music can be seen in the context of the entire jazz tradition. He represents a cultural heritage with roots extending back to Africa. Okay. Why not? After all, this is Rahsaan ROLL ON Kirk.

"One Ton?" Well, how about one ton of white oppression? How about one ton of suffering from blindness? How about one ton of sex? All the above? None of the above? How about—perish the thought—one ton of musical fun? Could it be that old Rahsaan is blowing his butt off just for the pleasure of playing? Could it be that he's simply up there having a natural ball and would like to share his enjoyment of music with us? No more, no less? And that's plenty. Frankly, I don't know what one ton means. And I don't care. That's right, I don't care. I don't understand his story, but I sure do like the way he tells it. And in reply to the serious jazz writers, all I can say is ROLL ON, RahSAAN. ROOLLL OOOOOONNN.

And maybe that's the way to end it. Jazz IS. It's whatever you hear when you listen. It means this to me and that to you. It means something today and something else tomorrow. Jazz is, for me, all the things I've written. It's ecstasy, unity, joy, oppression, excellence. It is coolness, perfection, hard work, beauty, mysticism, strength. It is African-European and 100 percent American. It is—I most firmly believe—the triumph of the human spirit. It is, in short, freedom. And, guess what, it's FUN. It's everything all music is, because it's part of all music, which is an essential part of all people.

To enjoy jazz, you don't need to know a diminished 9th from a flatted 5th. You don't need to know the difference between bebop and hard bop. You don't need to know Louis Armstrong's real birth date. You don't need to know how William Basie got his nickname. You don't need to know diddly-squat. All you need to enjoy jazz are ears, heart, and soul. And we all have those. Put on the number of your choice—not necessarily my choice— and give it a fair hearing. Maybe you don't like it much the first time. Try again. Maybe you don't like after five tries. Okay. Try something else. Not all jazz is for all people. I love jazz but not all jazz. But this I do believe to my soul: Some jazz and maybe a lot of jazz is for you. Can you dig it? Yes, you can!

So... ... ... ROOLLL OOOOOONNN!

PART TWO
THE BLUES AIN'T NOTHIN'

The blues ain't nothin' but a good woman on
    your mind...
I got up this mornin', saw blues walkin' like a
    man...
The blues jumped a rabbit, run him one solid
    mile...
Gotta keep movin', blues fallin' down like hail...
You see me laughin', I'm laughin' to keep from
    cryin'...

The blues cannot be defined. No one can say when or where blues began. People can't even decide whether blues is singular or plural. The blues is/are full of joy. The blues is/are full of misery. Here's how Gil Scott Heron ran it down in his introduction to "Watergate Blues":

There are at least 500 shades of the blues

For example, there's the I-ain't-got-me-no-money blues
There's the I-ain't-got-me-no-woman blues
There's the I-ain't-got-me-no-money-and-I-ain't-got-me-no-woman
Which is the double blues

B.B. King put it more succinctly: "The Blues is like a Mother Tree."
Here's what three old time bluesmen told Giles Oakley in his book *The Devil's Music*:

"Blues is a feeling" (Booker "Bukka" White).
"It's a relief, for pressure" (Henry Townsend).
"The blues come from black people" (Houston Stackhouse).

We all get the blues, no question about it. Junior Wells said that "the blues automatically touches people because most of the things you sing about, people can understand... it's something everybody has." Blues guitarist Donald Kinsey agrees: "It's a music that has a reality to it." And every culture in the world has a music to express this feeling of "lowdown." We have on the East African coast a type of music called "Taarab." One of its great singers, Shakila, does a song titled "*Chozi Lanitoka*" (a tear falls.) She sings: "*Macho yanacheka, moyo unalia*" (my eyes are laughing, my heart is crying). That is pure Swahili blues.

The blues evolved in the last decade of the 19th century from field hollers, work songs, and ballads like "John Henry." The precursors to the blues were the string bands and songsters throughout the southern regions of the United States. The first songs called blues were published in 1912. The best-known among them was "Memphis Blues" by W.C. Handy, who is called Father of the Blues even though he wasn't. A more accurate title might be Popularizer of the Blues. Singer Mamie Smith cut the first blues record, "Crazy Blues," in 1920. Bandleader Perry Bradford wrote that song. All these musicians were African-American. Most, but not all, of the important blues musicians have been black.

The blues has several meanings. Certain notes on the scale are called blue notes. But a piece of music can have blue notes and not be blues, such as George Gershwin's "Rhapsody in Blue." These notes give a blues feel. Blues is a form—in fact several forms. Songs following those forms are sometimes called blues. The most common form has 12 bars and usually three chords. A lot of rock and roll follows that same format. (Brownie McGhee sings: "The Blues had a baby and they named it Rock and Roll.")

You may have heard that blues is about the easiest music around. Blues is very deceptive. Albert Collins puts it straight: "It's really simple music, but it's the hardest music in the world to play." B.B. King adds: "Now if you've got a Blues tune, and you don't have but three chords for 12 bars, you've got to be a magician to keep the listener interested." Lonnie Brooks reinforces Booker White's statement: "The blues is more of a feeling than it is anything else."

To do the blues well you have to feel it. I've heard many go through the motions but not the emotions of the blues. They know the blue notes, they know the forms. They know where the "ooowee" is supposed to go. You've got to pay your dues if you want to play the blues, as the saying goes. The "ooowee" will tell you if the musician has paid those dues. All the blues musicians I will write about paid their dues. Some paid extremely heavy dues. You'll hear that payment receipt when they sound the "ooowee."

Blues come in 500 shades, said Gil Scott Heron. Blues also come in many styles, though maybe not 500. Blues scholar David Evans lists 33 starting with Acoustic and ending with Zydeco. You've got soft blues and loud blues, country blues and city blues, Mississippi Delta blues, Texas blues, New Orleans blues, Chicago blues, Piedmont blues, big band blues, jump band blues, small band blues, lounge blues, bar blues, old time blues, modern blues, gospel blues, hillbilly blues, jazzy blues. However, as Buddy Guy points out: "You take everybody's electronics away from us, and put us back on the acoustic guitar, and we're all playing the same stuff." Forget the labels, it's all just blues.

The blues wind up in a lot of jazz and a lot of rock and roll. The blues wind up in pop music and in religious music. The blues even wind up in 20th century classical music. Otis Rush sums it up: "The Blues is the Blues. It's everywhere. The Blues is the foundation for all music, you know." The blues is everywhere, because the blues is about life. And we're going to get inside this music that comes from inside.

I listen to all kinds of music from Bach organ fugues to Spike Jones. You may have gathered by now that I love jazz. But when I hear the blues, it hits deep, deep inside. I can't explain it much beyond that. I wasn't born on a cotton farm or in a city ghetto. But I've had my share of joy and pain. The blues are about joy and pain. Maybe that's it. The blues came from black people, but the music is about people, period. Johnny Winter had this to say: "It seems like the blues is just there for anybody who can relate to it." I've turned a heavy metal freak from Louisville, Kentucky, on to the blues; I've turned a Danish hippie on to the blues; I've turned a Tanzanian yuppie on to the blues. And guess what? Now I'm going to try to turn you on to the blues.

I can say that blues is truly wonderful music, but that doesn't get us very far. You've got to listen to it and decide for yourself. Just sit back, close your eyes, and let the blues fill you up. The music comes in through your ears, goes all around your insides, and lodges itself in your soul. That's right. Blues is soul music, as is all music. The blues will take you all the places, all the venues, that the very word "blues" calls to mind, from the Mississippi Delta and the swamps of Louisiana and into such places as Deep Ellum Street in Dallas, Beale Street in Memphis, and to Maxwell Street on Chicago's Southside. They will tell you about love and hate, happiness and sorrow. They will tell you about life.

Lawrence Hyman, editor of *Going to Chicago*, from which many of the preceding quotes were taken, sums it up well: "The blues creates, in its delicate balance of the comic and the tragic, the transformation of common misery into poetic truth." You see, the blues ain't nothin'... the blues is everything.

CHAPTER 26
BIG WALTER HORTON
"TROUBLE IN MIND"

https://www.youtube.com/watch?v=b89Ja97Gp6s

When I was 18, I put away my rock and roll saxophone and bought a Stella guitar for $7.50. I struggled through the chord changes to "Tom Dooley" and "Michael Row the Boat Ashore." Then I felt ready for the big time. I learned a blues song, "Trouble in Mind." Now I was legit. I could go out into the big, wide world and claim to be a bluesman: "Check this out... 'Trouble in mind, Lord I'm blue...'"

Why, from all the possibilities, did I choose this particular blues? Well, mainly because it's easy to play and I was a beginner. But on a higher level, "Trouble in Mind" has become a standard over the years because it's everything a great blues should be. It's personal, universal, and timeless. It deals with a subject that concerned our first ancestor several million years ago in Olduvai Gorge, still concerns us every day, and will pass through the last human soul just before oblivion. I expect that's why "Trouble in Mind" has been covered by so many blues artists since it was composed by one Richard M. Jones and popularized by Chippie Hill in 1926. I know almost nothing about Richard M. Jones, but I know all about "Trouble in Mind." Everybody knows all about "Trouble in Mind," whether or not they've ever heard the song. Blues come in 500 shades. With this composition, Richard M. Jones tapped into the very core of the human condition.

Big Walter Horton's version of "Trouble in Mind" came as something of a surprise. I'd always thought of him as a bluesman whose approach was to roll up his sleeves and let it rip. I think of "Rockin' My Boogie," a harmonica *tour de force* duet with Charlie Musselwhite—that's Big Walter Horton, the master. "Trouble in Mind" is pure finesse. This is sweetness, lightness, goodness, and any other "-ness" you care to throw in. Doing this number the way Big Walter does takes more than skill. There are harmonica wizards nowadays who can run circles around Horton in terms of pure technique. But when you cut through all the notes and get down to the core of the blues, there's the sad-eyed Big Walter staring at you as if to say: "Boy, get yourself some soul."

Walter Horton was playing harmonica ("harp" to a blues musician) before he could recite the alphabet. He hung out with all the Memphis blues people in Handy Park in the 1920s. Some sources claim Horton recorded with his mentor Will Shade and the Memphis Jug band, and also did some shows with Ma Rainey in 1927 when he would have been nine years old. He didn't get around to recording on his own until 1950 when he cut sides for Sam Phillips (who a few years later came across a young Memphis greaser with the unlikely name of Elvis). Big Walter continued making sweet harp music under his own name or as a sideman with other blues artists until his death in 1981.

In 1969 Horton was doing a session with his protégé Carey Bell when "Trouble in Mind" got recorded, almost by accident. During a break Big Walter and his boyhood chum, guitarist Eddie Taylor, started messing around doing one of those good old songs from way back. The messing around became a masterpiece in one take.

Walter Horton plays "Trouble in Mind" in what harp players call "first position," way up at the top end of the harmonica, warbling like a canary. Eddie Taylor is underneath on electric guitar. (Taylor spent years underneath backing bluesman Jimmy Reed.) The two spend most of the first chorus getting in sync. That doesn't seem to affect Walter's playing one bit. Oh, it sounds good: the warbles, the vibrato, the bends, the octaves. By the beginning of the second harp chorus, Horton and Taylor finally get it together and they really run it down. Blues harp just doesn't come any better than this.

After two choruses of harp, Big Walter—a good singer but not a great one—is about to lay on you some of the most famous blues lyrics ever composed:

> Trouble in mind… Lord, I'm blue
> But I won't be blue always

Everything there is to know about the blues is wrapped up in those two lines. The way Walter sings "Lord, I'm blue," you know he's weighed down by a world of trouble—his mind is full of it. Then comes that shouted "won't": "I WON'T be blue always." It's the whole history of the human race. Trouble after trouble. Problem after problem. Several million years. But we survive, we persevere, we carry on. Why? Big Walter Horton has the answer:

> You know the sun is gonna shine
> In my backdoor one day

Not the sun "may" shine or "I hope the sun will shine." Big Walter is certain that the sun is gonna shine. But why the backdoor? My guess is that the good things in life sort of sneak up on you when you're not paying attention. Often you plan things that don't seem to go right and then they just fall into place... through the "backdoor." Or maybe Richard Jones happened to like the sound of backdoor more than, say, screened-in front porch.

Big Walter goes on to tell us how badly the blues have got him down:

> I'm gonna lay my head
> Lord, on some lonely railroad line
> I'm gonna let that 219
> Pacify my mind

Is Big Walter contemplating suicide by having a diesel locomotive separate his troubled head from his troubled body?

Not really. He just wants us to know how bad his troubles are. And if he really was considering suicide, he rejects that option in the next verse:

> I'm gonna buy me a rockin' chair
> Whoa, gonna take it and sit right down
> And when the blues overtake me
> I'm gonna rock on away from here

I think maybe Walter messed up the first two lines (remember, he was just fooling around when this got recorded). It's usually sung "I'm goin' down to the river/Take along my rockin' chair." But it really doesn't matter much. After that harp break, he can sing anything he wants as far as I'm concerned. In addition, Big Walter sings another verse about his mother that I've never heard used in this song. Well, it's a free country, and blues, within its confines, is free music. There is one thing almost all blues tunes that invoke mothers have in common: If you don't heed their advice, you wind up in trouble. And that's exactly what happens to Walter which, of course, leads to the blues which, of course, is what "Trouble in Mind" is all about.

Big Walter inserts three choruses of harp between verses. Each is a gem. Now you may be wondering how someone could get so worked up about a simple bit of harmonica playing a simple eight-bar blues. Skip the fact that it was this simple blues song that started me on a quest over 60 years ago. The blues, done well, is only superficially simple, and if you think it's simple then you've only listened superficially. The more you listen, the more you hear. The more you hear, the more you appreciate what you're listening to. For me, every time I hear Big Walter Horton blow that first high warble, I ascend into harp heaven. And I know, for sure, I won't be blue always.

CHAPTER 27
MUDDY WATERS
"MANNISH BOY"

https://www.youtube.com/watch?v=bSfqNEvykv0

Oh yeah... (Guitar echoes oh yeah)
Oh yeah... (Guitar echoes oh yeah)
Everything gonna be alright this mornin'

And right away, you know it. You have no doubt that everything gonna be alright. So begins "Mannish Boy" by Muddy Waters, and that's just an appetizer.

It would be unthinkable, virtually impossible, to write, talk, or do the blues without reference to McKinley Morganfield. He got the name Muddy Waters from his grandmother because he liked playing in a creek near his home in Rolling Fork, Mississippi. Rolling Fork is in the Delta, which is not really a delta but rather an area around the junction of the Mississippi and Yazoo rivers at Vicksburg that runs north up to Memphis, Tennessee. The Delta gave birth to an amazing number of great bluesman. And one of the greatest of these greats was Muddy Waters.

Muddy Waters learned his music from country blues great Son House who also heavily influenced the master, Robert Johnson. Waters described his music as one-third Son House, one-third Robert Johnson, and one-third Muddy Waters. We might debate the proportions, but we can't argue with the results. Muddy Waters took country blues to the city in the mid-1940s. He certainly wasn't the first. Neither was he the first to use a group with electric instruments. But Muddy Waters, unlike others before him, incorporated electricity into his music. He played loud, he sang loud, his blues was really loud.

Muddy Waters performed his music in small clubs on the south side of Chicago. People came there to meet their friends, have a good time, drink, talk, shout, and sometimes fight. Intricate music full of sophisticated subtleties would simply get buried under an avalanche of noise in such establishments. If you wanted to get people's attention, you had to grab their attention. And Muddy Waters knew how to grab.

First, he grabbed them with the most basic, and most essential, element of his music— rhythm. His band would whip you with a beat that would not quit, that didn't know how to quit, that was—in a word —irresistible. Once he grabbed you, Muddy Waters delivered his message loud and clear. It might be: "There's another mule kicking in your stall," or "I wish I was a catfish swimmin' in the deep blue sea/I'd have all you pretty women swimmin' after me," or "I'm ready for you/I hope you're ready for me," or "I got my mojo working but it just won't work on you," or "I can't be satisfied and I just can't keep crying," or "I got a rich man's woman but I'm living on a poor man's pay."

Because they'd been grabbed by the rhythm and the message came out loud and clear, listeners knew exactly what Muddy Waters was singing about. It was something they could all relate to. So let's dispense with the subtleties and say it, plainly and only once: Around 90 percent of his songs dealt with sex. Percentages will vary, but that subject will figure prominently in the work of other blues artists, blues rhythms, and blues lyrics. Whether you concentrate on the words to "Mannish Boy," or concentrate instead on the beat, Muddy Waters makes the subject clear. "Mannish Boy," was first recorded in 1955. It completes a trilogy, if you will, or maybe serves as the last chapter in a saga that began the year before with "Hoochie Coochie Man." In the middle of it came "I'm a Man" by Bo Diddley. He hailed from McComb, Mississippi, and Muddy Waters introduced Bo Diddley to his record company, Chess Records. Willie Dixon, another son of the Delta (Vicksburg, Mississippi), wrote and produced all three numbers. (See what I mean about Mississippi and blues? I could add that Muddy Waters got his start in Chicago from Big Bill Broonzy, another transplanted Mississippian.)

Willie Dixon deserves a whole chapter to himself. Since he won't get one, I'll put in a few inadequate words now. Dixon wrote a number of blues classics for Muddy Waters, Howlin Wolf, and others. He produced a number of great recordings for Chess Records. He also led the Chess house band and played bass. He was instrumental in the careers of rock-and-rollers Bo Diddley and Chuck Berry. Willie Dixon's autobiography, "I Am The Blues," is less a boast than a pretty accurate description.

Back to Muddy Waters. He was blowing musicians off the stage from the 1950s. His original group was called the Headhunters and they would cruise the Chicago bars looking for bands to blow off the stage.

The original "Mannish Boy" seemed strong for a record in 1955. However, recording technology being what it was, the number doesn't come across as powerfully as it would if heard in a live performance. The drummer has to use brushes instead of the sticks he would have used in a club. The original recording isn't the complete song either because some of the lyrics might have been considered risqué or because it was too long to put on a three-minute 78 or 45 record for potential radio play.

If you want to hear "Mannish Boy" in all its glory, you can go to the Muddy Waters' performance on The Band's *The Last Waltz*. The Last Waltz was The Band's farewell concert. They collected an all-star group for the last hurrah, folks like Neil Young, Joni Mitchell, Eric Clapton, Paul Butterfield, and of course their old running mate, Bob Dylan. This was a big deal put on film by Martin Scorsese. The 61-year-old Muddy Waters gets up there and blows them all off the stage.

But even that performance of "Mannish Boy," as good as it is, pales in comparison to a version Waters laid down with Johnny Winter on the album *Hard Again* in 1977. That version, with modern technology, has assumed its true power. The drummer, Willie "Big Eyes" Smith, can let loose and not worry about drowning out the rest of the group. He is aided and abetted by Charles Calmese on heavy-duty electric bass, Pinetop Perkins on piano, and James Cotton on harmonica properly amplified. After the "Oh Yeah/Oh Yeah/Everything gonna be alright this morning," Big Eyes kicks into Force 10 beat that doesn't vary even a micro-point throughout the song. And the group, led by Johnny Winter's guitar, sets up a single drone—Doo-doo-doo-doo DOOP—which acts as a preface and comment on the outrageous claims Muddy Waters puts out. The group is saying, "You better believe it; you know it's true; he's right on it." In "Hoochie Coochie Man," Muddy Waters sang:

> Gypsy woman told my mama
> Before I was born
> You got a boy child comin'
> Gonna be a son of a gun

"Mannish Boy" dispenses with a gypsy woman talking about this boy in the third person. Here, we go right to the point, no messing about:

> Now when I was a young boy
> At the age of five
> My mother said I'm gonna be
> The greatest man alive

Unwilling to risk even the possibility that "son of a gun" could be misconstrued, Waters lays it straight on you—"the greatest MAN alive." No sentient human could possibly question what he means by "man." But, as the saying goes, a thing worth doing is worth overdoing, so he explains it again:

> Sittin on the outside
> Just me and my mate
> You know I'm made to move, honey
> Come up two hours late...
> Wasn't that a maaan?
> I spell M... etc.

And on the off chance there might be someone out there with the IQ of a lead pencil, he enumerates what a man or maaan is:

> That means *mannish* BOY...
> I'm a *full*-grown man...
> I'm a natural born *lover's* man...
> I'm a *roooolin'* stone
> (And if you happened to miss part one of the
>   saga)

I'm a Hoochie Coochie man

He continues to expand on the powers of this mannish boy:

The line I shoots
Will never miss
When I make love to a woman
She can't resist

When Muddy Water shoots a line, the women can't resist. I would add that nobody else can resist either. He then sings about his "second cousin little John Conqueroo," a voodoo charm used to increase a man's sexual potency. With the assistance of Little Johnny Conqueroo, Waters can take care of business in "five minutes time."

Looked at in cool objectivity, "Mannish Boy" is a series of fantastic claims. Little Johnny Conqueroo or no Conqueroo, could anyone possess that kind of power? My reply? It's irrelevant. That beat and Muddy Water's total conviction, supplemented by the band's affirmation—Doo-doo-doo-doo DOOP—prove to the listener beyond the shadow of a doubt that Muddy Waters knows exactly what he is. He asks, "Wasn't that a man?" The answer comes back a resounding yes!

Muddy Waters was a man. He came from poverty in the Mississippi Delta to bring his message to the big city ghetto. We (black people) are men (and women). We count for something. Muddy Waters was saying, I represent you. And I sing my message loud and clear. As he stated in "Hoochie Coochie Man," "I'm here/everybody knows I'm here." "Everybody knows I am." Muddy Waters was a MAN.

And everything gonna be alright. Oh yeah.

CHAPTER 28
LEAD BELLY
"BOURGEOIS BLUES"

https://www.youtube.com/watch?v=DT6lmhxXV_M

f you want to go back to the roots, I mean the very deep roots of the blues, just run out and buy everything you can find by Huddie Ledbetter, a.k.a. Lead Belly. When you listen to Lead Belly, he can take you back to the days of slavery. He came from Louisiana and East Texas; he was born in the 1880s, some sources have it 1885, others 1889. He grew up on an isolated cotton farm in Caddo Lake County, Texas. He played accordion, then 12-string guitar. He called himself "king of the 12-string guitar players." Eventually he added piano and harmonica to his arsenal.

Lead Belly had a phenomenal memory for music. Much of what he played pre-dates blues. He entertained his rural community as a teenager with jigs, reels, breakdowns, field hollers, and shouts. He also could do children's songs, lullabies, work songs, even cowboy songs and spirituals. Forced to leave East Texas in the early 1900s, he wound up on the notorious Fannin Street in Shreveport, Louisiana where he learned barrelhouse piano and early blues. He did several sentences in prison where he learned chain gang chants. Moving to Dallas, he met the younger Blind Lemon Jefferson who specialized in country blues. They would play together in Dallas on Elm Street (called Deep Ellum in song), attracting large crowds. In 1933, back in a Louisiana prison, he was recorded by John and Alan Lomax for the Library of Congress. These two managed to secure his release and they took him to New York to begin a recording career.

White audiences loved Lead Belly. Here was a genuine folk hero, only just this side of illiterate. He was a cotton picker and a brawler. His nickname allegedly comes from a bullet lodged in his stomach. Lead Belly was a convicted murderer and an honest-to-goodness chain gang refugee. He also possessed a treasure chest of music going back to the Stone Age.

Most black people had little use for Lead Belly. His records sold poorly in the "race" market, as it was called in those days. Lead Belly's music reminded them of things they had left behind: Uncle Tom's Cabin, handkerchief heads, and white men called Massa. Given this state of affairs, it's not surprising that the songs for which Lead Belly is best known—"Goodnight Irene," "The Rock Island Line," "The Midnight Special," "Poor Howard"—are not blues. Neither is it surprising that Lead Belly exerted more influence on white folk singers than on true blues artists. It took a black man, very sure of himself and what he was after, to return Lead Belly to his proper perspective—Taj Mahal.

So much for history. Let's get into the music. Lead Belly was a powerful musician; a big strong man, with a big strong voice, who played a big strong 12-string guitar. His claim to be "king" of the 12-string is not far off the mark. Mr. Ledbetter could definitely play that monster. He picked up a lower string, rolling boogie rhythm from his days in the barrelhouses on Fannin Street in Shreveport. He no doubt added blues licks by playing with Blind Lemon Jefferson.

Pressed to name my favorite Lead Belly song, I would plead a toss-up between "Black Girl" and "Bourgeois Blues." "Black Girl" is not really blues, but it is close, and it truly haunts your mind:

> Black girl, black girl, don't you lie to me
> Tell me where did you sleep last night
> In the pines, in the pines, where the sun don't
>   ever shine
> And I shivered the whole night through.

"Black Girl" is the poignant story of a man who very much loves this black girl. The black girl admits she's been out in the pines. The words never explicitly tell you what she was doing out there besides shivering, but there are plenty of hints. With a little reading between the lines, you can deduce that she was selling her body. She takes men out to the pines. But you don't blame her: She's had a hard life; her husband was killed in a railroad accident. You have the feeling Lead Belly doesn't blame her, either. First, because "the pines" is a place where the sun never shines; second, and more exactly, because of the way he sings the word "shivers." His voice literally shivers. Unfortunately, the version I have from 1939 is so cleaned up, I have to tell you about it rather than recommend it to you. Lead Belly sings "my girl" instead of "black girl." He also omits a key verse:

> Black girl, black girl, tell me where'd you get
>   that dress
> Tell me where'd you get them shoes so fine

I got that dress from a railroad man
And them shoes from a man in the mines

So much for "Black Girl."

You don't have to read between the lines on "Bourgeois Blues," except perhaps to substitute "racist" or "bigot" for "bourgeois." You get the point with no sugar-coating:

Me and wife was standin upstairs
We heard a white man shout
I don't want no niggers up there

I find it somewhat ironic that Leadbelly could sing explicitly about racism but chose to back off on an inferred allusion to prostitution. "Bourgeois Blues" deals with its subject in a manner that leaves no question about Lead Belly's anger, but I hear more than a little disgust in his voice. The further he gets into his story about trying and failing to find a house to rent in Washington, D.C., the faster his guitar playing becomes. The adrenaline must be really flowing.

He plays his guitar like a ragtime piano. Where a country blues guitarist would use lower strings for rhythm and upper strings to echo his voice or respond to his vocal call, Lead Belly simply rolls along on the lower-string rhythm. Only during his first solo does he move up on the neck, but his second solo is a bottom-string boogie. Lead Belly was never a finesse player, but the 12-string guitar of his day was not an easy instrument to play. The action—the space between the string and the fret board—on an old 12-string Stella was more appropriate for archery than arpeggios. You needed a goodly amount of strength just to depress the strings enough to sound a chord. Lead Belly could get a bit fancy as he plays bottleneck on "C. C. Rider," but even there it wouldn't be classified as delicate. On "Bourgeois Blues," he powers the strings into submission.

Lead Belly recorded the song in 1938, many years before the U.S. Supreme Court's landmark 1954 decision in Brown v the Topeka Board of Education decision which began to dismantle segregation laws in the United States. But even now it comes across as a powerful statement:

> Home of the brave
> Land of the free
> I don't want to be mistreated
> By no bourgeoisie

Not much different from the messages of Martin Luther King or Malcolm X. Lead Belly is truly offended by this bigotry:

> The white folks in Washington
> They know how
> Call a colored man a nigger
> Just to see him bow

Leadbelly will not take this kind of treatment from anyone. He may have done songs from the days of slavery, but Mr. Huddie Ledbetter was no slave. No, this affront to human dignity requires action:

> Tell all the colored folks
> To listen to me
> Don't try to find no home
> In Washington, D.C.
> Cause it's a bourgeois town... EEEEEE
> A bourgeois town
> I got the bourgeois blues

And I'm gonna spread the news

And so he did. What Lead Belly sang about more than 80 years ago might apply just as well today. Colored folks still got the Bourgeois blues. I wrote earlier that great blues are timeless. Just this once I wish I was wrong.

CHAPTER 29
BESSIE SMITH
"NOBODY KNOWS YOU WHEN YOU'RE DOWN AND OUT"

https://www.youtube.com/watch?v=HJLAwV_3dnY

When Bessie Smith died in a car accident outside of Clarksdale, Mississippi in 1937, some 7000 people attended her funeral. A decade earlier, the Empress of the Blues was the highest paid black performer in the world. Bessie Smith was orphaned at age eight. From a childhood of poverty in Chattanooga, Tennessee, Bessie Smith rose to the heights of fame and fortune, then fell again with the Great Depression. In between she created some of the greatest blues you will ever hear in your life. An Englishman compared her "Empty Bed Blues" to a Verdi opera.

Bessie did her apprenticeship in the Southern tent shows of Gertrude "Ma" Rainey, the "Mother of the Blues." By 1920, she had her own show and began recording in 1923. The 1920s was the heyday of great female blues singers and Bessie Smith towered above the lot. Her recording career spanned a mere 10 years, but in that time she sold nearly 10 million records. That is amazing when you consider that four of those years fell after the Wall Street Crash. Every side she cut is, at worst, very good and some are of classic stature. Her rendition of W.C. Handy's "St Louis Blues," accompanied by Louis Armstrong on cornet and Fred Longshaw on harmonium, ranks as one of the great moments in recorded music.

The power of Bessie Smith comes from more than a superb voice. Other singers had pipes that were just as good, if not better. Bessie, even when she was wined, dined, and celebrated by the cream of society, never ever forgot her roots. White folks might come to see her shows and buy her records, but black people had put her where she was. Her music went directly to the core of their lives. In her 1928 recording of "Poor Man's Blues," she lays it out straight:

> While you're livin' in your mansion
> You don't know what hard times mean
> Poor workin' man's wife is starvin'
> Your wife is livin' like a queen

In addition, Bessie Smith had an inner strength that was evident both in her voice and in her life. Black people got pushed around— they still do—but nobody messed with Bessie Smith. One time she stood off a whole group of Ku Klux Klan single-handedly and sent them packing. Who could help but admire such strength? For black people, Bessie Smith was a source of great pride.

Choosing a single Bessie Smith song from among my eight hours of Bessie Smith's music requires almost more will than I can muster. I could go for Bessie's first record in 1923, "Down Hearted Blues." How about those classic sides with Armstrong including, "You've been a Good Ol' Wagon." Or perhaps the great "Young Woman's Blues," a tribute to women's equality recorded with Fletcher Henderson in 1926. Or I might select "Empty Bed Blues." I would again roll my musical dice except for one thing—I've played one Bessie Smith song for almost as long as "Trouble in Mind." "Nobody Knows You When You're Down and Out" represents everything Bessie stood for. Those three minutes encapsulate not only her whole life but the lives of millions in 1929.

"Down and Out," composed by pianist Jimmy Cox, is not your 12-bar, three-chord country blues. This number is eight bars a verse, with no fewer than 12 chord changes. For rudimentary pickers like me, the song offers innumerable challenges. Bessie begins by telling the listener how it used to be:

> Once I lived the life of a millionaire
> Spendin' all my money, I didn't care
> I carried my friends out for a good time
> Buyin' bootleg liquor, champagne and wine

Bessie combines a blues sense of melody with a jazz feel for rhythm. She rushes ahead of the beat on "millionaire," then extends the word "time," and drops her pitch. She speaks rather than sings, "bootleg liquor." In 1929 the Halstead Act, which prohibited the production, sale, or consumption of alcoholic beverages, was still in force. Her spoken "bootleg liquor" comes out as a little secret shared between Bessie and her listeners—hey, we all drink the stuff, don't we?

The first verse takes her to the top; then cruel fate takes over:

> When I began to fall so low
> I didn't have a friend and no place to go

The fall, sung "faaall," doesn't bother her half as much as not having a friend—you know it from the ironic way she sings the word. How many people in 1929 felt the same way? Millions. But that situation could apply to anyone at any time—people who seem to be your friends when everything is going well but watch out when it all comes apart:

> But if I ever get my hands on a dollar again
> I'm gonna hold on to 'em till the eagles grin

People knew exactly what she meant, including the humor. Bessie was so strong she could make a joke out of being broke.

Now comes the crux of the message:

> Nobody knows you
> When you down and out

The way she extends Noooobody (almost four beats) and then does the same on "knows;" it's jam-packed with irony. Bessie purposely goes off pitch for the word "out." Now that's a master vocalist. That one word ought to put her directly into the Hall of Fame:

> In my pocket not ooonne penny
> And my friends I haven't any

For sure, Bessie Smith has the double blues. Still, no situation is so bad that you can't learn something:

> But if I ever get on my feet again
> Then I'll meet my long-lost friends

It's mighty strange, without a doubt
Nobody knows you when you're down and out
I mean, when you're down and out

Her emphasis on "long lost friends" leaves no question what she thinks of them. She practically growls "down and out." Has Bessie Smith thrown in the towel? That growl as much as proclaims: NO WAY. If anyone in the world is going to get on her feet again, it's Bessie Smith. And if she can growl "down and out," we can too. Speaking personally, whenever I feel down and out, I listen to Bessie Smith tell me all I need to know about human fortitude.

Bessie Smith was 33 in 1929 and her best days were behind her. With the stock market crash and advent of talking pictures, fewer people went to live shows and hardly anyone spent what little money they had on records, particularly the hardest hit: black Southerners and ghetto dwellers who formed the bulk of her audience. By 1931, she lost her recording contract and was drinking and fighting more than ever. She finally split from her worthless husband and manager. She made her last records in 1933 with backing from Benny Goodman, Chu Berry, and Jack Teagarden. The next year she was playing second bill to another major league blues singer, Ida Cox. Music impresario John Hammond was looking for her to help stage a comeback when she died. Whether she would have made it back to the top is moot.

We can debate Elvis as "King" or Springsteen as "Boss." There is no question that Bessie Smith was "Empress of the Blues." In her prime, she could move people like few others could. Her raw power, her personal feeling for the music and the people she sang it to, her inner strength were all without equal.

Her unmarked grave in Sharon Hill, Pennsylvania, was finally given a headstone in 1970, financed by her great admirer Janis Joplin, and by

Juanita Green, who worked for Bessie at one time. The inscription says it all:

Bessie Smith
The greatest blues singer in the world
Will never stop singing

CHAPTER 30
ROBERT JOHNSON
"ME AND THE DEVIL BLUES"

https://www.youtube.com/watch?v=YYsnRc09csQ

Are you prepared for a journey into the heart of darkness? Joseph Conrad took his readers upriver in search of the demented Kurtz. We have to go down the river to Morgan City near Greenwood, Mississippi, a hot August night in 1938. The horror: a young man down on his hands and knees barking like a dog. He's been poisoned; he's been stabbed; he's the victim of voodoo magic. So ended the life of the "King of the Delta Blues Singers," Robert Johnson. And so began the legend.

You see, Robert Johnson was no ordinary bluesman. No, sir. Ol' Bob achieved his greatness through a pact with Satan—like Dr. Faustus. Here's the story: Young Robert Johnson hung around joints where Delta bluesmen like Son House and Willie Brown entertained. Johnson didn't play or sing very well but he was always begging the big boys to let him sit in. They, quite naturally, just laughed him off. Maybe because he got tired of being the butt of their jokes, he disappeared for a while. One night he showed up begging once again to sit in. As usual, Son House turned him down. Then while Son was on a break (maybe quaffing a bit of liquid corn), he heard this strange and wonderful music coming from inside. Lo and behold, Robert Johnson, new King of the Delta Blues. And the word went out that during his disappearance, Johnson had met the Devil down at a crossroads and he'd sold his soul in return for the gift of great blues.

Whether any of this is true, two things about Robert Johnson are indisputable: He made some of the finest blues on record and he also made the gloomiest songs preoccupied with sin and evil. He is credited as composer of such blues classics as "Crossroads Blues," "Sweet Home Chicago," "Walkin' Blues," "Love in Vain," "Come on in My Kitchen," "Terraplane Blues," "Ramblin' on My Mind," "Stop Breakin' Down," and "Dust My Broom." All these have been covered by various other bluesmen and rock and rollers. If you add "Hellhound on My Trail" and "Stones in My Passway"—among his gloomiest—you have about a third of Johnson's total known output, currently pegged at 29 tracks, excluding 12 outtakes. He only recorded in 1936 and 1937 and was dead at the age of 26.

I must confess that trying to write about Robert Johnson fills me with as much fear and dread as the themes of Johnson's songs. The task is daunting, like writing something on Louis Armstrong. What can I write that hasn't been written before and better? Well, I can only try.

Let's start with the legend: Robert Johnson sold his soul to the Devil. You can take that literally or not, as you wish. You can also deal with it on two other levels. Gospel music and blues can be thought of as opposite sides of the same coin. The one is concerned with the spiritual; the other with the worldly and often profane. From this angle, *all* blues musicians have sold their souls to the Devil. Blues is called the Devil's music, after all. Many bluesmen have had a constant internal battle raging—to sing the Devil's music or to sing the Lord's music.

Some have done both. So, on this level, simply by choosing to do blues, Robert Johnson sold his soul to the Devil.

Then there's the technical level. As stated in the introduction, I believe we all have a natural inclination toward music—we are born to boogie. But to go beyond that—to develop the skills to boogie—requires serious effort. And no matter how good they become, musicians would do most anything to be better. That might include a deal with Satan. In 1960, I would have probably sold my soul to the Devil to play Harry Haller's sax part on the Viscounts' "Harlem Nocturne." So here's young Robert, who is mediocre at best. But within a very short time (six weeks? six months?) has achieved unmatched proficiency as a guitarist and singer. How do you explain it?

Here's how I explain it. Robert Johnson did what thousands of aspiring musicians did before and after him—he practiced his butt off. He played until his fingers bled. He sang until he lost his voice. And maybe he didn't seem to be getting anywhere. But he kept at it. And then either suddenly or slowly, the fog lifted. He hit a certain plane and it all opened up. From there on he could play and sing anything. That which had been locked up inside him was free. He could now execute any musical idea, sing exactly how he felt.

If you ever see one of the two existing photographs of Robert Johnson, the first thing you'll notice is his long bony—almost skeletal—fingers. Every guitarist I've read comments on Robert Johnson's fingers. Long skinny fingers are ideal for guitar and piano. Johnson had the perfect equipment to play as he did. On closer inspection, you may note the strange eyes. They don't match. The right eye is wide open and bright; the left one a narrow slit—in one photograph drooping, in the other slightly arched. Is it the camera angle? Is it my warped imagination? Or do I see a schizophrenic? Since most of what I've read on Robert Johnson is either speculation or interpretation, I might as well join the crowd.

The right side: Robert Johnson, young dude about to take on the whole world. He's got it and he knows it. People love his music. Musicians are in awe of his prowess. Women are scratching on his door. He has a couple of recording sessions under his belt. Fame and fortune await.

The left side: Robert Johnson, full of gloom and doom. Raised in poverty, racism, violence. The root cause of it is man's inherently evil nature. And here is this skinny little black man totally overwhelmed by a world of sin and moral corruption. He will drown in the slime and muck of this cesspool called life.

The right side and the left side. The outside and the inside. The illusion and the reality. The superficial glory and the ultimate terror. These I see in the eyes of Robert Johnson.

Let's look at Robert Johnson first as a blues guitarist. He took the two-fingered Delta style picking about as far as it could go, several steps beyond what anyone else had done. But don't take the word of a rudimentary picker. Let's consult a few experts on the subject of Robert Johnson the musician:

"To me, he's head and shoulders above anyone else. I mean, I can figure out everybody else's licks, just about. But not this one." Keith Richards (Rolling Stones)

"I got a little bit of it. Nobody can really get it. You can play it, but you don't get it. You can study this stuff till Hell freezes over, but there's no way you can sing and play with that kind of emotion." Robert Cray (the latest greatest bluesman)

"I'm telling you, it's hard to do. It is very hard to do. I can't play like him. I can play around, in the zone. But I don't play Robert Johnson's music, cause I can't get in the door.... When you get up into that kind of rarefied atmosphere of eccentricity, forget it." Ry Cooder (Every guitarist's favorite guitarist)

"I mean, the guy was brilliant, way ahead of his time, sophisticated in chord structure and rhythm. His guitar technique was phenomenal... I just don't think there's ever been a guy that good." John Hammond Jr. (Blue-eyed Delta bluesman from New York City)

"... It was too much to cope with. When I did his songs, I would simplify huge chord shapes that he could play with his fingers into one line and make it easier. Robert Johnson could accompany himself so simply that it was evasive. If you tried to pick it up, then you realized it wasn't that simple. I've always wanted to do 'Kind Hearted Woman' and also 'Come on in My Kitchen'. But you have to do all this stuff with the greatest of care. 'Hellhound on My Trail'?—forget it. That one's impossible." Eric Clapton (who some call "God")

Then there's Robert Johnson's rather high, almost whining, voice. The more scared his songs became, the higher the pitch. He'd jump into falsetto with an "OOOOO," or drop into a lower-register growl occasionally. His singing was not your ordinary, laid-back Delta blues. Johnson was often way out in front of the beat, so intense he might go totally out of control at any second.

Finally, there's his lyric content. His images come right at you:

> I got to keep movin', got to keep movin'
> Blues fallin' down like hail, blues fallin' down
>   like hail…
> And the days keep on 'mindin' me
> There's a hellhound on my trail...
> Hellhound on my trail...
> Hellhound on my trail

On "Hellhound," Johnson's voice is so far ahead of his guitar that it's like the two have set up a cross-rhythm. The beat is unsteady, the lines uneven. I find it impossible to count it. I also find it impossible to make sense out of what he's singing. I have to agree with Clapton:

"Forget it. That one's impossible." On "Hellhound," it seems poor Bob has lost it altogether. I can't imagine him doing that song in a Delta juke joint where people have come to drink, carouse, and have a good time. The folks are standing around, ready to get down and boogie, and here's this little skinny fellow singing, "There's a hellhound on my trail." You have to go home, lock your door, and pull the blankets up over your head.

Though I find "Hellhound" beyond my limited capacity, I can just about manage "Me and the Devil Blues." You can approach it as Robert Johnson sowing the seeds of his own legend, or as an ode to schizophrenia. In this blues, Johnson plays a nice steady four-to-the-bar, unlike in "Hellhound." He seems to be in control here. But as with much of Johnson's music what seems to be and what actually is can be miles apart. This song raises the question of who, exactly, is in control? Johnson wastes no time getting into the subject:

> Early this morning
> You knocked upon my door...
> And I said, hello Satan
> I believe it's time to go

You are immediately chilled. Not "he knocked," but "*you* knocked." And Bob knows his visitor well. He needs no introduction. It's amazing to me that anyone in the 1930s would acknowledge a close relationship with Satan. Maybe you could get away with it in New York City where weirdos come in droves, but not in the Deep South where most people were faith-professing, God-fearing, and even more Devil-fearing. Such an admission could get you killed. And this is just the first verse.

> Me and the Devil
> Was walkin' side by side...

> I'm going to beat my woman
> Till I get satisfied

Say what? Is Robert Johnson telling us he gets his jollies beating up women? Even if he was a sadist, why would he be so open about it? But then again, "beat" may mean something else and we move into Muddy Waters' Hoochie Coochie territory. Or we may go to the next verse for enlightenment.

> She said you don't see why
> That you be dog me 'round
> (Spoken: Now baby you know you ain't doin
>   me right now...)
> It must be that old evil spirit
> So deep down in the ground

Here is the key: It's that old evil spirit. It helps make some sense out of lyrics that seem to make none. And it unlocks the meaning of "Me and the Devil Blues." But first we have to agree that Robert Johnson was a poet. That the contents of his songs weren't just any old words that fell out of his mouth. That though he may have been illiterate, he carefully crafted his music. That he consciously formed the images in his lyrics. If we can't agree that Robert Johnson was a true poet, then most of what I've written (and what many others have written) is nonsense. I submit that Me and the Devil are not two separate characters, but rather the Jekyll and Hyde of Johnson's personality. Johnson doesn't even know why he's doggin' his woman 'round. His baby ain't doin' right and that old evil side of him beats her till *it* is satisfied. So, to go back to who is in control, poor Bob concedes that it's his old evil spirit, the Devil inside him. What to do? What to do?

You may bury my body
Down at the highway side
(Spoken: Babe I don't care where you bury my
    body when I'm dead and gone...)
So, my old evil spirit
Can get a Greyhound bus and ride

Note that the old evil spirit has now become *my* old evil spirit. Greil Marcus, in his superb essay on Robert Johnson in his book *Mystery Train*, calls the last verse of "Me and the Devil Blues" "... his most satisfied lines, a proud epitaph." Johnson may indeed be satisfied, but it's a grim sort of satisfaction—that he knows his true nature and the nature of the world. He doesn't care where his body is buried because his evil spirit will always find him, for he carries it with him always. His small hope of redemption is death. Then and only then will he rid himself of that old evil spirit who will, hopefully, ride on.

Fair warning: Robert Johnson takes you to the edge. His blues push the envelope of musical possibilities. His lyrics drag you into the abyss. He walks side by side with the Devil. He finds stones in his passway. He tries to escape from the hellhound on his trail. This is not the sort of stuff you play at parties. These are not good-timey tunes. But this I do believe: Once you get into Robert Johnson's blues, you'll never want to get out.

CHAPTER 31
B.B. KING
"CHAINS AND THINGS"

https://www.youtube.com/watch?v=7cPw959KBwc

I f you climb to the pinnacle of Blues Mountain, you may find there a Gibson ES355 electric guitar named Lucille in the hands of one Riley B. King, originally from Indianola, Mississippi. B.B. King may well claim the title of "King of the Blues." He didn't inherit that title from his father or forcibly take it in a palace coup. He earned it.

B.B. placed a song in the Billboard Top 20, "The Thrill is Gone," in 1970. He recorded with various pop superstars including U2 with "When Love Comes to Town." He performed at the top spots in Las Vegas and starred in television specials. Singer Ruth Brown speculated that more Americans knew the name of B.B. King's guitar than the name of their own congressional representative.

No one can dispute B.B. King's blues pedigree. His cousin Booker "Bukka" White was one of the great Delta bluesmen. B.B. studied with Robert Jr. Lockwood, stepson of the "master," Robert Johnson, and a fine blues guitarist/singer in his own right. King's initial influences on guitar were Lonnie Johnson and T-Bone Walker (whose style was derived from Blind Lemon Jefferson). B.B. King in turn influenced practically every electric blues guitarist who followed him. If there was a blues crown, it would fit very comfortably on the head of Riley B. King.

B.B. King's music combines low-down and refined. His singing hints at gospel and blues shouters like Roy Brown and Wynonie Harris. His single line guitar playing sometimes goes beyond Johnson and Walker and shows the influences of jazz greats Charlie Christian and Django Reinhardt. Unlike Howlin Wolf, who boasted that his blues never changed, B.B. King developed over the years from his first recording, "3 O'Clock Blues" in 1951, incorporating, modifying, fine-tuning. Yet to me he never sounds slick, never comes across as anything other than genuine. B.B. lays out his philosophy in a song called "Why I Sing the Blues":

> Father time is catchin' up with me
> Gone is my youth
> I look in the mirror every day
> And let it tell me the truth
> I'm singin the blues
> Um um I just have to sing the blues
> I've been around a long time
> Yes-yes, I've really paid some dues

King recorded steadily from the early 1950s until 2008. So many of his songs have become blues standards, it's difficult to single out just one. I could choose Robert Nighthawk's "Sweet Little Angel." But why not "How Blue Can You Get," "Worry Worry Worry," or "Help the Poor," or one of my all-time favorites, "Sweet 16"? There's the 1965 *Live at the Regal* album that ranks as a blues classic. Jeff

Hannusch, writing in *The Blackwell Guide to Recorded Blues*, had this to say about that album: "If you had a place for only one contemporary blues album in your collection, this should probably be it." However, at the risk of contradicting an expert, I'm going to reach back to Mississippi. One B.B. King song haunted me for years. I heard it on the radio late one night in the early '70s. I looked and looked for it with no luck. After a while I began to think it didn't really exist, that I'd only dreamed it. Then in 1990, I came across the album *Indianola Mississippi Seeds* and there it was: "Chains and Things."

"Chains and Things" contrasts the low-down and refined sides of B.B. King's music. On the one hand, it's a typical 12-bar, A-minor blues. On the other hand, it employs unusual instrumentation for blues songs—electric piano and strings. King—or maybe the producer Bill Szymczyk—uses violins and cello on this number much as others would a horn section. And it works, yes indeed.

"Chains and Things" begins with bassist Bryan Garofalo playing on the first beat of each bar. Underneath, Carole King's electric piano (yes, THAT Carole King) lays down a cross-rhythm. Over the top come B.B. and Lucille doing some simple but bluesy two-three-four note clusters. B.B. King demonstrates almost every time he picks up his guitar Lucille that it's quality that counts, not quantity. The gunslingers go for two million notes to the bar; B.B. hits one note and the hotshots pack up and leave. After Lucille does the blues, there just ain't no more to add. The strings enter in the fourth bar on sustained chords. Violins on a blues song? It takes someone of B.B. King's stature, confidence and, above all, good taste to pull this off. So, in the intro chorus we hear the bass play one beat to the bar, Carole King's electric piano doing a cross-rhythm; we hear sustained strings, above which Lucille softly cries the blues.

As B.B. begins to sing, the bass picks up the rhythm, the strings drop out, and drummer Russ Kunkel finally enters on his cymbal, while Carole continues the cross-rhythm underneath:

> Woke up this morning
> After another one of those crazy dreams
> Oh nothin' is going right this morning
> The whole world is wrong it seems
> Oh, I guess it's the chains that bind me
> I can't shake 'em loose—these chains and things

From the way B.B. sings "those" in the second line, we know this is not the first time he's had this particular crazy dream. The dream is about chains. The way he increases the volume and holds that word leaves no doubt. His voice conveys worry about these "chains and things."

The second chorus sees a return of the strings and Kunkel kicking in with snare and bass drum. Carole King maintains the cross-rhythm:

> Got to go to work this morning
> Seems like everything is lost
> Got a cold-hearted wrong-doin' woman
> And a slave-drivin' boss
> I can't lose these chains that bind me
> I can't shake em loose—these chains and things

Now we know what these chains and things are: a woman and work. B.B. has the old double blues. But there's blues and there's blues. B.B. manipulates the rhythm, uses his voice to emphasize "cold-hearted wrong-doin' woman and a slaaave-drivin' boss." That's *real* blues singing, the kind you might be able to learn by going on the road 250 to 300 days a year for a couple of decades.

Lucille takes over for a chorus. If you think this sounds like almost every other blues guitar solo you've heard since 1960, you're right. Only this time you're getting it from the source. All those other guitars were imitating this one. This is the original. Nothing fancy here except a consummate sense of rhythm, use of dynamics, space and silence. B.B. King is to blues guitar what Miles Davis is to jazz trumpet.

> Oh, you talk about hard luck and trouble
> Seem to be my middle name
> All the hurt that gets me
> Yes, I can only play the losin' game
> These chains that bind me…

Now B.B. is wailing in misery, but he brings it back down for:

> These chains that bind me
> Ah, these chains and things.

He seems to be resigned to carry them as he goes into the final verse:

> Oh, I would pack up and leave today, people
> But I ain't got nowhere to go
> Ain't got no money to buy a ticket
> And I don't feel like walkin' anymore
> Oh, these chains that bind me
> (Lucille comments) Oh, oh, can't lose…
> I can't lose these chains and things

On the refrain he's so overcome by the chains that bind him, he can't even sing the second line; Lucille has to help him out. You've just heard how a master of the blues takes one of the simplest forms of music and molds it into high art.

But don't go away because it's Lucille's turn again. B.B. starts his final solo with a wrong note (the fifth one), an absolute clinker. Does he stop and do it again "right"? Not B.B. He just lets Lucille lead him out of the mess with a superb four-bar passage that sounds almost classical, which fits right in with the fiddles. Then she gently cries through the remaining eight bars of the chorus. Carole King goes back to her cross-rhythm, the strings go back to their sustained chords, and Lucille softly sobs her way to the end.

Now the blues purists might puke all over their walkin' shoes listening to "Chains and Things." It is without debate highly produced —some might call it contrived. I won't argue that *Indianola Mississippi Seeds* was an effort to follow up on the success of "The Thrill is Gone." Phil Patton, in an *Esquire* magazine article, considers B.B. King too "prettified." He writes that B.B. is like Elton John when compared to a "real" bluesman like Charley Patton, who may be Phil Patton's distant cousin. (It seems Phil's great-great grandpappy may have *owned* Charley's grandpappy so somehow they're related.) I believe B.B. King's links to Charley Patton through the blues are a lot more genuine than Phil Patton's links to "cousin" Charley through slavery. Proto-bluesman Charley is blues developing while B.B. King is blues developed. I suppose the purists like their blues dead and stuck in some musical museum. To purists, if it wasn't done before World War II by someone born in the 19th Century, it's not "real" blues. Such a purist once told me that when jazz left New Orleans, it lost its integrity. The way I look at it, music "works," or it doesn't. And my ears and soul believe "Chains and Things" works. So the purists won't like it. Their loss is our gain. I doubt that up on top of Blues Mountain, Lucille and Riley B. King are much bothered.

CHAPTER 32
BIG BILL BROONZY
"BABY PLEASE DON'T GO"

https://www.youtube.com/watch?v=JttvoGmGijU

Folk music came out of the closet wearing button-down shirts when the Kingston Trio's "Tom Dooley" hit No.1 on the pop chart in 1958. Being a serious rock-and-roller at the time, I wasn't much impressed with such sanitized and lifeless presentations. The best you could claim for the Kingston Trio and their ilk was that it might lead to harder stuff like, say, Pete Seeger and The Weavers.

Folk singers had a curious relationship with the blues. They resurrected old black artists who hadn't cut a record in maybe 35 years. Mississippi John Hurt sang the 1928 classic "Stack-o-Lee"; folk music brought him out of the mothballs at the age of 71. The folk wave tracked down the even older Furry Lewis in Memphis where he worked as a street sweeper. Huddie Ledbetter, having long since passed on in 1949, was canonized. Young folkies interested in the blues said their prayers to Saint Lead Belly. Folk blues had one major taboo: Electricity. Lightnin' Hopkins was a folk blues guitarist just so long as he didn't plug in. Son House and Robert Johnson of the pre-electric Delta were deemed genuine folk singers. Muddy Waters and Elmore James, their logical heirs doing Chicago electric blues, would have to wait until the mid-1960s to receive their just recognition.

This irony must have been a source of great amusement for Big Bill Broonzy. Born in Mississippi in 1898, or maybe 1893, he was just as old as Hurt and Lewis and had started out doing pretty much the same country blues as they had in the late 1920s. However, when the depression hit and the others went back to chopping cotton and sweeping streets, Broonzy continued to cut records in Chicago. Along with Georgia Tom Dorsey, he was one of the Famous Hokum Boys. (Hokum was jug-band music without the jug.) He recorded with pianists and then added bass, drums, horns, and eventually electric guitars. Big Bill Broonzy was one of the founders of Chicago electric blues. (Meanwhile, Georgia Tom went the other direction, morphing into Thomas A. Dorsey, the father of gospel music.) Come the 1950s folk boom, Broonzy became the epitome of the down-home country bluesman. He liked money as much as the next fellow, and if college kids would pay big bucks to hear that old-fashioned acoustic sound, he'd turn back the clock 30 years. After all, he'd grown up on that stuff.

I didn't know any of this when I first heard a Big Bill recording in the early 1960s. Like most young folkies, I assumed Broonzy had always played acoustic blues. I can only write of Big Bill Broonzy from a very limited perspective. Yet I write of him anyway because he's simply too important and too good to leave out. Broonzy was a fine guitarist and singer. But more than that, he was one of the all-time great blues stylists. Style—like most important aspects of music—is next to impossible to define. Either someone has it or doesn't have it. Big Bill Broonzy had it by the bushel. When he does the blues, you know it's Big Bill in about 10 to 20 seconds. He's not a shouter or a growler or a crooner. He sings with power, right enough. But, more importantly, he sings with authority. His voice and guitar have charac-ter. Behind his most miserable low-down blues is the strength of will to carry him through.

These qualities of Big Bill's blues are all evident on "Baby Please Don't Go." This number maybe pre-dates blues. Maybe you can trace it back to Africa. It's a work song, also called "Another Man Done Gone." It was a field holler and sung by prison chain gangs, to keep their work going at a slow steady pace. If you're out in a hot sun, you don't want to overdo it while you're busting rocks, digging ditches, or cutting trees. So you get your leader out there singing at about 60 beats per minute...

> Leader: Baby please don't ... ...
> Group: Go! (and down come the
>   axes/picks/hammers)
> Leader: Another man done ... ...
> Group: Gone! etc.

Big Bill Broonzy doesn't do "Baby Please Don't Go" as a work song. He does it as a fairly straight-ahead blues:

> Baby please don't go... Baby please don't go
> Baby please don't go... Back to New Orleans
> You know it hurts me so

Did she want to return to the bright lights in the Big Easy? Where is Big Bill?

> Babe I'm way down here... Babe I'm way
>   down here
> Babe I'm way down here... in old Rollin' Fork
> Baby please don't go

If you're not up on your blues geography, Rolling Fork, Mississippi is the birthplace of Muddy Waters. It also had another landmark that Big Bill is about to explain:

> Babe I'm way down here... Babe I'm way
> down here
> Babe I'm way down here… On old Parchman's
> farm
> Baby please don't go

Why doesn't he ask old Parchman for a short leave of absence and then go along with her? Well, since you may not have had the opportunity to hear Bukka White sing about Parchman Farm, I'll clue you in: This is a prison farm. Bill goes on to tell his baby that:

> "It's cold down here..." and
> "I'm half-fed down here..."

When you listen to Broonzy sing "Baby Please Don't Go," you may wonder how anyone could write over 1000 words about it. On the surface, music just doesn't get any simpler. But as with most good blues, the surface is just the starting point. I won't get into a socio-political dissertation on Southern prison farms. I won't even get into the rather obvious conclusion that conditions on Parchman Farm don't bother Big Bill half as much as the fact that his baby is going to New Orleans. (And if you think she might be going there to do a little shopping… oh brother where art thou!) And I certainly won't get into the metaphorical and metaphysical concept of "prison." Rather I'd point out that Big Bill Broonzy is doing a very rootsy song in a very un-rootsy way.

First, he cranks the beat up from work song tempo to a rather brisk trot. You might jog to this rhythm; you couldn't bust rocks at this speed for more than a minute. Second, he jazzes up the number by adding an extra chord in the second line you don't normally hear in more traditional versions of the tune. Third, he plays in the same two-finger picking style that Charley Patton, Blind Lemon Jefferson, and Hudie Ledbetter all used, but he's a lot more swinging than any of them. All those years in Chicago playing with groups had altered his sense of rhythm. His tempo and chord changes are perfectly regular throughout the song. Plus, his vocal approach is much less "rural Delta," more modern. Broonzy had done John Hammond's "Spirituals to Swing" Concert at Carnegie Hall with Count Basie and Joe Turner. He'd played in front of Chris Barber's Dixieland band in London. He wasn't really down-home anymore.

But if he wasn't down-home, he was still Big Bill Broonzy. He delivers the song very differently than a victim of a chain gang. I have a field recording (perhaps made by John and Alan Lomax, musicologists and folklorists) of prisoners doing "Baby Please Don't Go" acapella; the two versions are worlds apart. The prisoners are sad, beaten-down, full of woe. Broonzy is... well... he's Big Bill. He sounds even a bit cocky like: "If you think I'm gonna let a little time on Parchman Farm get me down, then baby, you're a bigger fool than the people who put me here." And what is that but character and style. And style, in the blues, in all music as in all of life, is everything.

Broonzy was a pivotal figure in the transition of the blues from the country to the city. But more than that, the man had style. And that's why I write 1000 words on Big Bill Broonzy.

CHAPTER 33
HOWLIN WOLF
"SMOKESTACK LIGHTNIN'"

https://www.youtube.com/watch?v=9Ri7TcukAJ8

To howl or not to howl: That is NOT the question.

The question is: Who can out-howl the Wolf?

To begin to answer that question, I have to take you back to 1965, the first time I heard Chester Arthur Burnett a.k.a. Howlin Wolf. Someone had bought one of those new-fangled gadgets called a cassette recorder. I was like one of the apes in the movie *2001* discovering weapons. Gently I inserted a tape into the machine and pressed the play button. Out came the most raucous distorted wail I'd heard in my life. "HOLY MOLY, I broke it." No, said the owner, that's what it's supposed to sound like. And after listening to that raucous, distorted wail a few more times, I fell in love with the raw blues of Howlin Wolf, just as I'd fallen in love with Little Richard doing "Tutti Frutti" in 1955.

Born in Mississippi in 1910, Chester Burnett played on street corners and in juke joints until he was past 40. He did his first recordings at Sun Records for Sam Phillips in 1951. Phillips would later say that he thought Wolf had more raw talent than Elvis Presley.

From Memphis, Wolf attacked Chicago. I mean exactly that: he *attacked* Chicago. Here's how Giles Oakley described it at some length in *The Devil's Music*:

"With his massive frame lurching round the bandstand, crawling and rolling on the floor, blasting out searing bursts on his harp and moaning and shouting his blues till the veins stood out in his neck and the sweat poured off him, he was one of the most menacingly forceful singers of his time, and one of Muddy's biggest rivals in the Chicago clubs."

Charlie Gillett, in *The Sound of the City*, describes Wolf's first record, *Moanin' at Midnight*: "... [guitarist] Willie Johnson sounded as if he was twanging bailing wire with a six-inch nail... Wolf's mournful vocal... sounded as if he might swallow the microphone and jump out of the juke box speaker at any moment."

If you've never heard Howlin Wolf, you may think Messrs. Oakley and Gillett are exaggerating a bit. But just one listen to any Wolf blues and you'll become a believer. Wolf's vocals make a bare-chested, leather and chain heavy metal singer sound like a limp wimp. Howlin Wolf's influence on 1960s blues-rock goes beyond power vocals. His whole attitude towards music made a massive impact. Cream did his "Spoonful" (by Willie Dixon). Jimi Hendrix did his "Killing Floor." Johnny Winter did a blistering "Forty-Four." And then there was "Little Red Rooster."

"Little Red Rooster," also composed by Willie Dixon, was a Rolling Stones showstopper. In 1972, Howlin Wolf did a recording session in London, cleverly titled *The London Sessions*. On it we hear such superstars as Eric Clapton, Stevie Winwood, Ringo Starr, and Rolling Stones' Bill Wyman and Charlie Watts begging the 62-year-old Mississippi cotton picker to show them how the song is *really* supposed to be played. Would Wolf please-please-please do a bit of slide guitar so they could make the changes better? This comes from Eric Clapton, the greatest blues guitarist in Britain. And the results make you forget all about the Rolling Stones' version of "Little Red Rooster." Mick who?

(In fairness, I should note that the Stones always acknowledged and, more importantly, promoted their sources of inspiration. They did much to acquaint young British and American fans with authentic blues.)

As good as "Little Red Rooster" is, for Wolf at his howlin best, I direct your attention to "Smokestack Lightnin'," a single vamp classic. This vamp (a repeated musical phrase) by Hubert Sumlin, has appeared again and again in various songs since "Smokestack" was cut in 1956. It forms the basis for an otherwise forgettable tune by Sanford Clark called "The Fool." If you listen to this two-bar vamp, you'll notice that a lot is going on in the background. Sumlin's lead is juxtaposed with a second guitar counterpoint by Willie Johnson. Another counterpoint comes from the piano of Hosea Lee Kennard. Bassist Willie Dixon and drummer Earl Phillips throw in a little hitch-beat at the end of every second bar. To bring all this off requires precise timing. The vamp becomes something like an oriental drone, almost hypnotic. Then the Wolf begins to howl:

> Oh-oh Smokestack Lightnin'
> Shinin' just like gold
> Why don't you hear me cryin'
> OOO-OOO-OOO-OOO
> OOO-OOO-OOO OOOOOO

Those falsetto howls were the Wolf's trademark. They come as an aural shock. The Wolf growls in his natural growly voice and jumps an octave into a falsetto howl. Very eerie. And Wolf is not really singing all that low. He's usually at the top of his vocal range, which produces those rumbling undertones. He is simultaneously singing with his chest and throat, bouncing the sound back and forth. The effect is like one voice emitting two sounds. I am not making this up. I've been trying to howl like the Wolf for over 50 years. I know what he does; I just haven't quite got it down yet. Maybe someday...

> Oh-oh, tell me baby
> What's the matter here
> Why don't you hear me cryin'
> OOO... ... ...

Wolf feels something is wrong at home, that appearances usually deceive. The rhythmic tension between Sumlin's vamp and Wolf's voice make the irony all the more potent. So, they chew on it while Wolf does a few bars of harmonica dialogue with Sumlin's guitar:

> Oh-oh, tell me baby
> Where did you stay last night
> Why don't you hear me cryin'
> OOO... ... ...

Now we know what the howling is all about—Wolf's baby is running around on him. There's only one thing he can do:

> Oh-oh, stop your train
> Let a poor boy ride
> Why don't you hear me cryin'
> OOO...

It seems that verses two and three are flashbacks while Wolf was waiting for Smokestack Lightnin'. "Shining just like gold" may be the sun's reflection off the train engine as it pulls into the depot. But it might also metaphorically represent a new life on down the line. He's made his decision:

> Fare you well
> Never see you no more
> Why don't you hear me cryin'
> OOO... ...

Notice that Wolf omits the previous introductory "Oh-oh." This is a flat-out goodbye and "*never* see you no more." For all the howlin' pain, Wolf is determined to leave. You can hear that determination in his harmonica as the vamp slowly fades out.

Now we go back to that question: Who can out-howl the Wolf? A lot of folks have tried. I remember around 1970 when I heard Leslie West of the power trio Mountain doing "Mississippi Queen." I was thinking that maybe he was trying to out-howl the Wolf. West was certainly big enough and loud enough. Axl Rose sounds like he may be trying to out-howl the Wolf a couple of octaves higher (more like out-screech). To out-howl the Wolf, it helps if you're around six-foot-three and weigh close to 300 pounds, but it's not absolutely required. To begin with, you should spend the first 40 years of your life chopping cotton and playing in dives surrounded by bigots. Then move to Chicago and go up against the finest blues band there ever was—Muddy Waters, Little Walter, and Jimmy Rodgers. Later on, have a couple of heart attacks; get in a near-fatal car accident that wrecks your kidneys. And when the world counts you off as a goner, get back up on the stage and do the blues so hard that you have to be physically restrained. Then maybe... just maybe... you'll be ready to howl like the Wolf. Because to howl like the Wolf, you only need Chester Burnett's fierce determination... you only need his soul.

Here's what Howlin Wolf had to say about doing the blues:

> Now listen; peoples, everybody said they don't like the blues, but you wrong. You see, the blues come from way back. And I'm gonna tell you somethin' again: the things that's goin' on today is not the blues. It's just a good beat the peoples is carryin', but now when you come down to the blues, I'm gonna show you how to play the blues. Now you just sit here and watch me... ... ...

The Wolf then launches into a lethal version of "Back Door Man." And if it's late at night and there's a full moon, you may feel the urge to go out in the backyard, get down on all fours and howl:

OOO OOO-OOO-OOO OOO-OOO-OOO
OOOOOO

CHAPTER 34
SONNY TERRY - BROWNIE MCGHEE
"CHANGED THE LOCK ON THE DOOR"

https://www.youtube.com/watch?v=ZToHPVhL_sE

'm down at the crossroads late on a moonless night. A shrouded figure approaches from the darkness:

"Why are you here?" it asks.

"Would you believe looking for the ghost of Robert Johnson?"

"Cut the crap, Mr. Wise Guy. You know and I know you came to play Let's Make a Deal, right? So, you tell me what you want and I'll tell you what you'll pay."

I have to think quick: Do I want the chops of Charlie Parker, the voice of Howlin Wolf, the fingers of B.B. King? Then I blurt out: "Okay, give me the tone of Sonny Terry."

"Sorry," comes the reply, "even *I* can't do that."

To write that Sonny Terry could play blues harmonica like the Devil is gross understatement. He could play *better* than the Devil (assuming there is a Devil, and it plays musical instruments). The first time I heard Sonny Terry I had to run down to the local music shop and blow most of my savings—around five bucks—on a Hohner Marine Band harmonica. Before long I could bore family and friends alike with hot renditions of "Oh Susannah" and "Streets of Laredo." I could even do a few bars of Tchaikovsky's "1812 Overture." When Bob Dylan came on the scene, I found his harmonica stuff easy as country pie. But to save my soul, I couldn't play like Sonny Terry. How do you do blues on this thing? How do you bend notes? Years later, I came across a little book on blues harp by Jon Gindik. Epiphany! Within a week, I was wailing blues, bending notes like crazy. I still couldn't (and still can't) play like Sonny Terry. But then, in my opinion, nobody plays like Sonny Terry.

There are many types of harmonicas. The standard 10-hole diatonic model is no big deal. (The chromatic harmonica that Stevie Wonder and Toots Thielemans play is another matter altogether.) For someone aspiring to play music, a Hohner Marine Band is hard to beat. It's cheap, highly portable, and relatively easy to do tunes on. It also has the added benefit of protection against vicious canines. Just blow on the 10th hole and a snarling dog will run like hell. This little piece of chrome hardly qualifies as technology. But in the mouth of a master, it can produce marvelous music. The harmonica comes closest to that most perfect of instruments—the human voice. I characterize the harmonica in much the same way as I characterize people: an extremely limited instrument with almost unlimited potential.

Many have tapped that unlimited potential. A Who's Who of Blues Harp might fill several pages. Up at the top of my list—not necessarily others' lists—would appear the name of Saunders Terrell. Sonny Terry did not play fancy-fancy. For pyrotechnics you can check out Magic Dick Salwitz with the J. Geils Band on a tune like "Whammer Jammer." You'll know why he's called Magic Dick. Or you can go directly to the section on Sonny Boy Williamson. Sonny Boy could bend a note from the earth's core into outer space. Or listen to Little

Walter Jacobs play a 10-hole diatonic like it is a horn. Or get into the most revolutionary diatonic harp player to come along, Howard Levy, who can play notes that aren't there through over-blowing. I listen to these gentlemen and, to quote Chief Dan George, "my heart soars like a hawk." What Sonny Terry had in abundance were style, grace and, above all, tone. What a devilishly heavenly tone! That tone can charm honey from the bees and birds from the trees.

Terry played harp with many great bluesmen: Blind Boy Fuller, Lead Belly, Big Joe Williams, Lightnin' Hopkins, just to name a few. But for well over 40 years, his main man was singer/guitarist Brownie McGhee. Sonny was practically blind; Brownie had been disabled by polio in boyhood. On one album they go into a long rap about their times together. Sonny remembers a drunken pact they made. Brownie said: "Sonny, you walk for me, and I'll see for you." They became celebrities during the folk blues revival of the 1950s and '60s, and they recorded prolifically. They carried on a strange love-hate relationship until Sonny's death in 1986.

Theirs was a gentle, easy-rolling style, referred to as Piedmont Blues. Brownie McGhee had a smooth vocal delivery and, while not a great guitarist, he was a pretty fair picker and strummer. The two had a kind of mellow acoustic bounce. Even on a number full of misery like "Big Wide World," they can't seem to shake that laid back feel.

To hear Sonny Terry in all his splendor, I should take you straight to his version of the old spiritual "Beautiful City." Sonny sings and plays harp unaccompanied. It's guaranteed to set you free. But it doesn't seem right to give you Sonny without Brownie. It would be like red beans without rice; like Bugs Bunny without Elmer Fudd. My favorite Sonny and Brownie song is about a big problem Sonny has:

> My baby done changed
> She done changed the lock on the door...

> Well, she said that key you got, Sonny
> Just don't fit that lock no more

Very serious business here, but you'd never know it from the jaunty rhythm that Brownie lays down on acoustic guitar. Throughout the number, Brownie McGhee plays little more than simple chord changes. And that's a lesson for would-be six-string gunslingers. Anything other than simple chords would just get in the way. Brownie's job is to lay a foundation for Sonny's voice and harp. And the foundation he lays could support a skyscraper, only it's portable. Wherever Sonny goes, Brownie is right there underneath him chunking along. These two played together for so long, it must have been second nature.

Sonny tells us he doesn't believe his woman at first:

> I went home last night
> 'Bout half past ten
> Tried to get the key in the lock
> And I couldn't get in
> She done changed
> She done changed the lock on the door...
> Something is very definitely not kosher:
> I went round to her window
> To see what I could see
> She was kissin my best friend
> And I know it weren't me
> She done changed
> She done changed the lock on the door...

Most men would give up right then and there, but not Sonny Terry:

I called my baby up
Honey, what you want me to bring
You know she whispered low and easy
Don't bring a doggone thing
Cause I done changed
I done changed the lock on the door...

Well, that pretty much settles the matter. Then this lady adds insult to injury:

She moved the bed around
Even the carpets on the floor
She got a young man now
And I can't go there no more
She done changed
She done changed the lock on the door
She said that key you got Sonny
Just don't fit that lock no more

Here is yet another song about what Gil Scott-Heron explained as the I-ain't-got-me-no-woman blues. Why isn't Sonny Terry in sack cloth and ashes? Maybe he didn't care that much anyway. Maybe he had what bluesmen call a "sidetrack," another woman, all along. My guess: Sonny Terry, like a fine watch, is dust-proof, water-proof and shock-proof. Sonny is black and blind. What's getting jilted compared to that?

Let me state that if you've never listened to blues harp, it may not make much of an impression. Even if you listen to blues harp but not very carefully, it may not seem like much. I am certainly not better than an average harp player and I can blow some of Sonny Terry's licks almost note-for-note. But I won't sound like Sonny Terry. And really good harp players won't sound like Sonny Terry either. The only person who plays like Sonny Terry is, that's right, Sonny Terry.

But who knows. Maybe there's a 13-year-old kid somewhere right now playing "Oh Susannah" on a Marine Band harmonica and wondering why he can't play blues on it, why he can't bend notes. It is a very limited instrument with almost unlimited potential.

CHAPTER 35
PAUL BUTTERFIELD
"BORN IN CHICAGO"

https://www.youtube.com/watch?v=kCjFRNWN3o4

Sonny Terry and Brownie McGhee did a song with John Mayall called "White Boy Lost in the Blues." That fairly well sums up the life of Paul Butterfield. He got lost in the blues while still a teenager in Chicago, and stayed lost in the blues until the blues finally did him in.

Butterfield will not go down in history as Chicago's greatest harpist. He was plenty good, but he wasn't quite up to his model, Little Walter Jacobs. He won't go down as a great blues singer. He was better than okay, but not great. But still Butterfield deserves a place in blues history. He, along with a few others, instigated the Blues Revival of the 1960s.

Butterfield broke the electric blues taboo and opened the door for the whole Chicago blues crowd—Muddy Waters, Howlin Wolf, Junior Wells, Buddy Guy, Otis Rush, and the rest. Some may argue that they were the "real thing," and Butterfield was just an imitator. But I don't believe it. Yes, Paul Butterfield fashioned his sound on that made by the black Chicago bluesmen; he was also "real."

For Paul Butterfield had faced the same question from critics that many others had, from Bix Beiderbecke to Eric Burdon: How can white people do black music? There can be no debate that jazz and blues originated with black people. But music, whatever its source, belongs to everyone. I was listening the other day to a Louis Armstrong recording of the song "I Got a Right to Sing the Blues," written by the very white Ted Koehler and Harold Arlen.

So does Paul Butterfield. That doesn't mean it's easy. Most certainly, you pay your dues. All black people, by the very fact that they're black, pay their dues every day. But think about this: Here's this middle-class white teenager going to the Southside clubs to play harp with Muddy Waters. What are the patrons thinking? Well, ain't that cute. White boy thinks he knows the blues. Let's humor the kid a little. And pimple-face Paul is up there blowing and sweating as if his life depended on it. But his life doesn't depend on it. He comes from a well off family; he's got a nice home; he goes to a good school; he can be anything he wants because society will allow him to be anything he wants. But his life does depend on it because he wants to be a bluesman. So he has to overcome all the barriers—barriers that both black people and white people erected—to achieve that goal. In the end, he either makes it or he doesn't. Paul Butterfield, I believe, made it through the disdain and, even worse, the patronizing attitudes, to become a bluesman. In so doing, he helped many others. And in every song I've heard by Butterfield, I hear a man paying his dues. I've heard him play behind Muddy Waters and B.B. King; I've heard him do Junior Parker's "Mystery Train," Robert Johnson's "Walkin' Blues," and Memphis Jimmy's "Look Over Yonders Wall," and it's all the blues and it's all "real."

I go back to the first song I ever heard Paul Butterfield do which also happens to be the first track on Side 1 of the first album he ever put out in 1965. It grabbed me right away:

> I was born in Chicago
> In nineteen and forty-one...

It's not that I hadn't heard the blues before—I'd listened to it all my life. It's not that I hadn't heard white guys doing the blues—I did it myself. But I'd never heard this kind of power before. This, as a friend of mine says, is very serious stuff. It seems to me Paul Butterfield was always serious, even though he claimed never to be serious.

From the opening bar of "Born in Chicago," the group hits it hard and heavy. This bunch was geared for it. Drummer Sam Lay and bassist Jerome Arnold had backed Howlin Wolf before joining Butterfield so they knew a thing or two about hard and heavy. There was Mark Naftalin on organ and Elvin Bishop who played both rhythm and lead guitar before Mike Bloomfield joined up. Bloomfield was in a smaller way in the U.S. what Eric Clapton was in the United Kingdom. (Clapton was scared to death of Bloomfield until he found out that Bloomfield was scared to death of him.) Being the best white blues guitarist in America didn't do him much good. Bloomfield doped himself to death in 1981.

If you know the harmonica of Little Walter and listen to Butterfield, you'll hear that same horn-like sound. It may not be original with Butterfield, but he sure puts everything into it. Then he sings:

> I was born in Chicago
> In nineteen and forty-one...
> Yeah my father told me
> Son, you had better get a gun

Actually, Butterfield was born in Chicago in nineteen and forty-two, but that doesn't rhyme with "gun." The question is why would Paul's father—a lawyer no less—tell his son to get a gun? Maybe like 1941, we should chalk this up to poetic license or maybe the song's composer Nick Gravenites—another young Chicago white singer lost in the blues—was copying an old blues number that goes something like:

> I came to Chicago in nineteen and forty-one
> Big Bill told me, son you had better get a gun
> (The "Big Bill" is Broonzy.)
> Listen to the second verse:
> Well, my first friend went down
> When I was seventeen years old...
> Well, there's one thing I can say about that boy
> He's gotta go

Life is plenty tough in Chicago. (That's why you had better get a gun.) Hear Bloomfield put in those Albert King fills after each line: that's tough anywhere. And the rest of the group pounds out that riff: du-du-du-DU-DUT.

Then Butterfield blows his harp. Yes, yes, he blows. Can we call it something? How about intense? Now Paul wants to reinforce his father's admonition:

> Well, my second friend went down
> When I was 21 years of age...
> Well, there's one thing I can say about that boy
> He's gotta pray

Now it's Bloomfield's turn and he lets it rip. Today this may not sound like much. We're used to every leather-clad, long-haired kid with a designer-striped, spray-painted guitar playing through a stack of amplifiers and two dozen effects pedals. But take away all that high-tech and see what it sounds like. Then tell him to go lay flowers on Mike Bloomfield's grave. In 1965, Bloomfield was blowing some minds.

Finally we come to the moral of this tale:

> Well now rules are all right
> If there's someone left to play the game…
> All my friends are goin'
> And things just don't seem the same.
> No things just don't seem the same, babe

Butterfield and Bloomfield wail out a blues dual lead, interweaving their lines as the song fades.

I think about that line: "Well now rules are all right if there's someone left to play the game." It's just not possible that Butterfield could have known at the beginning of his career he would play the game for such a short time. He died, as did his old mate Mike Bloomfield, of a heroin overdose in 1987 at the age of 45. But there it is, literally, on the record. So this white boy, born in Chicago, got lost in the blues. I don't know much about him except what I hear in his music. And what I hear is a man in love. He was in love with a sound and with an idea. And the idea was that he, a white kid from the Northside, could cross over to the Southside to play black music. And the blues, like any great love, was all his glory and all his pain. And he finally got so lost in the blues, he disappeared. But some of us are still around to play the game.

CHAPTER 36
BLIND LEMON JEFFERSON
"MATCHBOX BLUES"

https://www.youtube.com/watch?v=BwtumOtcM3Y

A good name will not necessarily signify a good musician. Blind Lemon Jefferson had a great name and was a towering bluesman.

Yes, his real name was Lemon and that is what everyone, including his mother, called him. Maybe nobody called him blind, even though he was sightless from birth. And the experts call him one of the founding fathers of the blues. Back in the early years of the 20th century, Blind Lemon Jefferson was a Dallas-based street singer and guitarist. I doubt he consciously decided to become a founding father of the blues. In fact, he didn't sing just blues. He sang what people wanted to hear. He played music for money, to put food in his belly. If passersby tossed coins into the tin cup attached to his guitar and asked for blues, he'd give them blues. Which just goes to prove another old saying: Necessity is the mother of invention. Because Blind Lemon Jefferson came up with some truly fine blues.

Lemon Jefferson was born in rural Texas in 1893. As a teenager, he traveled around the south, playing at parties, picnics, and lowlife joints. He began his recording career in 1925. In fact, we might call Blind Lemon Jefferson the first male blues superstar. Blues on records began with Mamie Smith in 1920. Through 1923 women did not just dominate blues recording, they monopolized it. All blues records until 1923 were sung by women. The first male blues singer of any significance to record was one Papa Charlie Jackson. This elegant player of the six-string banjo did bouncy numbers like "Salty Dog" and "Alabama Bound." But for sheer blues power and record sales, Blind Lemon Jefferson was the man.

His blues were a world apart from the ladies' blues. Bessie Smith, Ma Rainey, Ida Cox, and the other popular females of the 1920s considered themselves "entertainers," much the same as the jazzmen of their day. They were part of the glamorous—and not-so-glamorous—world of black show business. While Bessie Smith was singing at the Howard Theatre in Washington, D.C., Blind Lemon Jefferson might be entertaining at a picnic in Waxahatchie, Texas, or a house party in Galveston. The ladies had left the rural South for the bright lights of the big cities. Bessie Smith had a private railway car. Ma Rainey wore a necklace of gold coins. Most of the male blues singers wore bib overalls in the daytime while they worked on their farms. Or they were, as Blind Lemon was, itinerant professionals living from hand to mouth. No bright lights. Probably no electricity or indoor plumbing. But Jefferson and a few others saved country blues from becoming the private domain of ethnomusicologists. They showed the businessmen, who decided what the public would hear, that this old-fashioned music had a market, and a profitable one at that.

Life, in the musical world of Blind Lemon Jefferson, is filled with bad whiskey, cheating women, and sometimes violence. You get through it with courage and wit. The music that depicted that life

struck a chord with its audience. It still does. Circumstances may have
changed, but the fundamental tools of survival haven't.

Some writers dismiss Jefferson's influence on the blues as insignificant. Others consider him nearly as important to the blues as another
Jefferson was to the Declaration of Independence. Blind Lemon
recorded before other early, great country blues singers, such as Blind
Blake, Charley Patton, Mississippi John Hurt, and Blind Willie McTell.
Almost all had the opportunity to hear and be inspired (if not influenced) by Blind Lemon. Two of his "lead boys" went on to become
stars—T-Bone Walker and Lightnin' Hopkins. T-Bone regularized,
electrified, and cleaned up Jefferson's style. Then B.B. King modified
and refined it and gave it to almost every blues guitarist who followed.
Jefferson's vocals influenced Son House who influenced Robert Johnson
who influenced Muddy Waters. Blind Lemon also made an impression
on a young fellow named Chester Burnett who would later change his
name to Howlin Wolf. The begats go on and on. Lemon used the term
"Booga Rooga" to describe his lower string rhythm in "Matchbox
Blues," which may have morphed into boogie woogie. And where
would we all be without boogie woogie in our lives?

Although Blind Lemon Jefferson recorded many blues and spirituals
before he died in a Chicago blizzard in 1929 at the age of 36, I do love
"Matchbox Blues," not only for the booga rooga but also the great first
line: "I'm sittin' here wonderin' would a matchbox hold my clothes." If
that's not poetry, what is?

For the modern listener, "Matchbox" may seem even more old-fashioned than it did in the 1920s. We're used to steady rhythms and
clearer sounds. There's little we can do about crude recording techniques used back then, except perhaps adjust our ears. The rhythm is
another matter. There's a difference between "proper" time and "steady"
time. Steady time is necessary for musicians playing together, especially
if they're playing for dancers. Lemon sang and accompanied himself on

guitar as he felt it, without fretting about confusing a rhythm section. He played as the music moved him, sometimes slowing it down, sometimes speeding it up. The mood dictated the rhythm. Son House pretty much summed it up to Giles Oakley, author of *The Devil's Music*: "Couldn't nobody never be lucky enough to dance by his music."

Lemon starts "Matchbox Blues" with an eight-bar introduction on guitar. He plays without a pick, using his thumb on the lower strings as a pianist uses his left hand while the first and second fingers create what will become a counterpoint to the melody. The thumb-finger combination was quite common with most country blues guitarists. The way Jefferson approached melody, harmony, and counterpoint was not. And rhythmically the song is complex almost beyond description. This 12-bar blues has not a single chorus of twelve bars, as best I can count, because the common four-four beat is hard to apply. Choruses vary from around 13 or 14 to 16 bars with the last chorus jumping to about 18 bars. The tempo speeds up from the intro's 120 beats per minute (bpm), which is about average march time, to 180 bpm in the third chorus and 205 bpm at the end. And if that wasn't enough, we get three— count 'em three—separate accompaniments on guitar. The intro and first three choruses have the thumb-finger counterpoint; in the fourth, Jefferson switches to his eight-to-the-bar booga rooga shuffle; in the fifth he lays on a little banjo-mandolin wrist tremolo; back to booga rooga in the sixth chorus; and he ends it as he began it with thumb-finger counterpoint.

It takes me longer to explain it than it does for him to do it. Which ought to tell us a few things. First, simple country blues isn't so simple. Second, I'm pretty sure Blind Lemon didn't sit down before he recorded "Matchbox Blues" and map all this out mentally. He had been playing for money since he was a teenager. By the time he started recording in his mid-20s, he had his act down cold. What's the difference between a black guy on Central Avenue in Dallas tossing a dime into his tin cup and saying, "Hey Lemon, sing me a blues," and a white guy in Chicago saying, "I'll pay you a hundred bucks plus a bottle of whiskey to sing some blues in a recording studio"? The money might be different but the music was the same.

Finally, can you enjoy (maybe even appreciate) "Matchbox Blues" without dissecting it? The answer is yes. I would hate to think anyone listens to music simply to analyze it. I recently happened across an article by Brian Eno (ex-Roxy Music, composer, synthesizer wizard, avant-muzak meister) titled "Resonant Complexity." In it, he rightly and righteously says, "… the interesting complexity is not so much in the music as in the listener… emotional resonances are entirely dependent on the audience's personal and shared histories as listeners." I agree. You can like—or not like—Blind Lemon Jefferson with—or without—knowing exactly how he goes about making his music. It depends on you—not me or some self-anointed expert.

I have two Blind Lemon versions of "Matchbox Blues." They are quite different in both feel and lyrics. Not being an expert, all I can tell you is that one starts with the line, "Up on the river, gonna walk down by the sea…" The version I'm writing about gets straight to the point:

> Sittin' here wonderin'
> Would a matchbox hold my clothes…
> I ain't got so many matches
> But I got so far to go

The rest of the song is of the she's-doin'-me-wrong variety of blues, not much different from Sonny Terry's lady who changed the lock on the door. After wondering about his matchbox, Jefferson asks his mama, "Who may your manager be?" By the fourth chorus, her infidelity has finally got to him: "I can't count the times I stole away and cried." But then in the last chorus he's got matters well in hand:

Now excuse me mama
For knockin' on your door...
My mind's okay
I'm lovin' my gal no more

A clue to the significance of the Blind Lemon's matchbox may be in the following line: "I ain't got so many matches but I got so far to go." Like Howlin Wolf some 30 years later waiting for Smokestack Lightnin' or The Clash in 1982, Lemon's wondering: "Should I stay or should I go?" (The Clash, for those wondering, is an English punk-rock group.) Suggesting a connection between Blind Lemon Jefferson and The Clash is not as far-fetched as it might seem; actually, as George Carlin would tell us, it is quite near-fetched.

From Blind Lemon Jefferson and his old-fashioned music would spring much of the blues that followed. That eventually led to music labeled rock-and-roll. In 1956 a young rockabilly singer and guitarist named Carl Perkins would make his version of "Matchbox Blues" for Sun Records in Memphis. A half decade later and on the other side of the Atlantic, a group of aspiring rock-and-rollers would copy the Carl Perkins "Matchbox Blues" practically note for note with their drummer Ringo Starr doing the vocal. It is reasonable to posit that without The Beatles, there would have been no Clash. Perkins regularized the beat, evened out the choruses to a steady 12 bars, added a nifty riff and changed the words. But the spirit of Blind Lemon Jefferson remained. Because Perkins was doing nothing more and nothing less than the down-home country blues. And of course, no one in his right mind would alter that poetic: "I'm sittin' here wonderin' would a matchbox hold my clothes."

CHAPTER 37
JANIS JOPLIN
"BALL AND CHAIN"

https://www.youtube.com/watch?v=d2L6vp_-0M8

A woman staggered over to me one night as I sat after a gig, trying to come down off the adrenaline, with generous help from the Scottish Highlands' peaty best. She had a gigantic head start on me.

"Ya know," she slobbered in my ear, "I jus' love the way you guys do the blues. Ya know, when I was 14 I jus' loved Janis Joplin, jus' loved her, I jus' wannid ta be like Janis. Ya know, she jus' dinnid give a fug. Like ever time she sang, it was jus' like a big 'fug you' ta the worl'. I jus' loved the way Janis sang the blues."

Flashback twenty-some years to a run-down hotel in Katmandu. A young, white American female with a beat-up guitar is singing what she thinks is heavy-duty blues. I am astounded by her vocal power but not much impressed with her feel for the music. Although I didn't know it at the time because I'd been out in the African bush since 1965 and was not up to date on the music scene, I was hearing an attempt to imitate the blues of Janis Joplin.

Janis Joplin recorded 3.9 albums in her all-too-brief lifetime, and the first one with Big Brother and the Holding Company hardly counts. Her big break came at the 1967 Monterey Pop Festival which led to a recording contract with Columbia Records and the album *Cheap Thrills*. Afterwards, she left Big Brother and the Holding Company and recorded "I Got Dem Ol Kozmic Blues Again, Mama." She died in 1970 before completing *Pearl*. Ironically, the track to which Janis hadn't put the vocal was "Buried Alive in the Blues."

Her celebrity rests mainly on an image, and not a very original one at that—the hard-drinkin' hard-lovin' blues mama with a heart of mush. Whether that image reflected the woman is beside the point. Whether she chose that image or it was foisted upon her by a male-dominated music business (with emphasis on "business") is not beside the point, in case you want to start a campaign, and more power to you. In the end what counts is the music. Janis Joplin was a musician. Symbols, no matter how important, will not alter that fact. I'll assess Janis Joplin as a singer.

Most people think of Joplin as a blues singer. In fact, she—like Billie Holiday—hardly ever sang a pure blues number. However, she could pulverize songs with blues feeling. She ranks among the very best screams on record. Along with Tina Turner, she perfected the fine art of screaming softly. That takes real talent. The girl can make you shiver with goosebumps on one of those quiet screams. She can work wonders on a two-bit piece of pseudo-profound hokum, namely "Me and Bobbie McGee." ("Freedom's just another word for nothin' left to lose." I guess Kris Kristofferson invoked poetic license, ignoring the 10,000 who died in Tiananmen Square.)

Janis Joplin, in my opinion, was a very uneven performer who sometimes did not exercise good musical judgment. But when she was good, like the girl with the curl in the nursery rhyme, she was very, very good. Unfortunately, the same can't be said of the Holding Company, whose members were for the most part second rate. Imagine Joplin in front of B.B. King's band. Good golly, Miss Molly, send her to New Orleans or Muscle Shoals or Memphis to work with The MGs.

Janis Joplin's magnum opus is, without question, the Big Mama Thornton song "Ball and Chain." This number was requested, demanded, hollered out, from the moment a Janis Joplin concert began until she finally consented to sing it. That this particular blues grabbed people—rather than any number of other songs associated with her such as "Piece of my Heart" or "Try"—goes a long way in explaining the reason I chose to include Joplin for this book. There are many versions of "Ball and Chain" out there. This one was recorded live at Winterland Ballroom in 1968.

On the surface, "Ball and Chain" is the old blues cliché: My man treats me like dirt, but I love him anyway. The metaphor of love as a ball and chain places Willie Mae Thornton as an inventive blues lyricist but there's nothing particularly outstanding about the performance I have of her at Newport. As Big Mama does it, "Ball and Chain" is a standard slow blues shuffle—good blues but not great blues.

Janis, with Big Brother and the Holding Company, radically changes the song and in doing so transforms good to great. The only similarities between the Thornton and Joplin versions are the title and most, but not all, of the first verse. Thornton sings the song in D major; Janis does it in gloomy G minor. The band alternates between Thornton's slow shuffle and triplets. This three-against-four cross-rhythm adds tension and intensity. But for even more intensity, Janis sings an approximation of Big Mama's second verse as a chorus in which she really whups it on you: "I say oh-uh, whoa-uh, whoa-uh..."

Joplin starts the song almost whispering (the less said about James Gurley's overwrought guitar intro and solo the better):

Sittin' down by my window
Honey, lookin 'out at the rain... lord-lord-lord
Something came along, grabbed ahold of me
And it felt just like a ball and chain

As the band hits that last line, the volume starts going up and Joplin leads into the first chorus with a spoken aside: "Honey, that's exactly what it felt like, and it's draggin' me down." The greatness of blues artists is determined by an ability to create within a fairly restrictive format. Here's Big Mama Thornton's second verse:

I say hey... hey baby
Why does everything happen to me
Ah, because I love you
And I'm sick and tired of being in misery

Now listen how Joplin embellishes Thornton's idea with strings of words conveying her frustration and pain:

I say oh-uh, whoa-uh, whoa-uh
Tell me why does every single-little tiny-little
      everything goes wrong... goes wrong yeah
I say oh-uh, whoa-uh, whoa-uh
Tell me why was eeeeeeeverything...
      everything…
Hey, hear you're gone today
I wanted to love you... I just wanted to hold you
      —I said—for so long yeah... alright... hey

Written words do not in any way convey the delivery. This is not some phony show biz slowed down "Happy Days are Here Again" vocal pyrotechnic hey-ain't-I-clever-and-marvelous ego trip. Janis Joplin is singing about the ball and chain of her life—the overweight teenager with bad skin who was teased by her classmates, the men who dumped her, the victim of her own turbulent emotions. You sense it in her trembling voice, in that first quiet scream on the word "everything," the way she almost cracks on the word "chain" in the second verse. She builds up intensity on the chorus, then backs off it on the verse, only to build up even more intensity on the next chorus. By the last lines of the song, Joplin is so far gone the band can't deal with it so they drop out and she finishes it acapella, repeating herself to the point of near-gibberish:

> Tell me whyyyyyyyyyy...
> Oh tell me why love is liiiiike...
> Is like a ba-a-a-aa-all...
> It's like a ba-a-a-a-a-all
> B A A A A A ll
> Oh daddy-daddy-daddy-daddy-daddy-daddy-
>   daddy-daddy...
> aAaand chai-ai-ain.

In "Ball and Chain," Janis Joplin takes blues right to the edge. Some claim she goes over it. Rock critic Dave Marsh dismisses her singing as "declamatory histrionics." My father called Janis "excessive." If Joplin is histrionic and excessive on "Ball and Chain," then Otis Redding practically self-destructs on "I've Been Loving You Too Long." Otis has a better band, the aforementioned MGs, but the subject matter and delivery of both numbers are same chapter, different verse. No doubt this is excessive. There are dangers in excess. One of them is winding up dead in Hollywood's Landmark Hotel with a heroin needle stuck in your arm. Understatement, as in the case of Billie Holiday, can kill you just as dead.

But let's not deny that "Ball and Chain" is also real. And we should remember, too, that the pain of love—for all the melodrama, histrionics, clichés, and excess—is real as well. Janis Joplin is exposing her anguish, stripping away the show-biz glitz, in public, before it destroys her. Like Greek tragedy, that process can be cathartic for listeners. We, too, are rid of our sorrow. And that's what the blues is all about.

Three things about Janis Joplin stand out in my mind. It was Joplin, and not all those true blues experts, who finally put a headstone on Bessie Smith's long-ignored grave. And when she was at her best, the lady could really sing. Yes, she could. And Janis Joplin stood for something, however misguided, in the lives of a lot of people. That includes that 14-year-old who told me that she "jus' loved Janis Joplin, jus' loved her." And I have to agree: I jus' love the way Janis sang the blues.

CHAPTER 38
T-BONE WALKER
"CALL IT STORMY MONDAY"

https://www.youtube.com/watch?v=ZfMguEHoKP4

Picture this: Three young guitar teachers at the Nairobi Conservatoire decide to jam. The Brit plays a bit of piano, the American knows a little harmonica, so the Frenchman (who claimed to have done studio work for the Beatles' Apple Corp) gets to show off on guitar. This one doesn't know that song, that one doesn't know this song, but they all know "Stormy Monday." After a tentative start, they jam on it for 20 minutes or so, because it sounds so good.

Fast forward 20 years: A gig in Dar es Salaam is running late into the night. The emcee asks the musicians in the audience to come up and play something. There's a Goan drummer, an American bassist, a Brit on keyboards, a Tanzanian on lead guitar, an Indian on rhythm guitar, and that same American from Nairobi on that same harmonica. So, what song do all six of them know? How about "Stormy Monday"?

After a tentative start, they jam on it for twenty minutes or so, because it sounds so good.

"Stormy Monday," full title "Call it Stormy Monday," is one of those cutting-edge numbers. Who knows how many times that song has been covered. "Stormy Monday" is to electric blues what "I Got Rhythm" is to beboppers and "Johnny B. Goode" is to rock guitarists. If Beethoven's Fifth Symphony is a classic, then "Stormy Monday" is a classic. If you say you know the blues and you don't know "Stormy Monday," your credibility goes down the drain.

On the strength of "Stormy Monday" alone, Aaron "T-Bone" Walker claims a spot in the blues hall of fame. But T-Bone had a lot more going for him than being composer of "Stormy Monday" and a cool nickname. He was inspired to do the blues from listening to his mother sing. He was inspired to play guitar from acting as Blind Lemon Jefferson's "lead boy" in Dallas for three years. He was one of the first, if not *the* first, to play blues on electric guitar. From Jefferson he took those chunky low-string rhythms and made a riff that formed the basis for thousands of blues and most of the classic Chuck Berry numbers, including the afore-mentioned "Johnny B. Goode." From Jefferson's high notes, Walker devised tremolos and sustains that B.B. King refined for all the blues guitarists who followed. I might add that T-Bone Walker wrote my personal theme song: "Too Lazy to Work, Too Nervous to Steal."

T-Bone had a lot going for him, but he was something of a musical schizophrenic. His music came from old-time country blues, but he played it with a very modern sound (for its time) and jazzy. He had a light, easy-going vocal style, yet on stage he turned into a wild man. Dressed in a gold lamé suit, he played behind his back, over his head, with one hand; he'd spin, roll on the floor, do the splits. Many of the rock and roll showmen from Chuck Berry to Jimi Hendrix simply imitated the routines of T-Bone Walker.

"Stormy Monday," recorded in 1947, starts out with a jazzy two-bar intro played by Teddy Buckner on trumpet, Bumps Myers on sax and commented on by pianist Lloyd Glenn. Right away, we are far removed from country blues. Walker toured at age 15 with Ida Cox, a classic blues singer in the Bessie Smith mold. He then played with big swing bands like Fletcher Henderson's. He much preferred the smooth urban type of blues to the raw electric style of a Muddy Waters.

T-Bone enters with Glenn and Myers noodling behind him:

> They call it Stormy Monday
> But Tuesday's just as bad...
> Wednesday's worse
> And Thursday's oh so sad

This is a variation on the "I ain't got me no money" blues. It describes how a poor working man spends his week. Note that Walker doesn't seem too perplexed by his monotonous job. He's cool about it. That's about what you'd expect from life. Things pick up a bit towards the end of the week. To emphasize the change, Buckner on muted trumpet takes over from Myers; it's payday:

> The eagle flies on Friday
> Saturday I go out to play...
> Sunday I go to church
> Then I kneel down and pray

T-Bone gives us a taste of that guitar style that, as described in the book *The Devil's Music* made B.B King go "completely nutty... I think that he had the cleanest touch of anybody I'd ever heard on guitar then." Clear and clean. Nothing low down and dirty about this guitar solo. Every note is well placed, nothing superfluous; the thinking man's blues.

So here's T-Bone in church praying:

> Lord, have mercy, Lord have mercy on me.
> (Is he praying for a pay raise? Maybe he's after a
>   less boring job? No sir.)
> Lord, have mercy, my heart's in misery
> Crazy 'bout my baby, yeah, send her back to me

T-Bone Walker's got the double blues. To emphasize the fact that we've moved from the sacred to more worldly matters, Buckner growls and T-Bone strikes a couple of chords with some power. It seems that while he can accept his menial job, losing his baby requires divine intervention. If this song has a moral, it may be that love is what counts. You can accept the drudgery of the daily grind, but losing love gives you the blues.

Once you've listened to "Stormy Monday," you may wonder why this particular song has assumed such classic proportions. It doesn't appear on the surface to be that special, just a typical 12-bar blues. For musicians, though, "Stormy Monday" has something they all search for —space to stretch, to play your heart out, to interpret the blues your own way. You can do it cool, like T-Bone, or you can infuse it with high emotion. That harp player doesn't "kneel down and pray," he sings: "I fall down on my knees and pray." Then he tries (and sometimes even succeeds) to make that harp cry and wail. And he totally changes the last verse and gives it a different meaning altogether:

> Lord, have mercy, Lord-Lord-Lord have mercy
>   on me...
> Tomorrow's Stormy Monday

Will I never-ever-ever be free

I don't know for sure if T-Bone Walker would approve, but I expect he might. After all, he took Blind Lemon Jefferson's blues and made them into something new. Maybe he'd get right in there and jam a few choruses in his gold lamé suit, playing that guitar between his legs, 'cause... ya know... it sounds so good.

CHAPTER 39
BIG JOE TURNER
— "CHERRY RED"

https://www.youtube.com/watch?v=kkMnWLkpFkc

Big Joe Turner was "Boss of the Blues" before the latest "Boss," Bruce Springsteen, was a gleam in his daddy's eye. And he was still Boss of the Blues when Springsteen recorded "Born in the USA."

Joe Turner was born in the USA—Kansas City to be precise—and even while still a teenager in 1929 he was the "Boss." Here's what Count Basie had to say about Joe Turner in his autobiography: "When I heard him that first time, I said to myself, Jesus, I *never* heard nothing like this guy. He was *the* blues singer in that town. Anybody who came to Kansas City talking about singing some blues had to go listen to *him*."

Others agreed:

"There is an authority to Joe Turner's brand of shouting that defies comparison" (Valerie Wilmer).

"His stentorian voice is still capable of blowing out windows and knocking down doors" (Peter Guralnick, from a 1977 Boston club date).

"... oceanic and commanding, resonant with that rumbling deep down in the ground... a voice of power" (Nick Tosches).

And finally at Tramps in 1982 when Joe Turner was 71 years old, Lee Jeske heard "... a voice so rich and clear and strong the walls shake, the plates rattle and the tables roll," a reference to Turner's 1954 R & B hit "Shake, Rattle and Roll."

Joe Turner and Howlin Wolf were roughly the same size and age. But their big voices were quite different from one another. Wolf sounded as if he lived on a diet of gravel wedged between two thick slices of coarse sandpaper. Howlin Wolf could out-growl a rutting lion. Big Joe Turner did not growl. His voice was more like a pipe organ, a bull elephant bellowing out clear, round sounds. Wolf's blues came out of the Delta. Turner's blues came out of Kansas City.

Kansas City in the 1920s and '30s was a wide open, anything goes town. In the many clubs that spread out from 12th and Vine, there issued forth a new romp-'em, stomp-'em music based on blues riffs. The teenage Joe Turner teamed up with pianist Pete Johnson to shout the blues over a boogie beat. At Piney Brown's Sunset Club in 1938, Count Basie took record executive John Hammond to hear, "*the* blues singer" in Kansas City: "... those two cats (Turner and Johnson) damn near killed him because they were swinging so much. He just sat there shaking his head and slapping his hands."

Hammond brought Turner and Johnson to New York to perform in his Spirituals to Swing Concert at Carnegie Hall. A few days later they recorded the classic boogie-woogie number, "Roll 'Em Pete." The Boss had arrived.

But it wasn't all smooth going. After his initial successes in the late '30s and early '40s, Big Joe hit a slump. Then came his Atlantic recordings from 1951 to 1956, beginning with "Chains of Love" through the immortal Jesse Stone classic "Shake, Rattle and Roll," to "Corrine Corrina," which crossed over from R & B to the pop charts. Turner never made the charts again, but that didn't seem to slow him down. He toured the clubs and sang his music. Whatever they wanted to call it—jazz, boogie-woogie, R & B, rock and roll—it was fine by him. Big Joe Turner was the Boss of the Blues.

Though his blues was different from the blues of Lead Belly, Bessie Smith, Howlin Wolf, B.B. King, and several hundred others, it was still the blues. As he told Valerie Wilmer, "Once I get started into a good blues song, I could carry on for hours... Blues I did mainly for the fun of it." The Boss, after all, was the Boss.

Joe Turner first cut "Cherry Red" with Pete Johnson in 1939. A lot of other people have covered that number. This version of "Cherry Red" comes from the classic 1956 album titled "Boss of the Blues." Pete Johnson—Big Joe's original partner—plays piano, along with Count Basie alumni Joe Newman trumpet, Frank Wess tenor sax, Freddie Green guitar, Walter Page bass, plus Lawrence Brown (ex-Ellington) trombone, and Pete Brown (no relation to Lawrence) on alto sax. They lay down that steady-rolling, four-to-the-bar, Kansas City rhythm. No delta blues sounds like this even though it can take the same eight-bar, three-chord form. From Blind Lemon Jefferson to Robert Cray, the blues come in many varieties. Turner's "Cherry Red" is classic Kansas City.

After the eight-bar intro, Big Joe begins to shout the blues. It doesn't sound like shouting. Recording studios can never do justice to this style of blues. Go to the clubs, then you may understand why it's called a blues shout. The music fills your ears, then your brain, then your guts, and your whole body vibrates from the sounds and rhythm. And like John Hammond in 1938, you're shaking your head and slapping your hands. The music can damn near kill you. And of all the shouters, Big Joe Turner was damned near a homicidal maniac.

> Right here, pretty mama
> Sit down on your daddy's knee
> I want to tell everybody
> How you've been sending me

This is no sad blues. Bouncy, not fast, is more like it. Big Joe feels fine as wine. And he's got some choice words for Pretty Mama, aided and abetted by the horns:

> Well, if that's your secret,
> You better keep it to yourself
> Cause if you tell me
> I might tell somebody else

If you don't pay attention, you might miss the point here. The secret, it seems, is how Pretty Mama "sends" Big Joe. He knows she sends him; how she does it and its implications is what the whole song is all about.

> I ain't never loved
> And I hope I never will
> Cause a lovin' proposition
> Is gonna get somebody killed

Now this makes no sense whatsoever until you listen to the next verse:

> Now you can take me, Pretty Mama
> And chunk me in your Hollywood bed
> And you can rock me baby
> Till my face turns cherry red

The subject is sex, and, as I interpret the third verse, Turner is telling Pretty Mama not to confuse sex with love. This not-exactly-original idea seems as valid today as it did in 1939. Turner calls trombonist Lawrence Brown to put out some blues which he does for three choruses with the other horns riffing behind him on the third. That riffing was what K.C. gave to the world.

Big Joe repeats his admonition about a lovin' proposition and then changes the last line of the song:

> I want you to boogie my woogie
> Till my face turns Cherry Red

Big Joe Turner packed it in in 1985 at the age of 74. For me The Boss of the Blues is still The Boss.

CHAPTER 40
SONNY BOY WILLIAMSON
"DON'T LET YOUR RIGHT HAND KNOW"

https://www.youtube.com/watch?v=0DrS72UUHXc

Music sometimes involves theft. Aretha Franklin stole "Respect" from Otis Redding. Otis Redding in turn stole "Pain in My Heart" from Irma Thomas. John Lennon used the intro to Chuck Berry's "You Can't Catch Me" for "Come Together," and the Beach Boys' "Surfin' USA" is Berry's "Sweet Little 16" with new words. Don't feel too sorry for Chuck, though. He took the tune from Memphis Minnie's "Me and my Chauffeur" for "I Wanna Be Your Driver." Minnie, in turn, had stolen the tune to "Good Morning Little School Girl." Bob Dylan built his early career on using traditional folk tunes to which he put original lyrics. But I know of only a single case where one person stole another person's name.

Aleck (or Alex) "Rice" Miller kicked around the south for many years singing blues and playing harmonica. In 1941, he and his guitarist partner, Robert Jr. Lockwood, became the King Biscuit Boys, doing a radio show from Helena, Arkansas, to advertise King Biscuit Flour. Rice

Miller started calling himself Sonny Boy Williamson. The "real" Sonny Boy Williamson, born John Lee Williamson in Tennessee in 1914, was a well-known singer/harpist based in Chicago and the composer of "Good Morning Little School Girl," mentioned above. This has caused confusion ever since. Usually, John Lee is referred to as Sonny Boy No.1 and Rice Miller as Sonny Boy No.2.

The bogus Sonny Boy and the King Biscuit Boys became hugely successful flogging flour. Sonny Boy even had a cornmeal named after him. "King Biscuit Time" spawned a number of other radio shows featuring bluesmen all through the 1940s. Williamson finally cut a record in 1951 called "Eyesight to the Blind." He was 52 years old... maybe. (His year of birth is given as any time between 1897 and 1912.) His records sold well among Southern black people to whom Sonny Boy was a big star. One of their own had a commercial product named after him. You couldn't buy Basie bread or Ellington oatmeal, but every rural grocer carried Sonny Boy Corn Meal.

After becoming something of a star, Sonny Boy decided to move into Chicago, the original Sonny Boy's territory. (John Lee Williamson, Sonny Boy number 1, had been fatally shot in 1948.) But what worked in the rural south didn't go over in the big city in the mid-1950s. Sonny Boy 2 was already a fairly old man playing an older style of music.

Then came the blues revival when old men and old styles were not only accepted but preferred; the older the better. Sonny Boy fit right in. Here was another genuine article: a gray-headed, sleepy-eyed, slurred-speaking, stoop-shouldered old fellow from Mississippi. If the American folkies loved him, young British blues-rockers like the Yardbirds venerated him. This mean, old, nasty-tempered Black American was a saint in their eyes.

I saw a video of Sonny Boy on a 1963 blues tour in England with several other notables, including Memphis Slim, Muddy Waters, and

Lonnie Johnson. Memphis Slim announces him as "Sir" Sonny Boy Williamson. (If he could steal a name, why not a knighthood?) And out he comes: tall, thin, slightly hunched forward, wearing a three-piece suit and bowler hat, carrying a briefcase and an umbrella. He sets the briefcase down, pulls a harmonica out of the breast pocket of his suit, takes off his bowler in acknowledgement of the lukewarm applause (What were nice middle class British teenagers to make of this?), hooks the brolly over his arm, and launches into a laid-back arrangement of "Keep It to Yourself," first recorded in 1955. Getting no crowd reaction, he lays on a little vaudeville by sticking the harp in his mouth like a cigar and playing "look ma, no hands." When Sonny Boy fulfills his three-minute obligation, the kids clap politely—more bewildered than entertained, it appears to me. The big star, Muddy Waters fared little better. Outside a sizable and fanatic cult, the Brits were as little prepared to deal with real blues as most of the white American middle class in 1963.

Whatever else—name stealing included—Sonny Boy Williamson could play the harp. He blew a 10-hole harmonica just about as well as it could be blown. He also is credited with composing "Bye Bye Bird," "One Way Out," "Don't Start Me Talkin'," "Fattenin' Frogs for Snakes," and "Help Me." So maybe the rest doesn't matter much. Williamson did much of his recording with electric bands which I don't like because they clutter up that beautiful harp sound. Even single acoustic guitar backing sometimes gets in the way. In my opinion, Sonny Boy at his best is Sonny Boy solo.

I selected a piece of blues gibberish titled "Don't Let Your Right Hand Know (What Your Left Hand Do)," off the album *Portraits in Blues, Volume 4*. The album was recorded in 1963, with Matt Murphy (future Blues Brother) on acoustic guitar, strictly for Sonny Boy Williamson on harp.

The lyrics, such as they are, don't amount to half a cup of cornmeal.

I'm not even sure Sonny Boy knows what his words mean. His woman has told him what they do should be kept secret. If not, everyone will be "doin what we tryin to do." I'll buy that including the cliché title. Later on, he says he can't explain what he's trying to get in your (her?) mind, which seems pretty obvious. And then he tells us that his money done run out and he's got nowhere to stay, so he better go home and make another start. All this is more spoken than sung. Not that Sonny Boy couldn't sing, he just didn't sing very well. But his vocal skills and the nonsense lyrics don't count. Once you hear that harp, you're gone, hooked, zonked, a believer.

On the surface, the harp playing seems simple enough. Sonny Boy blows single notes, also does a bit of "train time" on the lower end, uses a warbling vibrato, and bends notes from here till Tuesday. He could bend notes until they almost broke. Like the blues itself, Sonny Boy's harp is deceptive. Only a very few harp players could do what Sonny Boy plays on this number, and I doubt that even the best of the best could make it seem so effortless. Probably no acoustic harmonica player, including my main man Sonny Terry, had as much influence on harpists as Sonny Boy Williamson. Among his "pupils" were Howlin Wolf, Junior Wells, James Cotton, and even Little Walter although he didn't like to admit it. Many consider him the ultimate in acoustic blues harmonica. I once told a friend that if I could ever come close to doing "Right Hand," I would probably go directly to blues heaven.

Sonny Boy Williamson, cornmeal hustler and name stealer that he undoubtedly was, managed to achieve what many strive for and only a rare few attain: excellence. So maybe we can forgive him for breaking the 8th Commandment. When I listen to Sonny Boy, I hear what all those harp players he influenced heard. What we hear is the ultimate in harp mastery. So I honor Sonny Boy Williamson and I honor his achievement. One of his many disciples, British bluesman John Mayall composed a tribute to this "Mean Old Man":

I heard Sonny Boy blow
I heard Sonny Boy blow
He's a mean old man
But I love him so
I can add no more.

CHAPTER 41
BLIND WILLIE JOHNSON
"MOTHERLESS CHILDREN"

https://www.youtube.com/watch?v=ywTC7yt7XZw

One of the best of all blues musicians never did a blues in his life. Blind Willie Johnson would no doubt have been horrified if you called him a blues singer. He never ever, as far as I know, sang the Devil's Music. At least he never recorded a blues number. Johnson was committed 100 percent to the Lord's Music. But the way he did songs was also 100 percent blues. All you would have to do is change the words to be transported from paradise to purgatory.

I will confess that I know almost nothing about religious music of any sort. Once past Bach's "Jesu, Joy of Man's Desiring," I am wandering in the wilderness. I have a tape of Mahalia Jackson because she was one of the greatest singers of the 20th century. That she sang gospel is purely coincidental to me, although I'm sure it wasn't to her. She claimed that she was offered a pile of money to do an album of secular songs and she turned it down. I don't know if Blind Willie

Johnson was ever offered even a nickel to do a blues number, that's just
how his songs came out, usually referred to as "gospel blues." We'll get
to that shortly. What he did have in common with a lot of blues singers
besides his vocal and guitar style was singing on street corners for loose
change. But the bluesmen spent Saturday night entertaining in the juke
joints and Blind Willie spent Sunday morning evangelizing in the
churches around his hometown of Marlin, Texas, south of Dallas.

In his book, *The Land Where the Blues Began*, folk music archivist
Alan Lomax discusses spirituals and gospel music. His research brought
him to Professor Lewis Jones of Fisk University. Jones explained to
Lomax that the transition from old time spirituals to the modern gospel
style was the result of "a big power struggle in the church." Formerly,
the "sisters" and deacons ran the services principally by controlling the
singing. But then the preachers took over. They brought in "musical
directors" and choirs who were doing a new type of music called gospel.
These were songs the sisters didn't like and couldn't sing. "My guess is
that there's a tie-up between the big preachers and the publishers somehow," added Jones. "One thing for sure, there's a lot of money being
made out of the whole thing." How this affected Blind Willie Johnson,
I have no idea. His recorded output seems to me more like the old-time
spirituals than the "modern" gospel style, but what can a sinner like me
know.

What I do know is that many of Johnson's songs are classics. To
name just a few: "If I Had My Way," "Jesus Make Up My Dying Bed,"
"Let the Light from the Lighthouse Shine on Me," "John the Revela-
tor," "God Moves on the Water" (about the sinking of the Titanic),
"The Soul of a Man," "You'll Need Somebody on Your Bond," and
"Nobody's Fault But Mine." (This last is the story of my life.) That he
had so many hits is amazing considering that Johnson recorded a total
of only 30 sides between December 1927 and April 1930. Blues scholar

David Evans points out that Johnson's first release in early 1928 sold over 15,000 copies and that he regularly outsold popular singers like Bessie and Clara Smith.

The sources of information I have about Blind Willie Johnson's life greatly contradict each other, so details are unreliable. One source says he was born in 1890 and died in 1947. Another chops 11 years off his life, having him born in 1903 and dying in 1949. A third guesses he was born "around 1900" and died "around 1950 or 1951." There are at least three different accounts of how little Willie became "Blind Willie," the most dramatic being that his stepmother threw lye in the seven-year-old's face during (or maybe after) an argument with his father. All agree that he had a calling to the Lord early on and that he was a street singer and evangelist in adolescence. Several add that he learned his craft from another blind Texas street musician named Madkin Butler.

No one disputes Johnson's skill on slide guitar. Eric Clapton called it "probably the finest slide guitar playing you'll ever hear." Ry Cooder said, "I think this guy is one of these interplanetary world musicians—and there are only a few. Blind Willie Johnson is in the ether somewhere. He's up there in the zone." Who am I to argue with Ry Cooder, who some think is the best slide guitarist on the planet? For sliders, Johnson's magnum opus is the instrumental hum-along, "Dark was the Night, Cold was the Ground." Cooder, again, calls this "the most transcendent piece in American music." A copy of this song was sent into outer space along with Beethoven and Chuck Berry on board one of the Voyager II spacecraft. For all we know, there are E.T.s listening right now doing the intergalactic equivalent of wow, cool, far out.

While I highly recommend "Dark was the Night" to any music fan, my analysis would lean heavily, perhaps exclusively, on wow, cool, far out, because that song really defies description. On the other hand, I might be able to do something with "Motherless Children," sometimes wrongly titled "Mother's Children." First, it is as close to secular as Johnson ever got, and second, he really lays it on the line:

> Well motherless children have a hard time when
>   their mother is dead
> Motherless children have a hard time when their
>   mother is dead
> Well I don't have anywhere to go, wanderin'
>   'round from door to door
> Motherless children have a hard time when their
>   mother is dead

The above is not exactly how Blind Willie does it because he intertwines his guitar and voice so that the guitar completes some of the vocal lines and the voice completes some of the instrumental lines. You hear in the intro how his voice complements the guitar with "well well well" and "ah... ah." Let me transcribe the words again as it actually goes with "..." used for the guitar notes.

> Well Motherless children have a hard time... ...
>   ... ...
> Motherless children have a hard time... ... ...
>   ... ... (Mother is dead)
> Well, I don't have anywhere to go, wanderin'
>   'round from door to door
> ... ... have a hard time... ...
>   ... ...

Willie Johnson knows what he's singing about here. His mother died when he was very young and his stepmother blinded him...

maybe. The intensity of the vocal on this number leaves no doubt whatsoever that he believes every word he is singing and feels it deeply. The second verse reinforces not only the loss but his own feeling of guilt:

> Nobody on earth can take Mother's place when
> … … … when Mother is dead
> Nobody on earth can take Mother's place when
> Mother is dead
> Nobody on earth can take Mother's place,
> memory is startin' to fade away
> Nobody treats you like Mother will when… …
>
> … … … … … …

As to Johnson's vocal style, David Evans claims that Johnson really was a tenor but he sang in a "false bass." I have already explained a little about this vocal method in the section on Howlin Wolf—the oscillation between octaves from chest to throat and back. This style is very common in gospel, to wit Andre Crouch. You also hear it with Charley Patton. (This very important proto-blues singer will not make this book, sorry Charley.)

The most famous practitioner of this style is Louis Armstrong. Robert Palmer describes an African type of vocalizing called "voice masking." During religious festivals in West Africa, certain individuals assume the role of a god by putting on the god's mask, at which point the god's spirit enters them. Once the spirit takes over, these mortals also assume the god's voice, a low distorted rumbling sound. I have one song on tape titled "Toko" by a singer from Guinea named Momo Wando. He could be an African relative of Blind Willie Johnson. South African groaners such as Mahlathini with the Mahotella Queens bear a striking similarity to the American blues and gospel growlers.

Blind Willie needs to seriously testify so he begins to preach with his guitar and pocketknife (which he used as a slider):

> Your wife your husband may be good to you...
> ... ... when Mother is dead
> ... ... may be good to
>   you when Mother is dead
> Your wife your husband may be good to you but
>   there isn't nothin' in two by two
> Nobody treats like Mother will when ... ...
> ... ... when Mother is
>   dead, Lord

His voice becomes the congregation adding encouragement with "Lawd-lawd-lawd-lawd," then "Yeeeeeeeeeeah-well," and finally "Aaaaaaaah-aah." These are not just random noises spilling out of Johnson's mouth. The "Lawd-lawd-lawd-lawd" comes at the end of his first four-bar phrase, the "Yeeeeeeeeeeeah-well" is at the end of his second four-bar phrase, and the "Aaaaaaaaaaaah-aah" bridges the end of the third four-bar phrase and the beginning of the last four-bar phrase. These are vocal responses to his guitar's calls. They are rhythmic markers.

> Well, some people say that sister will do... ...
> ... ... (when Mother is dead)
> ... ... that sister will do
>   when Mother is dead
> Some people say that sister will do but soon as
>   she's married she'll turn her back on you
> Nobody treats you like Mother will... ... ...
>   ... ...

Having sought support from spouse and sister, there is one more person Willie can turn to:

> And Father will do the best he can... ... ...
>   ... ... (when Mother is dead)
> ... ... well, the best he can
>   when mother is dead
> Father will do the best he can but so many
>   things Father can't understand
> Nobody treats you like Mother will... ... ...
>
>   ... ...

Johnson is not criticizing father. He'll do the best he can. So will sister or spouse. It's just that, as he reiterates at the end of each verse: "nobody treats you like Mother will." To drive home his loss, he repeats the first verse and takes it out with a chorus on guitar. If I went through the mechanics of what Willie Johnson does on this last chorus, you would be really impressed with him and irritated with me for subjecting you to another 1000 words. While this may sound simple, it is really complicated to execute. Here is a condensed version: He does eight bars sliding on his lower strings, kind of moaning low, and then jumps to the high strings, using his thumb on the low strings to supply a rhythmic bass line, simultaneously flicking the chord changes with his fingers. For non-pickers, this is like rubbing your stomach and patting your head while walking backwards, all in a brisk and steady four-to-the-bar beat. I can tell you what he's doing, but have not a clue how he does it, except to repeat Ry Cooder: Johnson plays "up there in the zone."

A couple of ironies to ponder when listening to "Motherless Children": First, had Willie Johnson not lost his mother and gone blind (however it happened), he might not have become an interplanetary world musician. His losses are posterity's gain. Second, Johnson came to a strange and tragic end. He died of pneumonia from sleeping on the cold hard ground on a dark night after his house burned down. And Blind Willie's greatest song, recorded two decades before in 1927: "Dark was the Night, Cold was the Ground."

CHAPTER 42
ERIC CLAPTON
"HAVE YOU EVER LOVED A WOMAN"

https://www.youtube.com/watch?v=a73Lxi-o388

Around 1965, graffiti appeared on a wall in London declaring "Clapton is God." That's an impossible claim to live up to and not one Eric Clapton ever made for himself. He just plugged in his Fender Stratocaster and played some blues. He played at first in coffee houses around his home in Surrey. Then he went to London and joined the Yardbirds who were studiously copying American blues. That was when he got deified. He wasn't even that good yet, but he got better and better. Regardless, it's a giant leap from being good to being God.

Clapton attained deity status, in my opinion, simply by being English. In the U.S., he would have been good, but not a king like B.B. or a boss like Joe Turner. Eric Clapton was special because he was, I believe, the first (and one of the few) non-Americans to harness the full power and majesty of the blues. His style is no doubt derivative; it could not be otherwise. Very few musicians have ever created new music and even they had to start with what was already there. Music belongs to whoever can deal with it. Clapton began with the blues of B.B. King and went on. He added that which is distinctly Eric Clapton.

I've written about a white boy who got lost in the blues and a white girl who got buried alive in the blues. It seems to me that Eric Clapton lives on blues power (the title of one of his songs). He plays a mix of rock and pop, but when he's in need of inspiration, he always goes back to the blues.

That was the case in 1970 when he recorded the album *Layla*. The crowning glory of that double album was the title track. The song "Layla" is not blues in form, but most definitely solid blues in content and spirit:

> Layla... You got me on my knees
> Layla... You got me beggin' please
> Layla... Won't you ease my worried mind.

He even makes reference to Robert Johnson's "Love in Vain." "Layla" has to be one of the most magnificent pieces of music in the rock era. But for me, *the* track off that album is the blues classic "Have You Ever Loved a Woman." On this number, first recorded by Freddy King in 1960, Clapton demonstrates his mastery of the blues. I have several versions of "Have You Ever Loved a Woman." None even come close to capturing the intensity that Eric Clapton gives it, not even the original. The reason he could do this is because he was living the song. The album "Layla" was about his unrequited love for Patti Boyd Harrison. Talk about life imitating art: here it is.

From the very first notes off Clapton's guitar, you know you're in for a highly emotional experience. Carl Radle's bass goes sliding through the changes, while Bobby Whitlock on piano and drummer Jim Gordon lay down a solid slow shuffle. It's all Clapton can do to control the flurry of blues licks flying off the strings. In fact, they spill over into the first bar of the vocal chorus. It's as if he is reluctant to tell us about his trouble, but it has so consumed him that he just has to let it out:

> Have you ever loved a woman so much you
>   tremble in pain
> Have you ever loved a woman *so much* you
>   tremble in pain...

On the second "so much," Clapton jumps into a falsetto (a la B.B. King) to make his voice literally tremble. He has immediately established that this is more than just a song. This love has brought him so much pain his voice trembles even to mention it. Why?

> And all time you know, yeah
> She bears another man's name

This isn't just a pretty face he's in love with. No, she's a married woman. Listen to the way Clapton sings the word "she." You cannot doubt that this is a serious problem for him—even existential. It gets worse:

> But you just love that woman
> So much it's a shame and a sin...

Not a shame and a scandal; it's a sin, no bones about it. His voice has taken on the tone of a preacher with the falsetto and the rasp. The preacher is condemning the sinner for breaking one of God's Ten Commandments. The preacher and the sinner are one. As bad as it is,

Clapton has something to confess that makes his sin infinitely more damnable:

> But all the time you know (yes you know)
> She belongs to your very best friend

There it is, out in the open. To emphasize the gravity of his sin, he adds that second "yes you know": "You **know** (yes you **know**)." And that was exactly the reality. Patti Boyd Harrison wasn't just any married woman. She was the wife of Beatle George Harrison. Clapton had played guitar with Harrison on "While My Guitar Gently Weeps." Harrison had helped Clapton compose the song "Badge." They lived down the road from each other. Harrison was indeed one of Clapton's very best friends. And here he was in love with George's wife, just as the song says.

Having laid this revelation on us, the band takes the intensity level up several notches with the entrance of Duane Allman on slide guitar. Clapton switches over to rhythm and together with Whitlock, Radle, and Gordon, they pound out that slow shuffle. Allman, young and white, was in some ways the American counterpart of Clapton. He, too, chose to play the blues. And he chose to play slide, which very few white guitarists did at that time. If you listen to Allman's solo as he makes that guitar cry, moan, sob, and wail, you'll know how he got his reputation as a slide wizard. And you'll also know why so many of us mourned his loss in a 1971 motorcycle accident.

Then Clapton takes over for two choruses. It's B.B. King, Albert King, Freddy King, Buddy Guy, and Otis Rush. But it's all Eric Clapton. He had absorbed their blues, internalized them, and made them his own. He had gone far past playing all the right licks in all the right places. He was by this point playing himself—heart, guts, and soul. Blues done right leaves you nowhere to hide. Blues will expose you as a real artist or a poseur. On this solo, Clapton is playing his pain and sense of guilt and it's as real as any music... any music... can get.

Then he caps it off with the last verse:

> Have you ever loved a woman
> Ah you know you can't leave her alone...

The compulsion is evident in the way he sings the word "can't." There's a battle going on here between Clapton's personal demon and his guardian angel. The demon is telling him to do it, do it right now; the angel holds him back: You can't do this to your very best friend. The prize is Eric Clapton's soul. Who wins?

> Something deep inside you
> Won't let you wreck your best friend's home

So good triumphs over evil. The preacher exorcises the demon. And all's well that ends well, right? Not quite. Maybe as a substitute for Patti, Eric fell in love with heroin for a few years. After he finally kicked the monkey off his back, he asked Patti to divorce Harrison and marry him. She did. But even then, the sun refused to slink slowly in the West. Clapton hit the booze heavy for a number of years, and eventually he and Patti split up. Then his good friend and fellow musician Stevie Ray Vaughan died in a plane crash and Clapton's young son accidently fell to his death from a New York high rise apartment. Life has dealt Eric Clapton more than his fair share of suffering, rich and famous though he is. He returns again and again to his source of inspiration and strength, blues power, as he did on "Have You Ever Loved a Woman." And blues power is there for you too.

CHAPTER 43
JOHN LEE HOOKER
"BOOGIE CHILLUN"

https://www.youtube.com/watch?v=eM3PuXDpKiA

n 1990, John Lee Hooker came out with an album titled *The Healer*. Assisting him on various cuts are such luminaries as Robert Cray, George Thorogood, Charlie Musselwhite, what's left of Canned Heat, Los Lobos, and Bonnie Raitt. Bonnie and John Lee do an updated "I'm in the Mood," and it sounds as if they can hardly wait to get at each other. The album won a Grammy. Some must have thought it was way past time. John Lee Hooker was 73 years old.

The title track has Carlos Santana and the boys doing a nice easy Chicano cha cha with Hooker telling us that blues is the healer. It can heal you. It can heal me. Blues can heal the world. And that's about it: Blues is the healer. Leave aside the inherent contradictions, the possible truth. Leave aside even the cha cha beat. The song doesn't go anywhere, doesn't do anything.

Almost none of John Lee Hooker's best numbers go anywhere or do anything. Many of his songs have no chord changes. They are little more than a single riff constantly repeated. John Lee, let's face it, does not play guitar very well. John Lee doesn't bother much with such conventions as rhyme:

> Boom boom boom boom
> Gonna shoot you right down
> Right off your feet
> Take you home with me
> Put you in my house
> Boom boom boom boom

It doesn't rhyme, it doesn't make any sense, but I love it anyhow. What makes John Lee Hooker a great bluesman? Well, for starters he has the voice for it, that voice as big and wide as the Mississippi River. That voice draws everything to it. That voice is irresistible. Then he has that quintessential blues rhythm. John Lee lays that one-riff boogie on you, you know you've been boogied. That rhythm is the blood pulsing through your body. That rhythm can make the world turn. And finally there is the imagery:

> When I first started hobo-in',
> I took a freight train to be my friend

Or his song "Tupelo" about the historic 1927 Mississippi River flood:

> A dark cloud rolled way back in Tupelo
>   Mississippi
> Wasn't that a mighty time
> Wasn't that a mighty time

In "Tupelo" we hear the voice, the power, and the empathy of someone who has been there, who knows.

John Lee Hooker has created his own niche among the Delta bluesmen. There's a certain way of doing blues that's uniquely John Lee Hooker. As with other great musicians, his style, his special "voice," is immediately identifiable. That's John Lee Hooker or someone doing John Lee Hooker. Canned Heat built a career doing John Lee Hooker.

John Lee learned guitar early from his stepfather in Clarksdale, Mississippi, who had played with the early-bluesman Charley Patton. While a teenager he moved to Memphis, then Cincinnati, and finally Detroit where work could be had after World War II began. Nightlife centered around a group of clubs on Hastings Street. It was there that Hooker came into his own. And it is the subject of his most famous song with his most famous one-chord riff— "Boogie Chillun" (also written "Boogie Chillen").

The song begins with John Lee doing that riff on guitar accompanied by his foot tapping— the tapping is important. This goes on for somewhere between 12 and 13 bars. Why 12 or 13 bars? Well, you count it and see what you come up with. Various musicians have used that riff ever since. Canned Heat has any number of songs with the Hooker boogie riff. "Refried Boogie" immediately comes to mind. Canned Heat did an entire album with John Lee called *Hooker and Heat*. ZZ Top, in their song, "Le Grange," not only uses the Hooker boogie riff but also starts out imitating Hooker in the vocals. Our band would start "Le Grange" with that boogie riff and people would go bananas. After that 12 or13 bars of the boogie riff, John Lee explains what "Boogie Chillun" is about:

> Well my Mama didn't allow me
> Just to stay out all night long...
> I didn't care what she didn't allow

I would boogie anyhow

That's about the extent of the singing. The rest is spoken or something like chanted. So how could something that is not much more than nothing become so famous? We'll see, but first, John Lee wants to tell us about Hastings Street in Detroit:

> When I first hit the town, people
> I was walkin' down Hastings Street
> Everybody was talkin', about...
> Henry's Swing Club. I decided
> I'd drop in there at night.
> When I got there... I said
> Yeah people... they was really
> Havin' a ball. Yes I know it.

Then Hooker does four bars of nothing much on guitar and then here it comes: "Boogie Chillun!"

Then a little guitar-foot duet and back to that riff. It's like something folks might use for yoga meditation if they were seeking the nirvana of rhythm. Now we get to the crux of the matter:

> One night I was laying down
> I heard Mama and Papa talkin'
> I heard Papa tell Mama
> "Let that boy boogie-woogie.
> It's in him and it's got to come out"
> And I felt so good
> Went on boogie-in' just the same

And that's it. But of course, that's not it. That's not it at all. I'm about to lay on you the Hooker Philosophy of Boogie.

We have this young fellow whose mama won't allow him to stay out all night long, and rightly so; I didn't allow my kids to stay out all night long either. Parents make the rules and kids break the rules. John Lee hits Henry's Swing Club, takes one look around, and says, this is where I belong. This is where I can become the real me. John Lee Hooker wants what? He wants to boogie. Think freedom. He wants the freedom to make music, to express himself, to live it all.

I don't know if you've ever been in joints like Henry's Swing Club. Yes, people really have a ball. But you can also get hit over the head with a beer bottle or worse. Forget talking to people; just look at someone the wrong way and you may need an ambulance. Mama is concerned her little baby is heading for a world of trouble. But fortunately (for John Lee and us), Papa intervenes. The time has come for his boy to go out on his own. Yes, it's rough out there and yes, he may screw up. But Papa also sees that parental rules no longer apply. John Lee has to make his own rules now. And maybe Papa also senses that there is something special inside his son. By letting John Lee boogie woogie, he may make a small contribution to the fulfillment of that special talent. I hope Papa (and Mama too) were still around to witness what John Lee Hooker made of his boogie. I expect they would be most proud of their boy.

And I can't help but think of my own two daughters. They found their Henry's Swing Club. And I had to say, let those girls boogie woogie; it's in them and it's got to come out. And I gave them each a big hug and sent them on their way with this blessing: Boogie Chillun!

CHAPTER 44
JAMES BOOKER
"BLACK NIGHT"

https://www.youtube.com/watch?v=ysMTSBhkyjA

Around 40 years ago I borrowed a tape from an Australian truck driver. It had neither song titles nor artists' names. A very slow, haunting number at the end of Side 1 cut about halfway through. It was a singer accompanied by piano in front of an audience. From the lyrics I gathered the title was "Black Night." I had no idea who the singer was.

A few years later another copied tape included a version of "Black Night" by James Cotton, who once played harmonica for Muddy Waters. A year or so later, a friend sent me a Buddy Guy tape called *Damn Right I Have the Blues,* which won a Grammy and rightly so. It too had a version of "Black Night." Then I read a book by Nick Tosches, *The Unsung Heroes of Rock and Roll.* It mentions that "Black Night" was first done by Charles Brown in 1951. I went on a hunt for the original "Black Night." Without going into detail, I succeeded.

Then in 2012, I tuned into NPR's "Weekend Edition" toward the end of the program and there was a song on. WHAM! Two seconds into it I knew it was that cassette tape partial version of "Black Night"; the piano alone told me that and the voice confirmed it. I hoped NPR would identify the artist. It did: James Booker.

I knew nothing about James Booker other than his name. I'd heard him mentioned along with other post-WWII New Orleans R&B pianists, such as Tuts Washington, Huey "Piano" Smith, Fats Domino, Allen Toussaint, Mac Rebennack (aka Dr John), and the daddy of them all, Professor Longhair (Henry Byrd). I'd never heard Booker play piano or sing.

Thanks to the internet, research is easier than it has ever been. I soon had lots of info on James Booker and the full version of "Black Night" I had half-recorded 30 years ago. It comes off an album from a concert in Germany in 1977 titled *New Orleans Piano Wizard: Live!* However, before we get into this marvelous piece of music, we need to go back to down the river for a paragraph or so.

New Orleans is considered the birthplace of jazz, true or not. New Orleans also gave birth to a distinct style of Rhythm and Blues in the years after WWII. I don't like the term R&B at all—it is too vague, too general, and doesn't get us very far. But that is the term used to categorize this style of music, so I'll call it New Orleans R&B. There's blues in it, there's boogie woogie in it, and... what makes it special goes back to Jelly Roll Morton's insistence that the music has to have a "Spanish tinge." New Orleans pianist Allen Toussaint called it "that mambo-rhumba boogie thing."

Born in 1939, James Booker was younger than many of the first wave New Orleans R&B artists, but he cut his first record at the age of 14. His style was different in that he was schooled in classical music and had picked up on jazz pianist Erroll Garner (composer of "Misty"). All the other pianists knew Booker was special. (He went by his last name.) Dr. John covered it thoroughly in a single sentence. He said Booker is "the best black, gay, one-eyed, junkie piano genius that New Orleans ever produced." (He usually wore a patch with a star on it over his left eye.)

Now we come to "Black Night," composed by Jessie Mae Robinson. She wrote pop songs in the '50s for Patti Page, Jo Stafford, and Frankie Laine, but she also wrote "Blue Light Boogie" for Louis Jordan and "Black Night" for Charles Brown, a popular R&B singer, who recorded it in December 1950. It became a classic because you can do anything with it. Charles Brown does a very laid-back treatment. James Cotton and Buddy Guy dive deep into the blues with it. And Booker, who did nothing by halves, wrings every ounce of soul possible out of it.

As you listen to the first verse, you will know exactly where this feeling comes from. It comes from the church. That is not surprising, as Booker's father and grandfather were Baptist preachers and Booker's first gig was playing organ in his father's church. This is no mambo-rhumba boogie thing. This is rich, gospel piano... with a little blues thrown in.

If we changed the words, the vocal would sound as if it belongs in church. Booker employs a device commonly used in gospel and soul music called "melisma." Melisma means using several notes to sing one syllable. Booker sings:

> You know I've got no one to talk to
> To tell my troubles to-oo-oo.

That's melisma. Aretha Franklin uses it. The great blues singer Bobby Bland uses it. And even the very laid-back and totally cool Charles Brown, in his original "Black Night," used it. Melisma adds tension. "I've got no one to tell my troubles to" is a statement. "... to tell my troubles to-oo-oo" is a big problem. The reason?

> I don't even know that I'm livin'
> Since I-I-I lost you-oo-oo

And with almost no break he goes into the chorus:

> You know that that… black night is fallin'
> Weeeell you know I hate to be-ee alo-one
> Well I just keep on cryin for my baby-ee yeah
> Well well well well well-ell-ell you know another
>   day has go-o-o-o-one
> Another day has gone right now…
> The pause after "that that…" adds emphasis to
>   "black night is fallin'."

Booker is testifyin', no other way to describe it. If you compare Booker's "Black Night" to the Charles Brown's original "Black Night," you are listening to the same melody with the same words done so totally differently that they may as well be two songs. Which goes back to what that old-fashioned, down-home country bluesman Bukka White said at the beginning: "The blues is a feeling." Charles Brown felt "Black Night" as quiet desperation; James Booker felt "Black Night" as insufferable pain:

> Nobody cares about me
> I ain't even got a frien-n-n-nd
> My baby's gone away and left me
> When will my troubles en-n-n-n-nd
> You know that…
> Black night just keeps on a-fallin'… keeps on a-
>   fallin'
> Weelll you know I hate to be alo-o-o-ne

> Well I just keep on cryin for my babe-e-e
> Well-well-well-well weeellll another day has
>   gone...
> Another day has gone right now

Then comes some piano—half church and half saloon—for two choruses. There's some Chopin in there mixed with Ray Charles. In New Orleans they call it gumbo.

> My mother had her problems
> My father's got 'em to-o-o-o
> My sister's on a corner somewhere
> And I just don't know what to do-o-o-o
> Because that...
> Black night just keeps a-fallin'...

Line 3 is a divergence from the original and other versions of the song. Charles Brown in 1950 sang:

> My mother has her troubles
> My father has his too
> Brother's in Korea
> And I don't know just what to do

In the '60s James Cotton sang "my brother's in Vietnam." In 1991, Buddy Guy sang "my brother's in Iraq." But Booker has a sister on a corner somewhere—he's not sure where, but he knows what she's doing there. However, all four singers are in the same boat: They "don't know what to do."

Actually, they know exactly what to do. They sing and play the blues to rid themselves of the blues. Many of us are alo-o-o-one.

Listening to a blues artist is a sort of catharsis: the blues singer taking on our burdens for us. There may be a message in that last line, "But now another day has gone." It's not exactly hope, more like determination. With all this trouble and loneliness, I somehow made it through today. And if I did it today, I can do it again tomorrow, black night and all. I will struggle, I will persevere, and in it I will earn my dignity.

When I discovered the Booker version of "Black Night" after looking for 30 years, I sent my daughters a message.

Some lessons learned today:
One—never give up
Two—patience will be rewarded
Three—you just never know when something fantastic will
happen

CHAPTER 45
SON SEALS
"GOING BACK HOME"

https://www.youtube.com/watch?v=y2BqrCMNYis

n 1989, a Chicago club called B.L.U.E.S. celebrated its 10th anniversary by bringing in 10 groups to play for 10 hours. I happened to be in Chicago for a few days before returning to Tanzania and I was not about to miss this event. I was the first customer when the doors opened at 2 p.m.

"Music doesn't start for an hour," said the man.

"Doesn't matter," said I. "What's the best seat in the house?"

The "house" turned out to be about the size of a large sitting room, 15-20 feet wide by 40-50 feet long, and the best seat was a barstool where I parked my bony butt until 1 a.m., except for two *in-extremis* trips to the men's room out back. Some might consider perching on a tiny stool for the better part of 11 hours physically debilitating, even torture. Ah, but the music. That's what I came for and that's what I got.

The program started with an old bluesman named Smokey Smothers. After a while Sunnyland Slim, who had played piano with most of the great first generation Chicago bluesmen, entertained. Now Sunnyland Slim is somewhere between 80 and 2000 years old and can't move without crutches—he had to be hoisted onto the tiny platform that passes for a stage in B.L.U.E.S.—but put that ancient human wreck at a piano and watch out. There's still fire in the furnace.

My main reason for sitting through 10 hours of blues was to catch Son Seals, who along with Otis Clay, was the headliner. I knew almost zip about Son Seals. I had two tracks by him on one of my blues tapes. Those two songs were all I needed. He came on between 11 and midnight, and once he got started, all the aches and pains of that barstool disappeared. I just floated away on a blues cloud.

Frank "Son" Seals was born in 1942. He spent most of his time at home in Osceola, Arkansas, until his father died in 1972. He wasn't just hanging out, though. Son began music playing drums and took a lesson or two from another Osceola resident, left-handed blues guitar king Albert King, no relation to right-handed blues guitar king B.B. Then he lit out for the Blues Mecca, Sweet Home Chicago. And it didn't take him long to make an impression. Within a year or so he had his first album out.

Son is a pretty fair picker in the Albert King mold, but it's his voice that will get you—the vibrato. I haven't heard that much quaver since Billy Eckstine and Edith Piaf. Those first two tracks—"All My Love" and "Cotton Pickin' Blues"—just blew me out. It will make the hair in your ears stand up.

I chose "Going Back Home" from the 1977 album *Midnight Son* for several reasons. First and foremost, we hear Son Seals in all his glorious vibrato. Second, he plays some great guitar. Third, this is one of those blues about the country boy come to the city and it contrasts the current tough times with the idyllic past. Finally, I chose it for the horns. I find it strange to say the least that someone who loves horns as much as I do hasn't included more blues that feature them. Horns done properly can add real flavor to the blues. B.B. King and Albert Collins use them to great effect. But I chose a song with strings for the B.B. King chapter and just didn't have space for Albert Collins. (I sometimes think about all the superb musicians who got left out of this. It really gives me the blues.)

The drama of "Going Back Home" begins with the first notes of the 12-bar intro. The horns zap you with a minor blues lick. Seals comes wailing in during the third bar with his slightly distorted guitar. It's a Chicago blues equivalent of German opera *sturm und drang*. You don't know what all this is about yet, but it has an apocalyptic feel to it. The wait is a short one because Son gets right to the point in the opening verse:

> Sometimes I wonder
> Why'd I ever leave home...
> I had a few dollars in my pocket
> Oh, now that old change has gone

Son has got a version of the "I ain't got me no money" blues. But the twist is that he has also pulled up his roots. Note that as Son starts to sing, the horns drop out, leaving drums, bass, keyboards, and rhythm guitar to accompany Seals, who adds lead guitar responses after each line. Then in the ninth bar as he starts to sing "I had a few dollars..." the horns return to add emphasis and heighten the drama. This is that tension-and-release effect I've mentioned before. Almost all good music from Mozart to Marsalis has it, and the blues is chock full of it. The way a vocalist holds or cuts his words, the way a guitarist or harpist bends or sustains a note, the way horns punch or float their phrases—those are all part of tension-and-release. It is also the very essence of life.

> I didn't think a city
> Whoa, could be so dog-gone mean...
> Oh, but this is the meanest place
> Lord, I've ever seen

Having built the drama, the horns sustain it by continuing their little bit through the entire second verse. Son adds a small chuckle after singing "meanest place." The city has got him down but he's far from out. He can still laugh at his own problems.

> I used to have a job
> Doin' spot labor everyday...
> But when I got to work this mornin'
> Lord, they'd packed up and moved away

I find that "spot labor" a brilliant touch. Son doesn't give himself any sort of fancy employment. No, he's just a simple country boy who took the first menial job that came along. He wasn't after anything more than surviving in the mean city, and he's lost that now.

As if this is very much on his mind, Seals launches into an "oh-woe-is-me" guitar solo, a bit of down and dirty business, wails and runs, exactly right for the mood he's in.

> I called my boss
> I wanna know can I come back home...
> He said, you know I'm sorry, Son
> Boy, your job is gone

Now Son is really in a fix. He's lost his job in the city and he can't get his old job back at home. This brings on the Um-Um-Um blues:

Um-Um-Um...
What in the world am I gonna do...
I guess it's just all wrapped up in a nutshell now
Oh, it looks like old poor Son is through

Seals soars into an "end-is-nigh" guitar solo, flying and falling all over the fret board. The horns punch and hold, and they all together come up with a high-drama finish.

I come back to Son's quaver, his vibrato. Once you've heard Son's quaver-quaver, you'll know why I like him so much. And you'll also know why a grown man with a fairly responsible job and two lovely children would park his bony butt on a bar stool in Chicago for 11 hours to hear it. And I'll tell you one more thing: bad back and all, I'd do it again. Want to join me?

CHAPTER 46
JOSH WHITE
"ONE MEAT BALL"

https://www.youtube.com/watch?v=po5rUasUWIg

I learned "Trouble in Mind"—the first blues I wrote about—from a Josh White album. "You Don't Know My Mind" was also on the album. I learned that one too. Those songs are two sides of a single coin. "The sun's gonna shine 'round my back door someday" is akin to:

> You don't know my mind
> You see me laughin'
> I'm laughin' to keep from cryin'.

Josh White is seldom mentioned anymore, but in the 1950s and 1960s he was one of the leading bluesmen, like Big Bill Broonzy. And like Broonzy, Josh White was not just a down-home blues singer. He started recording in the late 1920s. In addition to blues, he did traditional folk songs, gospel, pop tunes, and jazz.

At the age of seven, he became the "lead boy" for a street singer named Blind Man Arnold. He danced, banged on a tambourine, and collected coins from passersby. Over time he learned to play the guitar. By 13, he was a session musician in Chicago and first recorded gospel songs in 1928 as Joshua White, the Singing Christian. He also did blues under the names of Pinewood Tom and Tippy Barton. In the late 1930s, White moved to New York. He starred with Paul Robeson in a Broadway musical called *John Henry* in 1940.

Josh White's biggest hit, and my favorite, is "One Meat Ball." It has a very strange back story. In 1855 a Latin professor at Harvard, George Martin Lane, wrote a humorous little ditty he called "The Lone Fish Ball." It was extremely popular at Harvard and became part of a mock operetta. From there, the song went through several iterations and eventually morphed from fish to flesh as "One Meat Ball" by Tin Pan Alley songwriters Hy Zaret and Lou Singer.

I'm only guessing that when Zaret and Singer presented the song to Josh White about a poor hungry fellow desperate for a meal, it may have reminded him of his own hardscrabble upbringing. White recorded the song as an A minor blues. He begins with a catchy intro phrase used in a number of songs such as in Ray Charles' "Hit the Road, Jack." After the six-bar intro, White sets the scene:

> The little man walked up and down
> To find an eating place in town
> He read the menu through and through
> To see what 15 cents could do
> One meat ball
> One meat ball
> He could afford but one meat ball

In 1944 when this song came out, a lot of people had struggled

through the Depression and could relate to the "little" man's predica-
ment—many firsthand. But the situation gets worse:

> He told the waiter near at hand
> The simple dinner he had planned
> The guests were startled one and all
> To hear the waiter loudly call
> One meat ball, everybody,
> One meat ball
> Hey this here gent wants one meat ball.

Oh, the embarrassment. Furthermore, the waiter did it on purpose:
This fine establishment doesn't need paupers like you! The humiliation
worsens even more:

> You know, the little man felt ill at ease
> He said some bread sir if you please
> The waiter hollered down the hall
> You gets no bread with one meat ball
> One meat ball
> One meat ball
> Well, you gets no bread with one meat ball.

The waiter shows disdain for the little man's privation: the nerve of
this wretch, asking for complementary bread. The little man's distress
haunts him:

> The little man felt very bad
> One meat ball was all he had
> And in his dreams he hears that call
> You gets no bread with one meat ball

One meat ball… and no spaghetti
One meat ball
You gets no bread with one meat ball.

Josh White could empathize with the little man. At the age of seven, he was left on his own. He didn't have decent clothes to wear or a bed at night until he was 16. I expect he often went to sleep hungry. Josh White sings about a have-not butting up against the haves; possibly a black man confronting segregation. Consider "One Meat Ball" a subtle protest song.

When I explained "One Meat Ball" to a Tanzanian, she responded: "Why didn't the waiter sympathize? He's not much better off than the little man." A very well-known East African Swahili song by Orchestra Makassy loosely translates as "Going Broke is Not a Joke." One line warns, "Don't laugh: today it's me; tomorrow it may be you."

In my view, "One Meat Ball" is as relevant today as it was almost 80 years ago. And it's a joy to hear Josh White sing it.

CHAPTER 47
MEMPHIS MINNIE
"ME AND MY CHAUFFEUR"

https://www.youtube.com/watch?v=rD2GUKwqliU

My usual Sunday routine used to include tuning in BBC World Service on shortwave to catch "Jazz for the Asking." One Sunday, a request came in to the now-departed Peter Clayton (R.I.P.) to play Memphis Minnie's "Kid-Man Blues." I found it not too strange that Memphis Minnie should wind up on a jazz program. Bessie Smith regularly got requested and I've seen jazz anthology albums with Robert Johnson tunes. The distinction between jazz and blues is sometimes rather fine. It's all music. If there was strangeness in this request it was because the listener also wanted Clayton to explain the meaning of "kid-man." Even stranger, Clayton didn't know. This led me to conclude that neither the host nor the listener had really gotten into the blues. So, for Peter Clayton, who is now doing his A-B-Cs (Armstrong, Basie, and Coltrane) in the afterlife, and that listener hungry for erudition, a kid-man is a young fellow notable for his sexual prowess.

Though I now have a Memphis Minnie double CD, at that time, I only had three songs by Memphis Minnie. But those three cuts told me everything I needed to know. Ms. Minnie could really get down on the blues. "Nothin' in Ramblin'," "Kid-Man," and "Me and My Chauffeur" will do a number on you. Three out of three is about as good as you can get.

Memphis Minnie, unlike Memphis Slim, was not originally from Memphis. She was born Minnie (or Lizzie, depending on the source) Douglas in Algiers, Louisiana, across the river from New Orleans in 1896. Her parents gave her the nickname "Kid" and she was called Kid Douglas until her first record came out in 1929. When she was eight, her family moved to Memphis. She took up the guitar as a teenager and became part of the Beale Street blues scene.

Beale Street was a major center of blues development. W.C. Handy had become the first "blues star" as composer of such hits as "Memphis Blues," "Beale Street Blues," and most especially the classic "St. Louis Blues." No doubt all these tunes were inspired by the music Handy heard on Beale Street. Down on Beale Street you might find a jam including Furry Lewis, Gus Cannon of Cannon's Jug Stompers, Will Shade of the Memphis Jug Band, Walter Horton (in those days called "Shakey," a nickname he detested), and Kid Douglas.

While women were the city blues stars (Ma Rainey, Bessie Smith, et al.), country blues was still a man's world... except for Minnie Douglas. Women could sing the blues, but if they played an instrument it had better be piano... again, except for Minnie Douglas. She was the exception to all the rules. When she played with Will "Casey Bill" Weldon, lead guitar in the Memphis Jug Band, or Kansas Joe McCoy (who was actually from Mississippi), or Ernest "Little Son Joe" Lawlers, it was usually Minnie who took lead and did the solos while these fine guitarists supported her. And sing? Minnie might have described her size but not her sound. She was a five-foot lady with a six-foot voice.

Poet Langston Hughes, reporting for the *Chicago Defender* in 1942, wrote, "Memphis Minnie sings through a microphone and her voice—hard and strong anyhow for a little woman's—is made harder and stronger by scientific sound.... The rhythm fills the 230 Club with a deep and dusky heartbeat that overrides all modern amplification."

I have chosen "Me and My Chauffeur," recorded in 1941, over "Kid-Man Blues" or "Nothin' in Ramblin'," principally because of what Giles Oakley, *The Devil's Music* author, describes as Minnie's "emphatic swing." This number will practically swing itself off your music machine and dance around the room. As with other great swing tunes, it's difficult to remain still. You just have to move something. The emphatic swing on this number is supplied by Minnie, Little Son Joe Lawlers, and a bassist. As the rhythm guitar is at least as important as the lead in establishing the swing, my guess would favor Minnie on rhythm and Little Son Joe on lead. Whatever and whoever, both really crank it up in the introduction. This swing is somewhat different from Basie's four strong beats to the bar: Chunk-Chunk-Chunk-Chunk. On "Chauffeur," the accent falls on the second and fourth beats, so we get more of a... ring-CHUNK-ring-CHUNK. Meanwhile the lead plays a catchy little two-bar figure. For me, the intro is the best part of the song. And I'm not the only one who liked it as we'll soon discover.

Most blues are eight, twelve, sixteen, or occasionally thirty-two bars. All, you will note, are divisible by four. If you count "Chauffeur," you will come up with 18 bars. That's because Minnie sings the second line of each chorus twice as in...

> I wants him to drive me...
> I wants him to drive me downtown

This repeat—the musical term is "delay"—adds two bars to what would otherwise be a 16-bar blues. It also adds emphasis to that particular line, which is what Minnie was after.

> Wants to see my chauffeur
> Wants to see my chauffeur
> I wants him to drive me...
> I wants him to drive me downtown
> Says he drives so easy
> I can't turn him down

You may think this song is about the driver of an automobile. Chauffeur is derived from the French word for "warm" and comes from "stoker." This is also where Memphis Minnie is coming from. The song has nothing to do with cars.

> But I don't want him
> But I don't want him
> To be ridin' his girls...
> To be ridin' his girls around
> Cause I'm gwine steal me a pistol
> Shoot my chauffeur down

Are you getting the idea? Maybe you need another verse:

> Well I'm gon find him
> Well I'm gon find him
> A brand new V8...
> A brand new V8 Ford
> Then he won't need no passengers
> I will be his load

With a "yeah, take it away," they move into the instrumental. The rhythm guitar shifts from a ring-CHUNK four to a "beat-me-daddy-eight-to-the-bar" boogie woogie. The solo barely manages to hang on and ends after 12 rather than 16 or 18 bars.

> Gwina let my chauffeur
> Gwina let my chauffeur
> Drive me around the...
> Drive me around the world
> Then he can be my little boy
> Yes, I'll be his girl

Minnie has written a little ode to female liberation. If her chauffeur messes around, he gets a lesson with lead; if he provides good service, she'll reward him with a brand new V8 Ford. This is an altogether different attitude toward men than that expressed by Janis Joplin in "Ball and Chain." Joplin sang, "Hear you're gone today, all I wanted to do was hold you for so long." Minnie is very much in command on "Me and My Chauffeur," if not exactly in the driver's seat.

The first time I heard this song it sounded somehow familiar. Too many years on malaria pills have played havoc with my memory. Then I remembered the Sonny Boy Williamson classic from 1937, "Good Mornin' Little School Girl." Chuck Berry also used it: same tune, same riff, somewhat different rhythm, different lyrics, highly amplified, on the same subject matter, called "I Wanna Be Your Driver." However, neither Sonny Boy nor Chuck can match Minnie for that emphatic swing.

CHAPTER 48
LITTLE WALTER
"KEY TO THE HIGHWAY"

https://www.youtube.com/watch?v=FoAV-Axey90

have tried to keep down the number of harmonica players in this book. Little Walter Jacobs did not make my original list. For all of that, I still must do a little something on Little Walter.

Little Walter is to the blues harp what Charlie Parker is to the alto sax. He started a style of playing that many others have emulated. You can play hard like Little Walter or not play hard like Little Walter, but in either case you have to consider Little Walter. Walter played with Muddy Waters until he struck out on his own after an R&B hit in 1952 titled "Juke." He produced what is described as a horn-like tone, since many of his musical models were sax players like Louis Jordan. Little Walter would put his harmonica right up on the microphone, making the amplification become part of his sound. He wasn't after a pure harp tone as Sonny Terry sought. Walter didn't bend notes like Sonny Boy Williamson, which, given the closeness of the microphone, might have made the sound too mushy. He was after a more modern sound, sometimes so loud it often seemed distorted. He had to play loud because he played with Muddy Waters in those Chicago bars.

Here's what I think he did to produce his sound… at least it's what I do to produce a similar sound. I use a special microphone called a Green Bullet, because it's a kind of pea-soup green and shaped a bit like a bullet. Originally, Little Walter used a taxi dispatcher's microphone. Its shape fits nicely in your hand. You cup the device with your right hand to control the tone—open, muted, or in between. The microphone plugs into a small amplifier cranked up full volume. Another microphone connection runs to the mixer that controls the overall sound coming out of the P.A. system. Even though the amp may be full volume, the volume on the mixer can be adjusted so that the harp blends in properly with the rest of the band. In my case, I have a distortion pedal connected to the amp, so if I want a "purer" sound I disconnect the distortion. I step on the distortion pedal and I'm ready to do "The Walkin' Blues," "Spoonful," "Back Door Man," "Rock Me Baby," "Born Under a Bad Sign," and so on.

"Key to the Highway" is a blues standard recorded many times. Big Bill Broonzy and Chas Segar composed it, and both recorded it along with another harp player, Jazz Gillum, in 1940. The number rolls right along, just the way a song about highways should.

And like most of the songs I've written about, there's a story attached to Little Walter's version of "Key." A former musical colleague sent me a tape copied off a radio program in 1970. The disc jockeys were Mick Jagger and Keith Richards. Apparently, somebody from the radio station asked them what music the Rolling Stones listened to when they are on tour. It's a remote broadcast from their hotel room. They play along a musical spectrum from Mississippi John Hurt's 1928 "Stack-O-Lee" through 1960s Motown. They make a few mistakes, among them telling listeners that "Goin' Down Slow" is sung by Howlin Wolf with "comments" by Willie Dixon, when in fact it's sung by Wolf, Muddy Waters, and Bo Diddley, and if Willie Dixon is anywhere in the studio, he is probably playing bass with his mouth shut. But still, that is not too bad for a couple of British art school boys. They had a lot to say about Little Walter but Little Walter says it all on "Key to the Highway."

From the first note of the four-bar intro you hear that distinctive Little Walter harp and you'll know why so many copied his horn-like sound. You would never confuse Walter with Sonny Terry. It would not be a sign of ignorance to confuse him with Junior Wells or Paul Butterfield or a couple of hundred other harp players. But in Walter Jacobs, you are hearing the original.

When Walter left Muddy Waters in 1952, he took over the Junior Wells band, called the Aces. Turnabout being fair play, Junior Wells took over harp for Muddy Waters. Walter recorded "Key to the Highway" as a tribute to Broonzy shortly after Big Bill died in 1958. Backing Jacobs were the Muddy Waters' tinny guitar and Otis Spann's piano.

> I got the key to the highway
> Billed out and bound to go
> I'm gonna' leave here runnin' because
> Walkin' is most too slow

Little Walter is without argument one of the great blues harpists, but he's not a bad vocalist, either. He placed a number of songs in the R&B Top Ten; all but "Juke" were vocals with harp. The way he growls "billed out," and especially how he moves "because" from its natural place at the beginning of the last line up to the line before—these are the ingredients of good blues. He wants to emphasize "**Walkin** is most too slow." Once again, blues may seem simple, but it's not. Anyone can play or sing "Key to the Highway." It involves straight three-chord eight-bar blues. I used to do it at almost every gig I played. But to do it well takes talent, skill and, most important, feel. You have got to feel the blues to play the blues.

> I'm goin' back to the border
> Where I'm better known
> Because you haven't done nothin' but drove
> A good man away from home

Here, too, he moves the "but drove" up a line to emphasize what a **"good man"** he is. This speaks to how you feel the song. Another bluesman might start the last line with "drove." If you can, listen to how Big Bill Broonzy does "Key" or Eric Clapton on his "Layla" album. They are entirely different. The Delta Cross Band does it another way. The point is that "Key to the Highway" is one of those great songs that people constantly come back to because it lends itself so well to different styles and interpretation.

> Give me one more kiss Mama
> Just before I go
> Because when I leave this time girl I
> Won't be back no more

Here it comes: Little Walter's harp. I can dream on that sound. I can fly over continents on that sound—a sound so funky yet so fine you can go straight to blues heaven upon hearing it.

Little Walter changed everything. You simply cannot discuss blues harmonica after 1950 without mentioning Little Walter Jacobs. Muddy Waters, not usually given to hyperbole, said, "So all I can say is that he is the greatest I ever heard." Mick Jagger calls him the best electric blues harp player ever. Giles Oakley writes, "But the greatest of them all was

Little Walter." You can decide for yourself whether he was the best or greatest.

> When the moon peep over the mountain
> Honey I'll be on my way
> I'm gonna run this highway
> Until the break of day

Note the way he extends the word "I'll" and that he doesn't move "until" up a line. Why? Because of the way he sings the word "Hi-I-way." Feel, Feel, Feel.

> Well, it's so long, so long baby
> I must say goodbye
> I'm gonna run this highway
> Until the day I die

The day he died came ten years later in 1968 when he got hit on the side of his head in a brawl. It is unclear whether he started it. Little Walter was 37 years old.

CHAPTER 49
TAJ MAHAL
"OH MAMA DON'T YOU KNOW"

https://www.youtube.com/watch?v=QoD-AQNDsII

met Taj Mahal one night back in 1972 in Wichita, Kansas. He was in town for a concert and decided to mellow down at an eastside club I used to hang out at. I chose this place because it featured a fairly fine group called the Bear Valley Blues Band. Taj Mahal may have chosen it for the same reason. I felt comfortable approaching him because he had been the neighbor of friends of mine in San Francisco. As I remember we talked about the blues. We talked about the roots. We talked about carrying on a tradition.

Two things stand out about Taj Mahal. He is totally committed to black music and he is a consummate musician. He doesn't perform blues exclusively. He goes back beyond blues. He does rags, he does jazz, he does reggae, and he even does cakewalks. He'll do blues to a reggae beat. He'll do blues to a rock beat. He'll do songs that aren't blues and make them into blues. He'll resurrect an old Lead Belly number like "Bourgeois Blues," because he rightly knows that things haven't changed much. And he always adds something, no matter how ancient, to give it a fresh sound.

Taj Mahal plays more instruments than I can name. The list would include various acoustic and electric guitars, banjo, double bass, piano, and harmonica. Playing all these instruments is no big deal; playing them as well as Taj Mahal does is a big deal. His sense of phrasing is both idiosyncratic and immaculate. I could continue at an embarrassing length about Taj Mahal's musicianship. But I suppose his greatest strength is to make whatever music he chooses to do, however he chooses to do it, sound right. I don't like absolutes. To me there is no right or wrong way to play a song. It either works or it doesn't. Taj Mahal's music works. He did Robert Johnson's "Walkin Blues" as a dirge and it worked. (Paul Butterfield did it as a stomp and it also worked.) He's recorded with a tuba choir and it sounds great. And his message to me seems to simply be: This music is alive.

Taj Mahal didn't come out of the typical blues breeding grounds of the Delta or rural Texas or New Orleans. Born Henry Saint Clair Fredericks in 1942, he grew up in Springfield, Massachusetts. He is probably the only blues musician in the world with a degree in animal husbandry. While at his university he became interested in black folk music. The first time I heard Taj Mahal on the radio, he was not doing black folk music but that truck driver classic, "Six Days on the Road." He didn't sing it anything like Dave Dudley sang it. Part of discovering Taj Mahal is discovering that he almost never does anything like anyone else. Another Robert Johnson standard, "Sweet Home Chicago," is usually done as a fast shuffle. Taj Mahal, with help from the Pointer Sisters, turns it into a bump and grind:

> Two and two is four
> Four and two is six
> I'll be back tomorrow night

As soon as I get my business fixed

On "Oh Mama Don't You Know," Taj chooses to play a steel-body National guitar which lends an even more haunting sound to this slow eight-bar blues. From the first notes, this Taj Mahal composition takes us back to the primordial blues. This is basic roots music, as deep as the bayou whence mankind emerged. Its subject, the relationship between a man and woman, has been with us since humankind emerged from the ooze. All the joy and pain that men and women give each other is contained in this five-and-a-half-minute lament:

> Now you know when I first met you baby
> I was in the lost and found
> And I did promise you I would chase away all
>   the bullets
> Whoever bothered you here in the town
> Cause you're a real good dough maker baby
> And you really know how to make your biscuits
>   soft and brown
> Mama, don't you know

The man was down and out; he met a woman—what sort we don't know—and exchanged protection for companionship. That seems fair enough. If you listen to the way he draws out "found," you are getting a lesson in singing blues. Note his timing on the guitar with that thumb going thump-thump-thump-thump on the bass strings. Note, too, how he phrases his lines so that even when he's cramming all those words in lines 3 and 6, he doesn't sound rushed in the slightest. That's a musician at work and, perhaps, at play.

Oh, you know I do love you baby

And I do know you're bound to love me some
Oh, you put your arms around me baby
Like a circle round the sun
Please do me baby
You know the easy rider is the one
Mama now don't you know

Again, mark that phrasing on words "Oh" in line 1, "some" in line 2, "around" in line 3, "baby" in line 5, and especially "easy rider is the one" in line six. That is not learned. You have to *feel* it. It's there or it's not, and you can't fake it. From protection and companionship, we move to love. But things don't go smoothly:

Sometimes I get lonesome, baby, you know
And I do go downtown
I stand on the street with all the lights, baby
And just take a look around
And I come back home to you, baby,
With a lonesome frown
Baby, don't you know

We don't know if he's lonesome because his woman is running around or maybe he remembers his younger wilder days when he was in the lost and found. But the key word, repeated twice, is "lonesome." Something is bound to happen. It probably occurs during the guitar solo. After his solo excursion, the guilt sets in:

Please come here, darlin'
Put your hand in mine
Likes to have his ways sometimes
And I know I have left you cryin'

> I ain't no angel, baby
> And there ain't no denyin'
> Baby, don't you know

So he's "fessed up," as we used to say in the Ozarks. Now comes the difficult part—getting her back. It's time to plead:

> Oh pleeeease, baby
> Won't you give me one more chance again
> To save my life, baby
> From sadness and sin
> I know it ain't easy
> To try and try again
> Mama, don't you know

"To save my life from sadness and sin": this is down to the core of a man's soul. Without love, what is there but sadness and sin? To reinforce just how crucial this woman is to saving his life, he adds:

> I ain't got no money, baby
> And I don't mean to cop a plea
> But I would sure be doin, better, baby
> If you were sleepin' next to me
> O O O Lord
> O Lord indeed
> Baby, don't you know

He gives her time to think this proposal over by doing another solo on guitar, very short (four bars), very plaintive, very insistent. I guess it works because he reminds her of how they started out together by repeating the first verse, implying she has agreed to try and try again.

Taj Mahal created this song from his vast knowledge of traditional blues with lines like dough maker and biscuits, circle 'round the sun, and easy rider. I've never heard another song quite like "Oh Mama Don't You Know." The structure, the chord changes, the delivery all speak to me of something very rare and very, very fine. And it is one of my treasures. And in this age of synthesized schlock and sound bites, it is music like this, and musicians like Taj Mahal, that help save my life from sadness and sin. Oh, Mama don't you know.

CHAPTER 50
CLIFTON CHENIER
"BLACK GAL"

https://www.youtube.com/watch?v=SeJY5KIKrZ4

My first instrument was the violin. I grew to hate it. In the hands of a master, it can make beautiful, beautiful music, but in the hands of a beginner, it produces the most god-awful racket. I'll listen to any instrument played well with one exception—the accordion. Just say "Lady of Spain," and I run from the room. No matter how well played they are, I can't stand accordions. Or didn't think I could. That was before I heard Clifton Chenier do "Black Gal." When it comes to the blues on the accordion, this gentleman gets it done.

Clifton Chenier plays a style of Louisiana music called zydeco—a combination of traditional Cajun, blues, and country, with a bit of rock and roll mixed in, sung in French or English or both. It's a sort of musical gumbo—whatever you have, throw it in. I didn't know at the time, but Clifton Chenier is to zydeco what Charlie Parker is to bebop. Chenier, practically on his own, originated it, perfected it, then took it out of the bayou and spread it around the world. I first heard zydeco about 50 miles west of Tanzania's Mt. Kilimanjaro.

Chenier did not get off to an auspicious start in 1954 when he recorded "Cliston's Blues" by "Cliston" Chenier. But he quickly got on track with a number of regional hits in the late '50s and early '60s. He became "The King of Zydeco," complete with crown, cape, and gold-capped tooth. John Broven, British musical historian, claims (and proclaims) that "Clifton Chenier was the best accordion salesman ever." (Chenier favored a chrome-studded model himself.)

Chenier cut "Black Gal" in 1966. It's an updated zydeco version of a blues recorded by one Joe Pullum in 1934. Chenier's got a very serious problem with his Black Gal:

> Oh, Black Gal, Oh, Black Gal
> What makes your dog-gone head so hard

Those hard headed women, to quote Elvis Presley, "been causin' trouble ever since the world began." There's a Parchman Farm chain-gang chant that goes:

> I don't want no hardheaded woman
> She's too mean, Lord, she's too mean

Louis Jordan, Woody Herman, B.B. King all sing:

> Caldonia... Caldonia... what makes your big
>   head so hard

Chenier's "Black Gal" is about as hard and basic as hard and basic blues can get. It is pure rhythm and sound. A harper plays along as does the drummer. Neither does a whole lot. Chenier renders any defects insignificant by wailing magnificently on his accordion. His sense of swing makes the drummer almost superfluous; his beautiful runs make you forget about the harmonica. As much as I hate to admit it, it's the accordion that makes this blues great.

"Black Girl" starts with Chenier whuppin IT on you for eight bars. It is the blues and there is no question about it. If it sounds like there are more than three instruments, it is because Chenier can do so much with his accordion. He uses those buttons on the left to furnish a bass part, while his right hand flies over the keys—part piano, part organ, part harmonica, and all accordion. Then he begins his complaint:

> Oh, Black Gal, Oh, Black Gal
> What makes your dog-gone head so hard
> I had my mind on seein' you
> Oh, your head's so hard

It seems Clifton is meeting some resistance from his gal, or more precisely, his prospective gal. He just wants to see her, whatever that might mean, but her head's so dog-gone hard. A little sweet-talk might do the trick:

> You know I love you, I love you baby
> And I'll tell the world I do
> I had my mind on seein' you, girl
> But your head's so hard-hard-hard

That "hard-hard-hard" tells it all. The lady won't budge. I can empathize with Chenier—about 95 percent of the women I had a mind on seein' were hard-hard-hard just like that. Clifton is nothing if not persistent. If sweet talk won't do it, maybe some sweet blues on the accordion will work. He asks the harp to help him out. He (I assume it's a "he") plays it straight, sticking pretty close to the melody line, while Clifton embellishes on his squeezebox. It has that down-home bluesy feel, that Cajun soul, that bayou funk.

Unfortunately, this strategy is no more effective than the sweet talk:

> Oh, Black Gal, Oh, Black Gal
> What makes your dog-gone head so...
> (He can't even bring himself to sing that word.)
> I had my mind on seein' you
> O-O-Oh your head's so hard

The "O-O-Oh" indicates to me Chenier has thrown in the towel. He's resigned to not seein' this hard-headed gal. And that brings on some really serious blues from the accordion—about triple the intensity of anything previously played. And the blues fade out.

Only the blues will be back. The blues are always there. "I guess the Blues is about as old as buttermilk," said Chicago bluesman Otis Rush. "Ever since people have been in the world, somebody's had the Blues." Because the blues is nothing but human emotion—all the joy and tears and hopes and fears. The blues are as real as life. And no matter how miserable, they somehow make you feel so good. You see, the blues are not only the disease; the blues are also the cure.

And here's how I look at it: If I can endure Clifton Chenier playing accordion—an instrument that usually makes me want to puke—then you can at least give this music a listen. And I will lay odds that if you open your ears, you're will get hooked, just as I got hooked on "Black Gal." Because I do believe to my soul, the music is in you and it's got to-got to-got to come out. So BOOGIE CHILLUN!

CODA

Webster defines "coda" as: 1) a concluding musical section that is formally distinct from the main structure; 2) something that serves to round out, conclude, or summarize. This is my coda.

All people everywhere have music within them. Charles Darwin believed song came before speech. Who am I to argue with Darwin? People say that babies babble and coo. *Au contraire*, say I. They are singing. They are expressing their thoughts and feelings before they have the ability to say "mama." Here's an example: A friend phoned one night very excited. She put on Ella Fitzgerald doing "On the Sunnyside of the Street," and sang along. Although I respect and admire this friend, she can't carry a tune in a bucket. But that didn't matter because she sang with such passion and conviction. She wanted me to know how she felt. Words couldn't do it. She used music (and Ella) to help her out.

Together we have listened to 25 jazz and 25 blues songs. You may not have liked all of them but I trust you liked some of them. I listen to jazz and blues programs every week and usually dig about 20 percent of what they play. I stated right up front that my purpose in doing this book is to hook you on jazz and blues… not necessarily *my* jazz and blues. I hope you're hooked.

For me, one of the best things about music is discovery, hearing something new that knocks my socks off. I wrote that, the first time I heard Charlie Parker as a teenager, it was like being hit by a brick between the ears. Since then I've been hit by hundreds, possibly thousands, of bricks.

My hope is that, having listened along with me to these 50 songs, you are ready to search out and listen to 50 more, then 50 more, and that you will get your socks knocked off. The music is out there waiting for you. With the internet, it's as easy as peasy. Better yet, check out the music live at a club or concert. Let those Noble Sounds become part of you.

To paraphrase John Lee Hooker: Noble Sounds are in you and they've got to come out.

—J Strauss
Dar es Salaam
Tanzania

AND IN THIS CORNER

Let's take a quick look at the corner bookshelf. In writing this book, I had to rely on the hard work of others. Rather than simply present a dry bibliography, it might be more fun to examine a few of the sources I used in case you want to read further on the music presented here. You can also check the internet. But being an old fuddy-duddy, I like books.

For jazz I might recommend you start where I started around 1961 with *The Story of Jazz*, by Marshall Stearns. It will only take you up through the mid-1950s, but you'll get a good grounding in where jazz came from and how it developed during its first half-century. More up-to-date and practical would be *The 101 Best Jazz Albums*, by Len Lyons. Lyons offers a very good general background on the various styles in addition to discussing specific jazz albums. This will take you up to 1980. If you get to the point where you feel ready for the big time, the most complete and up-to-date book on jazz (as of 2001) is *A New History of Jazz* by Alyn Shipton, all 888 pages. It's also good for building your biceps.

There is a quasi-comic book which is a good starting place—quick and easy to read—*Jazz for Beginners* by Ron David. (He errs now and then, such as writing that Gato Barbieri is from Brazil when he's from Argentina, but nothing too serious.) Martin Williams, one of the real authorities on jazz, has written extensively, and his primer is *The Jazz Tradition*.

I have two books I refer to frequently. The first is *Jazz: The Essential Companion* by three British jazzmen, Ian Carr, Digby Fairweather, and Brian Priestley. These gentlemen not only know their subject firsthand but also write well. The second is the *Penguin Guide to Jazz* by Richard Cook and Brian Morton. If you think another music guide might come in handy, there's *The Rolling Stone Jazz Record Guide*, edited by John Swenson. Finally, I borrowed a school library book and forgot to return it… accidently. It's titled, *The Blackwell Guide to Recorded Jazz*, edited by Barry Kernfeld. It is similar in format to the Lyons book.

For jazz from the musicians' view, I have three books on swing by Stanley Dance: *The World of Swing, The World of Duke Ellington*, and *The World of Count Basie*. My man Kevin Mulqueen gave me his copy of *Hear Me Talkin' to Ya*, edited by Nat Shapiro and Nat Hentoff, probably the most quoted book on jazz ever published… and rightly so. I might add *Notes and Tones* by drummer Art Taylor and *Talking Jazz* by singer and pianist Ben Sidran. In addition, I highly recommend two fabulous books by jazz bassists: *Jazz Anecdotes* by Bill Crow (some very funny stories in there) and *The Jazz Anthology* by Miles Kington.

Probably the best book on jazz I ever read is *The Best of Jazz* by British trumpeter Humphrey Lyttelton. He writes about great jazz musicians from the point of view of a jazz musician. In fact, it is laid out a lot like this is (I swear I didn't read it until most of this was already written) except it's a bit more advanced, but well worth a read even if you are not musically trained.

There are two books on jazz, highly opinionated books, by writers who have earned the right to be highly opinionated: *Blues People* by LeRoi Jones and *Stomping the Blues* by Albert Murray. If you like great writing which also happens to cover jazz, I unreservedly recommend anything by Whitney Balliet (who wrote pieces for *New Yorker* magazine) and Gary Giddins. I have Balliet's *American Musicians*, the title of which is not 100 percent accurate as one chapter deals with Stephane Grappelli [French] and Django Reinhardt [Belgian]). I also own his *Collected Works*, and *New York Notes*, and three books by Giddins: *Rhythm-A-Ning*, *Riding on a Blue Note*, and *Visions of Jazz*.

In addition, I took quotes from the following:

The View from Within by Orrin Keepnews
African Rock by Chris Stapleton and Chris May
The Penguin Encyclopedia of Popular Music edited by Donald Clarke
The Genius of Louis Armstrong by James Lincoln Collier
The Jazz Book by Joachim Berendt
In the Moment by Francis Davis
Jazz on CD by John Fordham
Jazz People by Valerie Wilmer
Blue: The Murder of Jazz by Eric Nisenson

Finally, here are three biographies that are worth your time: *Chasin' the Trane* by J.C. Thomas, and *Ascension: John Coltrane and his Quest* and *Open Skies: Sonny Rollins and his World of Improvisation*," both by Eric Nisenson. Two more that are worth reading are *Straight Life* by Art Pepper and *Good Morning Blues*" by Count Basie with Albert Murray.

As sparse as my collection of books on jazz is, I have even fewer books on blues. My one primer is *The Devil's Music: A History of the Blues* by Giles Oakley. This will give you a very good perspective on the blues and also the many trials and tribulations of Africans in America.

One of the groundbreaking studies on the blues (actually two in one) is *The Blues Makers* by Samuel Charters, not so technical that a non-musician can't follow. It deals with acoustic pre-WWII blues. I also recommend *The Land Where the Blues Began* by Alan Lomax.

The very best reference book I know is *The Penguin Guide to Blues Recordings* by Tony Russell, Chris Smith, et al. You will find everything you want to know about blues (even if some of it is wrong) in *Encyclopedia of the Blues* by Gerard Herzhaft.

And then there are the guides, of which I have several: *The Blackwell Guide to Recorded Blues* edited by Paul Oliver, a pioneer writer on blues; *The Big Book of the Blues* by Robert Santelli; and the *Music Hound Guide to Blues* edited by Leland Rucker.

I also recommend *Deep Blues* by Robert Palmer, which is about as good a book on Mississippi Blues as you're likely to come across. Gayle Dean Wardlow, another old boy from Mississippi, wrote *Chasin' That Devil Music*. A northerner, Peter Guralnik, did a little book, *Searching for Robert Johnson*. There is also *Chicago Blues* by Mike Rowe and *Urban Blues* by Charles Keil, which is more sociological than musical but interesting, nonetheless.

Although not specifically on blues, the books below mention blues to some extent and all are well written and entertaining:

The Sound of the City by Charlie Gillett
Mystery Train by Greil Marcus (essay on Robert Johnson)
Lost Highway and *Feel Like Going Home* by Peter Guralnick
Unsung Heroes of Rock and Roll by Nick Tosches
The Heart of Rock and Soul by Dave Marsh
White Boy Singin' the Blues by Michael Bane
Harmonicas Harps and Heavy Breathers by Kim Field
The Rolling Stone Encyclopedia of Rock and Roll edited by John Pareles and Patricia Romanowski

Two quotes on Big Joe Turner came out of the books I mentioned by Valerie Wilmer and Count Basie. I got most of the quotes on Robert Johnson from a feature by Tony Scherman in *Musician* magazine, dating from January 1991. The Phil Patton article on blues in *Esquire*, which I picked up in an airport, has long since flown away, so I can't cite the date of that issue. *Going to Chicago* is primarily photos with a few remarks by various blues artists, edited by Lawrence Hyman, and is more for fanatics like me than casual listeners. I also borrowed a few quotes from various album liner notes. I have one autobiography, *Big Bill's Blues*, by Big Bill Broonzy as told to Yannick Bruynoghe.